Cash, Clothes, and Construction

Diverse Economies and Livable Worlds
Series Editors: J. K. Gibson-Graham, Maliha Safri,
Kevin St. Martin, Stephen Healy

*Urbanism without Guarantees: The Everyday Life of a
Gentrifying West Side Neighborhood*
Christian M. Anderson

*Carving Out the Commons: Tenant Organizing and
Housing Cooperatives in Washington, D.C.*
Amanda Huron

The Solidarity Economy
Jean-Louis Laville

Cash, Clothes, and Construction: Rethinking Value in Bolivia's Pluri-economy
Kate Maclean

Reimagining Livelihoods: Life beyond Economy, Society, and Environment
Ethan Miller

Fair Trade Rebels: Coffee Production and Struggles for Autonomy in Chiapas
Lindsay Naylor

Building Dignified Worlds: Geographies of Collective Action
Gerda Roelvink

Practicing Cooperation: Mutual Aid beyond Capitalism
Andrew Zitcer

Cash, Clothes, and Construction

Rethinking Value in Bolivia's Pluri-economy

Kate Maclean

Diverse Economies and Livable Worlds

University of Minnesota Press
Minneapolis
London

Portions of chapter 3 are adapted from "Chachawarmi: Rhetorics and Lived Realities," *Bulletin of Latin American Research* 33, no. 1 (2014): 76–90, https://doi.org/10.1111/blar.12071; copyright 2013 Society for Latin American Studies; published by John Wiley & Sons Ltd. Portions of chapters 3 and 4 are adapted from "Gender, Risk, and Micro-Financial Subjectivities," *Antipode* 45, no. 2 (2013): 455–73, https://doi.org/10.1111/j.1467-8330.2012.01005.x; copyright 2012 Kate Maclean, *Antipode* copyright 2012 Antipode Foundation Ltd. Portions of chapters 3 and 4 are adapted from "Capitalizing on Women's Social Capital? Women-Targeted Microfinance in Bolivia," *Development and Change* 41, no. 3 (2010): 495–515, https://doi.org/10.1111/j.1467-7660.2010.01649.x; copyright 2010 International Institute of Social Studies. Portions of chapters 3 and 5 are adapted from "Evo's Jumper: Identity and the Used Clothes Trade in 'Post-Neoliberal' and 'Pluri-Cultural' Bolivia," *Gender, Place and Culture: A Journal of Feminist Geography* 21, no. 8 (2014): 963–78, https://doi.org/10.1080/096636 9X.2013.810607; reprinted by permission of the publisher, Taylor & Francis Ltd, http://www.tandfonline.com. Portions of chapter 5 are adapted from "Fashion in Bolivia's Cultural Economy," *International Journal of Cultural Studies* 22, no. 2 (2019): 213–28, https://doi.org/10.1177/1367877918821233. Portions of chapter 6 are adapted from "Envisioning Gender, Indigeneity, and Urban Change: The Case of La Paz, Bolivia," *Gender, Place and Culture: A Journal of Feminist Geography* 25, no. 5 (2018): 711–26, https://doi.org/10.1080/0966369X.2018.1460327; reprinted by permission of the publisher, Taylor & Francis Ltd, http://www.tandfonline.com.

Published by the University of Minnesota Press
111 Third Avenue South, Suite 290
Minneapolis, MN 55401–2520
http://www.upress.umn.edu

ISBN 978-1-5179-1595-7 (hc)
ISBN 978-1-5179-1596-4 (pb)

Library of Congress record available at https://lccn.loc.gov/2023021904

Printed in the United States of America on acid-free paper

The University of Minnesota is an equal-opportunity educator and employer.

UMP BmB 2023

For Alva and Vega

Contents

Acknowledgments   ix

Abbreviations   xiii

Introduction: Pluri-economy in Bolivia   1

1. The Vision of Pluri-economy   31

2. The Political Space for Pluri-economy   59

3. Andean Economic Femininities   89

4. Cash: The Culture of Capital and the Value of Symbols   117

5. Clothes: Nation, Production, and Contemporaneity   149

6. Construction: Aesthetics, Recognition, and Urban Mobilities   175

Conclusion: Processes of Plurality   201

Glossary   223

Bibliography   227

Index   251

Acknowledgments

More than sixteen years have passed since I first embarked on the research that has informed this book, and I have accumulated huge debts of gratitude over this time. First, to Florinda Henderson and her family in York and Bolivia, who introduced me to the beautiful valley of Luribay. In particular, Charo, Noemi, Remedios, Lucy, Freddy, Lineth, Jherry, Nardín, Horlinda, Brener, Catriona, and *comadre* Sylvia and *ahijada* Melany. Deepest thanks to Doña Maria and Don Pedro from Pocuma, Doña Cristina and Don Emilio from the Town, Doña Virginia, Doña Julia, and Don Ramiro from Mojon, and Doña Lidia from Peña Colorada. To the many people who showed me kindness, generosity, and forbearance in Luribay: I will never forget you. Many thanks also to the professionals from various NGOs whom I met in Luribay—Milton Macias, Calixta Choque Churata, Javier Rios, Miguel Salazar Olvea, and Tomas Choque.

In La Paz, I am forever grateful to Doña Baldomera Cussi Parrado and Alison Parrado for their kindness, advice, support, and extremely good company over the twelve years we have known each other. Alison also provided invaluable research assistance along with Natalia Casanovas and Sergio Marín. Many, many thanks to Alan and Lidia Shave, Winston Moore, Kate Ford, and all at the Anglo Bolivian Societies both in London and La Paz for giving me many opportunities to present and for your generous engagement with my work. My conversations with Edgar Pacheco, former director of the Municipal Government's Research and Data team, have been invaluable, both for his comprehensive knowledge of La Paz and for the extremely good coffee. Marvin Acebey's expertise in finance, enterprise development, and the textiles sector helped me immeasurably in the development of my research and fieldwork in El Alto and La Paz. Over the years I benefited from many insightful conversations with Susanna Rance and Amaru Villaneuva Rance, director for the Centre for Social Research and founder of Bolivian Express. Amaru passed away at a tragically young age just as this manuscript was being finished. His humor, wisdom, and generosity will never be forgotten.

My colleagues in the Social Communication Department of the University Católica were great to work with on the "Urban X-Rays from the Global South" symposium in 2018. Special thanks to Guadalupe Peres Cajías, whose expertise and energy made this an unforgettable event, and to Claudio Rossell Arce, Rafael Loayza Bueno, the brilliant students on the Social Communication degree, and to everyone who contributed to the conference, including Joana Barros, Fernanda Wanderley, and Virginia Manzano. Many thanks to Pablo Mamani for the opportunity to present at the Universidad Pública de El Alto and for the engagement of the students and staff there. I have also over the years benefited from the expertise of the La Paz–based international scholars Nico Tassi and Linda Farthing.

In the UK, deepest gratitude to Enrique Castañón Ballivián, who has been so much more than a research assistant over the past fifteen years. He has worked with me on research projects I have carried out in both Bolivia and Colombia, and as a native of La Paz his analysis and insights have been invaluable in the writing of this book. Many thanks to my mentors, formal and informal, in Latin American studies and feminist geography—Ann Varley, Nina Laurie, and Ruth Pearson—and to Roger Burrows, who now knows more about Bolivia than he ever thought he would. I appreciate the support of colleagues at King's College London; Birkbeck, University of London; Northumbria University; and University College London; and in the Development Geographies and Gender and Feminist Geographies Research Groups of the Royal Geographical Society. Many thanks for the opportunities to present research seminars at the University of Cambridge, University of East Anglia, University of Newcastle, and the University of East London.

Special thanks to my dear family and friends who have tolerated repeated requests to read chapters and "just think out loud"—John Maclean, Helen Edling, Lucinda Towler, Debby Potts, and Shahla Tizro. The wonderful David Green has accompanied me on many journeys, including two to Bolivia—thank you for your way of seeing the world. And of course my parents, Mary Maclean and George Maclean (1940–2019), for their unwavering support, belief, and curiosity about the mystery of things.

Research for this project has been supported by the following awards: ESRC Studentship Award (PTA 030 2004 00186), 2004–7; British Academy Small Grant (SG101208), 2009–10; and Leverhulme Trust Fellowship (RF-2015–331), 2015–17.

Unless otherwise indicated, all translations of quotations from interviews and texts from Spanish to English are my own. The responsibility for errors and omissions in this text is entirely my own.

Abbreviations

ALBA	Alianza Bolivariana para los Pueblos de Nuestra América (Bolivarian Alliance for the Peoples of Our America)
ASARBOLSEM	Asociación Artesanal Boliviana Señor de Mayo (Association of Bolivian Artisans Señor de Mayo)
BCB	Banco Central de Bolivia (Central Bank of Bolivia)
BDP	Banco de Desarrollo Productivo (Productive Development Bank)
CCSF	Comité de la Coordinación de las Seis Federaciones (Coordination Committee of the Six Federations)
CIDOB	Confederación de Pueblos Indígenas de Bolivia (Confederation of Bolivian Indigenous Peoples)
COB	Central Obrera Boliviana (Bolivian Workers' Center)
COCAMTROP	Coordinadora de Mujeres Campesinas del Trópico de Cochabamba (Coordinator for Peasant Women of the Tropics of Cochabamba)
COR	Central Obrera Regional (Regional Labor Federation)
CPESC	Coordinadora de Pueblos Étnicos de Santa Cruz (Coordinator for Ethnic Peoples of Santa Cruz)
CSCB	Confederación Sindical de Colonizadores de Bolivia (Union Confederation of Bolivian Settlers)
CSUTCB	Confederación Sindical Única de Trabajadores del Campo de Bolivia (Confederation of Peasant Workers of Bolivia)
EGTK	Ejército Guerrillero Túpac Katari (Túpac Katari Guerrilla Army)
FEJUVE	Federación de Juntas Vecinales (Federation of Neighborhood Boards)
FSL	Financial Services Law (Ley de Servicios Financieros)
FTG	Federación de Trabajadores Gremiales (Federation of Street Traders)

GC	Grupo Comuna (Comuna Group)
IFI	international financial institution
IMF	International Monetary Fund
MAS	Movimiento al Socialismo (Movement toward Socialism)
MCD	modernity/coloniality/decoloniality
MFI	microfinance institution
MNR	Movimiento Nacional Revolucionario (Revolutionary Nationalist Movement)
MSM	Movimiento sin Miedo (Movement without Fear)
SME	small and medium-sized enterprise
SUCRE	Sistema Unificado de Compensación Regional de Pagos (Unified System for Regional Compensation)
TIPNIS	Territorio Indígena y Parque Nacional Isiboro Sécure (Isiboro Sécure National Park and Indigenous Territory)
USAID	United States Agency for International Development

Introduction

Pluri-economy in Bolivia

On January 26, 2006, Evo Morales was inaugurated as Latin America's first indigenous president, an office he occupied until his resignation on November 11, 2019. His almost fourteen years in power saw remarkable—some would say revolutionary—changes in the political, economic, and social fabric of his country. Morales and the Movimiento al Socialismo (MAS; Movement toward Socialism) had been elected on a platform of anti-neoliberalism and pluriculturalism, and they promised to restore Bolivian sovereignty over the economy and natural resources, reduce poverty and inequality, and ensure cultural diversity and autonomy. To this end, the MAS, within six months of being elected, renegotiated contracts with international companies for the exploitation of Bolivia's significant hydrocarbon resources. The nationalization of oil and gas was announced on May 1, 2006, and the following day the papers were full of pictures of soldiers, mostly of indigenous, rural backgrounds, holding banners outside oil refineries and gas stations declaring "Nacionalizado: Propiedad de los Bolivianos"—"Nationalized: Property of the Bolivian People." The renegotiated contracts gave the Bolivian state a significantly increased percentage of profits from the sale of Bolivian hydrocarbons, which they promised to invest in a redistribution and welfare strategy. In the same year, the MAS government commenced preparations for a new constitution that would reflect Bolivia's diversity and redress the exclusions created by centuries of colonialism and decades of neoliberalism. The Constituent Assembly was formed in 2006 in order to debate and consider the possibilities of a post-neoliberal, decolonized order in which social movements would be directly involved in the country's government and indigenous peoples would have autonomy. Bolivia would then become a "plurinational state."

The new constitution was approved by referendum in 2009, and its opening paragraph reads:

> Bolivia is constituted as a Unitary Social State of Pluri-National Communitarian Law that is free, independent, sovereign, democratic, inter-cultural, decentralized and with autonomies. Bolivia is founded on plurality and on political, economic, juridical, cultural and linguistic pluralism in the integration process of the country. (Constitution of 2009, Article 1)

This is by no means the first time that plurality has been used to define a nation, but the meaning of plurality in the Bolivian Constitution draws specifically on the relationality at the heart of indigenous cosmology and Latin American scholarship on colonialism and modernity. The sense of plurality evoked here rests on the relational logic of the Andean cosmovision, in which "relationality is the main and fundamental principle of reality, everything is related, nothing can be an abstraction or exist on its own" (Querejazu 2016, 9), and the *pluriverse*, summed up by the Zapatistas in the phrase "un mundo donde quepan muchos mundos"—a world in which many worlds fit. The pluriverse has mutuality, reciprocity, and cooperation at the heart of its metaphysics, as opposed to the atomistic rule of noncontradiction that is the starting point of Western logic. It recognizes a plurality of epistemologies and hermeneutics and so goes beyond approaches to diversity that remain couched in liberal individual rational choice or Marxist dialectical logic. To contextualize this specifically Latin American approach to plurality, points of contrast include "cultural plurality," referring to the preservation of minority cultures within the dominant legal system, and multiculturalism, in which different cultural norms are valued equally within a liberal framework. The plurality of the Bolivian Constitution hence indicates a radical, penetrating vision of diversity and inclusion in which the very values and ways of knowing behind politics, jurisprudence, economy, language, and culture are called into question. The assertion specifically of economic plurality in the 2009 Constitution invites a rethinking of key economic notions of value, exchange, scale, time and production, as well as a reimagining of the cast of tropes that populate economic narratives and which frequently associate femininity with motherhood and indigeneity with the rural and traditional.

The idea of pluri-economy accommodates the MAS's dual aims of post-neoliberalism and pluriculturalism and goes beyond liberal approaches to diversity and inclusion by recognizing that the economy itself is culturally situated. Pluri-economy is defined in the 2009 Constitution as "composed of forms of community, state, private and public cooperative economic organization" (Article 306.II) and "based on the principles of complementariness, reciprocity, solidarity, redistribution, equality, legal security, sustainability, equilibrium, justice and transparency" (Article 306.III). This framework recognizes that cultural communities are composed of reciprocity, cooperation, and gift giving, and that as such communities can be corroded by liberal and neoliberal policies built on the utility-maximizing, competitive individual at the heart of orthodox economic theory. The recognition of the role of the state and the importance of public investment also represents a rejection of the neoliberal orthodoxy that seeks to maximize the private sector. However, the state is a colonial institution, and the power accorded to the state in the MAS vision, albeit with a view to decolonizing institutions of power, did not sit well with indigenous demands for autonomy.

Creating an indigenous popular hegemony based on community at the level of national governance posed one of the many "creative tensions" (García Linera 2011) the MAS faced in implementing its postneoliberal, pluricultural agenda. Intellectuals and activists involved in developing MAS strategy and theorizing pluri-economy sought a formulation that incorporated the Marxist, class-based rejection of neoliberalism as well as cooperative, reciprocal economic institutions and traditions that could underpin indigenous autonomy and demands for decolonization. This was achieved by bringing Gramscian ideas of civil society and cultural hegemony into dialogue with Bolivian theorists who had highlighted the importance of diversity and redress for the violences of colonialism. *Suma qamaña* or *vivir bien*—living well—the Andean vision of reciprocal community and human/nature relations, was adopted as the "articulating axis" of Marxist and indigenous ideas and was the unifying ethos of the new plurinational Constitution of 2009 (Avendaño 2009). However, tensions quickly emerged between this notion and the MAS's reliance on extractive industries, and between the pastoral construction of indigeneity implied by *suma qamaña* and the lived experiences of people of indigenous descent earning their living in popular markets based on community organization, and negotiating modernity on their own terms (Martínez Novo 2018; Stefanoni 2012).

The underpinning logic of pluri-economy theoretically provides a basis for the valorization of social reproduction and community labor—work that is generally performed by women and coded as feminine but is overlooked in orthodox economic policies focused on maximizing productivity and income generation (Stewart 1992). Care and community relations are not valorized in terms of utility to production or income generation, but they can have value via the principles of reciprocity and solidarity that underpin pluri-economy. The constitutional recognition that indigenous traditions underpin community and economic activity and therefore are of value in themselves rather than, for example, being of commercial value in craft markets, potentially valorizes the work in maintaining traditions and community bonds that typically falls to women. However, neither the text of the 2009 Constitution nor the theorizing behind pluri-economy explicitly discusses the gendered implications of this idea, as the focus was on the unification of class-based and indigenous agendas. The MAS addressed gender inequality as an element of decolonization, arguing that gender itself was a colonial imposition and that the international discourse of gender equality was based on a Western ideal of individual empowerment which perpetuated the exclusion of indigenous community and households. By contrast, the Andean notion of *chachawarmi*—complementary but equal gender roles—would frame the MAS's approach to the inclusion of women, girls, and femininity.

Nevertheless, from the moment the MAS was elected there were concerns that, in the words of prominent feminist critic María Galindo, "No saldrá Eva de la costilla de Evo"—Eve would not come from Evo's rib (Galindo 2006b). The de facto limits on women's attenuated participation in unions and social movements and the gendered construction of power on Bolivia's left, which is frequently deemed *machista,* were focal points of the Bolivian feminist critique of the MAS. The conservative framing of *chachawarmi* was summed up by Aymara feminist Julieta Paredes with the phrase "the woman cooks and the man eats, what lovely complementarity" (personal communication, May 2006); Paredes also pointed out the continued patriarchal exploitation and high levels of violence that were hidden by this idealized image of the Andean household. The heteronormativity of this ideal, the pressure it places on single women to be in a partnership, and the shame associated with single motherhood were all disputed by Bolivian feminist organizations. There were also concerns that indigenous women were integrated into the economy only on conservative terms that essentialized their position in the reproductive sector and their role as wives and mothers (Galindo 2006a).

Despite the fact that the markets of the Andes are known for being feminine spaces in which women of indigenous descent demonstrate their business acumen, the characterization of indigenous women in the Bolivian Constitution of 2009 identifies femininity almost entirely with the reproductive role and associates indigeneity with rurality. The everyday lives of the women in rural production who sell in the competitive markets of Bolivia's rapidly expanding cities, the indigenous woman selling secondhand clothes from the United States, the designer of new *pollera* fashions (the traditional Andean outfit of a pleated skirt, derby hat, and shawl) who shows her collection at New York fashion week, and the powerful, rich *chola paceña* whose real estate investments are transforming the cultural map of La Paz and El Alto, all defy these characterizations. Their livelihood strategies represent a reinterpretation of key economic terms—nation, production, scale, exchange, time, and competition—as they move from rural production and community relations to the markets of El Alto, negotiate the pressures of tradition and modernity, and, in the process, remap the assumptions about gender and indigeneity that are present in both orthodox and heterodox economic theory, as well as the MAS's vision of pluri-economy. Their experiences provide a conceptual framework by which to analyze the vision, conceptualization, and policies of pluri-economy in Bolivia over the course of Morales's administration.

The MAS in Power

The MAS's ascension to power was part of Latin America's *marea rosa*, the "pink tide" that saw the election of governments rejecting neoliberalism and adopting left-wing policies to varying degrees across the continent. The left-wing governments associated with the pink tide are often characterized on a spectrum ranging from the "populism" of Hugo Chávez in Venezuela to the "pragmatism" of Lula da Silva in Brazil, a distinction that has also been simplistically divided into the "bad left" and the "good left" (Ellner 2019). Associations are frequently made between Morales's Bolivia, Chávez's Venezuela, and Rafael Correa's Ecuador at the populist, and redder, edge of the *marea rosa*. Each of these countries implemented state-led reforms based on resources from nationalized industries, and both Bolivia in 2006 and Ecuador in 2009 became members of ALBA (Alianza Bolivariana para los Pueblos de Nuestra América; Bolivarian Alliance for the Peoples of Our America), a trading bloc initiated by the governments of Cuba and Venezuela to develop regional solidarity and integration. However, there are important institutional and economic differences between these nations. While both Ecuador and Bolivia adopted state-led modernization strategies and explicit constitutional recognition of indigenous institutions and cosmovisions, Bolivia did not centralize power to the same extent as Ecuador (Eaton 2014), and it adopted a more pragmatic approach to the renationalization of privatized industries (Webber 2011). The Bolivian state had to strike a balance between its revolutionary aims and confrontation with the power of economic elites in the wealthy department of Santa Cruz. Of the three countries, Bolivia had the largest "informal" sector in 2006, at over two-thirds of the economy, and it has grown since (Medina and Scheidner 2018). Although the characterization of "informal" disguises the multiplicity of activities involved in the country's popular markets, it does indicate the limited extension of the state and "formal" regulations (Coen, Ross, and Turner 2008). Contrary to speculation particularly from orthodox critics, Bolivia has not suffered the economic decline and hyperinflation that beset Venezuela, largely because of the checks on presidential power provided by the social movements upon which the MAS depended, the strength of indigenous resistance, and the need to find consensus with economic elites (Albro and McCarthy 2018).

Over the period in question the MAS had many successes—including the fastest-growing economy in the region and a reduction in inequality that exceeded that of comparable countries (Farthing and Kohl 2014). There was an upheaval in the country's social and political landscape that challenged the continued colonial construction of public institutions and the dominance of traditional elites. The MAS's key successes were to increase the state's share of hydrocarbon industries and reduce inequality and poverty by reinvesting this wealth into welfare and modernization programs. Redistribution of wealth to indigenous groups was demonstrably more effective than under previous governments (Hicks et al. 2018). There was substantial investment in infrastructure, including the striking alpine cable car, the Teleférico, which traverses La

Paz and El Alto (McNelly 2020b). Modernization projects provided work contracts for "unskilled" construction labor, which favored the indigenous, working-class population, and the social and spatial mobilities enabled by transport infrastructure changed the cultural map of Bolivia's cities. Greater distribution of wealth was accompanied by a powerful sense of confidence and entitlement to public space and power for those who were previously excluded. Measures to decolonize public space and government administration have been conspicuous in the symbolism of state institutions, which display the indigenous flag—the *wiphala*—alongside the Bolivian tricolor. Indigenous languages were made official in Morales's first term, and knowledge of an indigenous language became a requirement for public servants, a condition that challenged colonial epistemological hierarchies as urban elites had to learn from native speakers of Aymara and Quechua (Gustafson 2017).

The successes of the MAS are frequently attributed to its administration's coinciding with the best economic decade Bolivia had seen due to the global commodities boom at the beginning of the twenty-first century. Concern was expressed, however, that the revenues from these resources led to a greater centralization of power within the state and in the charismatic persona of Morales as president than had been anticipated in the 2009 Constitution. Critics feared that Morales and his party ruled by cabal, particularly given his decision to stand for a fourth term, despite referendum results to the contrary (Farthing 2019). The MAS also suffered numerous and damning corruption scandals, frequently involving high-profile women. Examples include the case of the management of the Fondo Indígena, in which eleven million bolivianos (approximately $1,592,000 U.S.) intended to support indigenous people's production in rural areas was put into the personal bank account of the fund's *directora*, Melva Hurtado, who was consequently detained and imprisoned (Puente 2015), and the only minister to resign and be charged was Nemesia Achacollo (*Latin News* 2015). There was also the much-sensationalized case of Gabriela Zapata, the woman who alleged that Morales was the father of her child and who was convicted of "influence peddling" for securing government contracts for the Chinese firm that employed her (Collyns 2016). These scandals gave succor to those who have always said that Morales's government lacked the technical capacity to govern—a judgment frequently expressed in racist terms. These incidents also raised questions about how women who were given positions of responsibility in the government were treated in the MAS administration.

Divisions that the notion of pluri-economy intended to unite—particularly in relation to the state and civil society and to indigenous autonomy—were at the crux of prominent controversies that marred the MAS's time in government. The highest profile of these disputes was the proposed road through the Territorio Indígena y Parque Nacional Isiboro Sécure (TIPNIS; Isiboro Sécure National Park and Indigenous Territory), which set modernization against the reciprocal vision of human-nature relations that was central to indigenous politics and activism, and national-level economic development against indigenous territorial governance. The national government defended the construction of the road in terms of access to social rights, including health care, for the indigenous communities living there. Activists in those communities objected, however, that constitutionally mandated consultation processes had not been carried out and that the road represented a developmentalist, masculinist vision of modernization which trumped the priority that had been previously accorded to *vivir bien* and community hegemony (Hope 2021). The case became iconic on the global environmental stage, and Vice President Álvaro García Linera responded by accusing foreign activists of "environmental colonialism" and of holding an essentialized, picture-postcard view of indigeneity (Hirsch 2019, 821). This conflict demonstrated the fault lines between the unification of a class-based redistribution strategy and indigenous autonomy that was at the heart of the MAS and its vision of pluri-economy. Feminist organizations were vociferous in their condemnation of the masculinist, developmentalist agenda that had become dominant over the community, relational, and decolonial approach to development that had been promised (Rivera Cusicanqui 2015). The government's defense of its actions, however, also demonstrated the inadequacies of the association of indigeneity and rurality present in its own documentation.

Support for the MAS in peri-urban areas had been crucial to its success in the 2005 elections. There is constant mobility between the markets of El Alto and rural areas as people go back and forth to sell their produce. Peri-urban areas and the popular markets that characterize them provided the space for rural unions to articulate with social movements and urban networks, and so extend MAS reach and support (Lazar 2008). However, over the course of the MAS administration the informal markets in these areas were also sites of controversy and conflict. One example was the protest in response to the *gasolinazo*—a sudden removal of state subsidies on fuel which increased the price of gasoline and diesel by 70 percent, the largest price increase in thirty years. This was enacted by decree on December 25, 2010, but the strength of resistance was such, including massive demonstrations involving the powerful transport unions, that the decree was annulled within a week. The removal of subsidies had been defended in terms of national sovereignty and preventing contraband across the border with Peru, where Bolivian fuel could be sold at a profit. However, critics pointed out that informal workers, who constituted around two-thirds of the population, would be hardest hit by the change (Achtenberg 2011). This particular incident was one of a number of controversies that demonstrated the lacunae in MAS theory and policy around urban indigeneity and informality in the development of pluri-economy.

Informality and Popular Markets

Structuralist analyses characterize the expansion of informal economic activities since the 1980s as evidence of the iniquities and exploitations of neoliberal capital. For the structuralist, informal economies are not excluded from capitalist modernity but are rather "the expression of the uneven nature of capitalist development" (Rakowski 1994, 504). The evidence demonstrating the lack of stability, minimal infrastructure, and high rates of inequality and poverty in informal areas is compelling (e.g., Davis 2006). The rapid growth in the late twentieth century of informal markets and settlements in El Alto and La Paz was indeed a result of the iniquitous impacts of the neoliberal reforms of the 1980s, as people, particularly women, were forced to turn to makeshift income-generating strategies as formal, stable employment was decimated. However, on this traditional Marxist account, those working in informal economies lack the potential for revolutionary organization that an industrialized proletariat could generate. This position is entrenched by the neoliberal romanticization of people's coping strategies as free-market self-sufficiency and empowerment, which overlooks the systematic patterns of exploitation that informal, peri-urban markets represent. However, the autonomy, resistance, and power that are frequently evident in the accounts of those—even the poorest—earning their livelihoods in this way can be conspicuous in their absence from structuralist accounts, and the assumption of the need for state regulation and safety nets is built on the experience of the state as developed in Western Europe. Theorizing the agency of those working in informal economies without losing sight of oppressive structural conditions or the implications of extending a state bureaucracy and regulation in a postcolonial context has been recognized as a crucial challenge for the left: "The key is to take seriously the subjective figures that appear when one avoids the all-encompassing pretense of victimization" (Gago 2017, 102).

The centrality of peri-urban areas and social movements, rather than proletarian movements, to Bolivia's overthrow of global corporations inspired the MAS's rise to power, as will be discussed in chapter 1. The conceptualization and vision of pluri-economy drew on autonomous Marxism and Bolivian political theorists to capture the diversity of actors that came together in the gas and water wars of the early twenty-first century. The words "motley" (Zavaleta Mercado 2002), "baroque" (García Linera 2008a), and "fractal" (Raquel Gutiérrez cited in Gago 2017, 46) were used to describe coinciding patterns of accumulation and dispossession, associated with different historical time periods, that had produced such multiple yet unified protests against transnational corporations. Building on this work, and in specific reference to Latin American informal markets, Gago proposed the term "baroque economies" to theorize "the type of articulation of economies that mixes logics and rationalities that tend to be portrayed (in economic and political theories) as incompatible" (2017, 14), hence complicating the core–periphery arguments that characterize structural analyses of informality. When these ideas were being developed in Bolivia, however, there was criticism that urban indigeneity, which finds its clearest expression in the popular peri-urban markets of Bolivian cities, was being overlooked, as were the gendered dimensions of Bolivia's "motley" diversity. What's more, the implementation of pluri-economy reverted increasingly to standard heterodox policies of modernization that relied on an extractivist state, which in effect replicated structuralist constructions of informality.

Much post-Marxist feminist research on informality centers on empirical and ethnographic work with those working in peri-urban, popular markets around the world and the epistemological and political challenge of using, but also abusing, theory (Gibson-Graham 1996, 2006).

This involves taking the multiple, contradictory interpretations of lived experiences and everyday realities—with all the complexities that those terms imply—as key parameters in the analysis. Despite accusations of this work not being "political" (e.g., Glassman 2003), such everyday strategies can "crack" capitalism (Holloway 2010), provide the space for new autonomous geographies (Pickerill and Chatterton 2006), and be true to the anthropologist's challenge that our theories need to be close to research participants' concerns (Moore 2011). The political potential of this work lies in rewriting the scripts and abusing terms of absence that place these views in alterity, without losing sight of consistent patterns of exclusion and oppression. In doing so, this approach can also reveal the conceptual biases that consistently render the feminine invisible, trivialized, underestimated, and a consistent lacuna in both orthodox and critical theories.

One such term of absence is "informality" itself. The word "informal" categorizes myriad livelihood strategies, mostly adopted by women, according to their lack of formality, hence continuing a pattern in which the feminine is placed in alterity. In doing so, the term accords "formality" more stability than is warranted given the contested nature of governance and the colonial history behind formal state institutions (Meagher 2013). While the formal/informal divide can still have its uses (McFarlane 2019), increasingly the phrase "popular economy" is favored, which "embodies the various efforts undertaken by those with no, partial or unsustainable access to wage labour not only to generate a viable livelihood but . . . to participate in larger circuits of sociality and to elaborate the semblance [of] a public infrastructure" (Simone 2019, 618). This approach draws the focus to the actually existing institutions, logics, and social relations that are obscured by dominant notions of formality. The inadequacies of the term "informal" are nowhere more evident than in Bolivia, where peri-urban markets have their roots in long histories of rural-urban migration and networks maintained by Andean institutions of cooperation (Tassi 2017). The term "popular" also represents the power of these markets vis-à-vis the Bolivian state, which historically has lacked the extension and legitimacy to make claims to formality.

To appreciate the radical potential of popular markets it is necessary to reconsider the narrative that constructs informal microbusinesses and petty commerce as the negative local effects of globalization, and therefore a threat to national production. This means playing with assumptions—both orthodox and critical—about scale. Challenging scale is central to decolonial epistemology, which seeks to overturn Western thought's universalizing tendencies, which render "other" forms of knowledge particular and local (Santos 2015). Abstractions to the global macro-economy, which place the benefits to global financial flows and the stability of the global macro-economy above the hardships generated "on the ground," exemplify this dynamic. Geographers and anthropologists, however, have observed how the local both constitutes and reworks the global and that analyses which assume vertical or nested scalar structures, typified by the "Russian doll" of global, regional, national, and local, can perpetuate the political hierarchies they seek to overturn (Marston, Jones, and Woodward 2005; Nagar et al. 2002). Hierarchies of scale that place the global above the local recreate gendered dichotomies of economy/culture, technical/natural, and universal/particular, as well as the gendered script of globalization that positions the global as the perpetrator and the local as the penetrated victim (Freeman 2001).

Alternative views of scale propose a flat ontology, which focuses on the flows of people, ideas, and things around the world, the networks, assemblages, and patterns of accumulation, dispossession, and exploitation that are created (Escobar 2007a). A flat ontology demands that "the largest entities, territorial entities like kingdoms, empires and nation-states, should be considered to be every bit as singular and unique as local communities and organisations" (DeLanda 2008, 166). This metaphysics allows a relational understanding of political and economic processes rather than a hierarchical one. These realist ontologies, which do not extrapolate or generalize to the reified abstract of the global, are associated with work on informatics and the virtual and with the interactions and networks that are possible without any meaningful direction from "above" (e.g., Gandy 2005). However, the activities of women trading in rural production and peri-urban markets on the Bolivian Altiplano also exemplify this relational, nonhierarchical approach to scale. Historically, the market women *de pollera* of the Altiplano—*cholas*—are renowned for the networks they have formed nationally and internationally as they travel to trade and exchange produce. These networks, as we will see, are recreated in contemporary La Paz and El Alto, where global flows of goods, enabled by transnational networks of local traders, are remade, resold, and reinterpreted in ways that demonstrate the simultaneity and inherent relationality of local and global. The challenge these women's livelihood strategies pose to analyses that postulate a hierarchical scale are all the more potent because their bodies—indigenous and feminine—are themselves coded "local," with accompanying assumptions of tradition, family, and household.

Implicit assumptions about time can also disguise the worth of women's work and feminized labor. The rhythms of repetition and recreation associated with reproductive labor are trivialized in a context that values progress, often represented by the metaphor of an arrow of time illustrating how technological advances produce order from chaos—in a word, modernity. Extractivism exemplifies this modernist view of time as energy is harnessed from nature for production. Indigenous people's resistance to extractive industries can fall into the trap of reinscribing them as modernity's other—the local, the traditional, the parochial. I seek to complicate this picture by focusing on the work of women in Bolivia's popular markets, and in particular those involved in selling and making clothes—items that are date-stamped with the ideas of the contemporary inherent in notions of fashion. Rather than directly opposing the exclusions of modernity, an empirical focus on the multiple rhythms and patterns of time represented by repetition, recycling, remaking, and reproduction can better diagnose the exploitations and exclusions experienced by those othered by capitalist modernity, as well as the West's self-appointed entitlement to decide what counts as the contemporary.

Despite the relative absence of discussion of the informal, popular economy in the theoretical vision of pluri-economy, and the ambivalence around the imbrications of indigeneity and urbanity in official discourse, the popular markets of El Alto have flourished since the MAS took power. Bolivia's new urban Aymara bourgeoisie made international headlines and introduced a trope that challenges some of the received wisdom of international development and politics: the wealthy, modern, indigenous *comerciante*. The spectacular architecture and fashions this new consuming class has developed have gained international attention; the eye-catching facades of Aymara architect Freddy Mamani were exhibited in Paris, and the *pollera* outfits of Aymara designer Eliana Paco Paredes were shown in New York. In Bolivia this conspicuous consumption was frequently associated with the political favors granted to indigenous markets from whom the MAS does not appear to collect as much tax as it does from formal enterprises. Accusations of involvement in narcotraffic are repeatedly leveled against the new Aymara bourgeoisie, and while there is evidence that involvement in cocaine production has increased, the assumption that their wealth is *necessarily* derived from illicit, as opposed to informal, trade is incorrect and overlooks the historical development of indigenous wealth (Toranzo 2020). Over 60 percent of the Bolivian economy remains "informal," the largest "shadow economy" in the world (Medina and Schneider 2018), a statistic that highlights how inappropriate it is to define these myriad livelihood activities by what they lack. The fact that the majority of Bolivia's economy falls into this category should itself call into question the imposition of the formal/informal divide, without losing sight of the vulnerabilities and exploitations that can be indicated by the word "informal." Although standards of living have increased, the percentage of the Bolivian population in poverty remains the highest in the region, and indigenous women are overrepresented among the poorest and tend to work in the most vulnerable and insecure sectors (Lundvall et al. 2015). Nevertheless, this period of rapid social and economic change, enabled by the MAS's approach to redistribution and decolonization, opened up the space for the gendered economic tropes underpinning scripts of marginalization to be challenged and renegotiated.

Methodology

This book develops an analytical framework based on the livelihoods of women whose everyday strategies demonstrate the inadequacies of the conceptual building blocks of even critical theories of the economy. The aim is to deconstruct the underpinning concepts of pluri-economic policies to bring out dynamics of gender and ethnicity, and consider which feminine economic subjects are "permitted" in the pluri-economic worldview. The book explores the livelihood strategies of those who are dealing not just with the formal processes of change initiated by the MAS and its commitment to pluri-economy but also with the ongoing influences of the globalized economy, the effects—intended and unintended—of the MAS modernization strategy, and the opportunities that the country's economic boom has brought to those working in popular markets. The focus of much recent research on Bolivia has been neo-extractivism (Anthias 2018; Gustafson 2020; Postero 2017), and the state's appropriation of hydrocarbons has had an influence on each of the sectors explored here. The strength of the boliviano was maintained via the foreign reserves accrued due to the high price of gas, which has in turn facilitated the import of clothing and textiles and a boom in construction. Some of the political discourses surrounding neo-extraction have created a simplistic dichotomy between rural indigenous communities and urban *comerciantes*. Using the everyday strategies of those working in popular markets as a basis to deconstruct the terms of political economic debate in Bolivia will add to the work that seeks to complicate the picture of indigenous tradition versus capitalist neo-extractivism.

The empirical chapters of this book focus on three sectors in which indigenous women have transgressed expectations, and so broken conceptual molds that associate indigeneity with rurality, and femininity with reproduction. These three sectors—finance, textiles and clothing, and construction—exemplify the challenges of balancing cultural, community, and economic exchanges and illustrate the tensions inherent in recognizing plurality and autonomy within a state-led economy. The artificiality of the divisions between capital and culture and between formality and informality are uncovered by exploring the institutions channeling financial flows and the role of cash in recreating networks and traditions of gift exchange. The importance to economic activity of cultural identity and the gendered burden of recreating tradition is made clear with an exploration of clothes. Clothes symbolize the national and indigenous identities that underpin plurality and illustrate Bolivia's position in global production chains via which textiles and garments flow. The exploration of construction, particularly in the context of a worldwide speculation-fueled real estate boom, brings out politicized and racialized definitions of laundering, speculation, and corruption. In the particular case of Bolivia, where the new rich are of Aymara, rural origin, the emerging urban landscape in La Paz challenges the division between rural and urban identities and aesthetic imaginings of future cities.

The empirical basis of this book is the research I have been conducting in Bolivia since 2006, the year Evo Morales was inaugurated as president and Bolivia's hydrocarbons were nationalized. I have had the opportunity to follow the remarkable transformations over the subsequent thirteen years, including the formal policies to build a more inclusive economy, developments in the macro-economy (notably the resource boom), and the continued influence of global capital, particu-larly from China. The three projects I conducted in Bolivia were on microfinance (2004–8), contraband in used clothes (2010–11), and the new Aymara bourgeoisie (2015–17). Although these projects were in-dependent from each other and separately funded, there is significant continuity between them, and they represent startling transformations in Bolivian society over this period. In 2006, Bolivia was the poorest country in Latin America and the recipient of significant aid and debt relief, but also a reference point worldwide for its microfinance insti-tutions. In 2016, some of the women recipients of microfinance loans I had met a decade prior introduced me to key informants among the Aymara bourgeoisie. It is also rumored that one Aymara woman, who now owns a shopping mall in a wealthy commercial area of La Paz, used to sell used clothes on the street. Not all have experienced such dra-matic upward mobility, but the successes and failures of these women demonstrate that the political and economic terrain has shifted seismi-cally over this period.

The underlying curiosity in each of these research projects was how women marginalized by gender, indigeneity, and locality earn a living. The political and economic strategies of the MAS toward achieving a pluri-economy and the radical rejection of neoliberal orthodoxy that this represented are critiqued on the basis of the wide diversity of eco-nomic strategies employed by indigenous women to survive and thrive. Their various understandings of the economy, the traditions that under-pin exchange, their priorities, their cultural values and identities, and their views of the local, national, and global all provide a penetrating critique of some of the fundaments of political and economic theory.

The formal methods used—interviews, focus groups, document analysis—anchored each project, but the interactions I had in the places where I stayed in Bolivia allowed me to become more aware of, and therefore challenge, the conceptual scheme by which I interpret the world: "to see the colonial difference, and emphatically resist [my] epistemological habit of erasing it" (Lugones 2010, 753). The aim of my research from the outset was to "abuse" (in the deconstructive sense; see Gallop 1994) powerful economic ideas on the basis of how they were being negotiated and worked "from below" by women marginalized in various ways. This process involved facing the limits of words and translation as well as the multiple ethical, political, and epistemological

challenges of cross-cultural research (Maclean 2007) in order to see the
coloniality of these global processes and how they are being "adapted,
adopted, rejected, integrated or ignored" as "global designs meet local
histories" (Mignolo cited in Lugones 2010, 752). This summary of my
fieldwork focuses on the places where I was based that were constructed
as "local" but where the "global" was recreated and challenged, resulting in dynamic political economic landscapes of which I was temporarily a part. I reflect below on how I was being perceived and interpreted,
how these interactions changed over time, and how, and to what extent, these experiences challenged my own assumptions. Research is
not static, and the way relationships with the people I have stayed with
in Bolivia have developed reflect my processes of "unlearning" (Spivak
1994) which formed the conceptual basis of this analysis.

My first period of fieldwork in Bolivia was for nine months in 2006,
during which time I stayed in the inter-Andean valley of Luribay. Luribay is an Aymara-speaking, fruit-producing valley in the department
of La Paz, and at the time of my research it had a population of just
over eleven thousand. In the middle of the valley is Luribay Town, from
which two roads lead to the southeast and northwest, connecting a total
of seventy-eight hamlets. The Town was the location of the colonial administration, and people there tend to primarily speak Spanish and describe themselves with the urban-inflected *vecinos*—neighbors—rather
than *campesinos*—peasants. The hamlets are administered by agrarian
unions rather than neighborhood associations, and the majority of
women there are *de pollera*. While most in the hamlets also speak Spanish, Aymara is the primary language. During the harvest months families travel to the cities to sell their produce in the markets or to stock up
their shops, guesthouses, and inns. The journey to and from the valley
is notorious, as there are only two steep roads leaving from the valley
to Highway 1 on the Altiplano, and while the drive to La Paz could take
as little as seven hours, it frequently took far longer. There are continuous
visits back and forth to the cities, and households extend to the various
properties where Luribayeños regularly stay in El Alto (Maclean 2014).

While in Luribay, I was lodged with an elderly couple whose adult
children I had met socially in El Alto on my first visit there via Bolivian
friends in England. Their mother was participating in a microfinance
scheme in Luribay, where the family had land, and she had kindly let me
stay with her. This first period of fieldwork formed the basis—both in

terms of access and theoretical framework—of my subsequent research in Bolivia. I stayed with Doña M. and Don P. in Pocuma, the first community encountered on entering Luribay from the winding, unpaved road down en route from La Paz. Doña M. and Don P. earned a living from their crops—potatoes, peaches, and peas—which Doña M. sold in the city, and they ran a small café and shop at the entrance to the hamlet from the main road. They also had a truck that provided transport for those in Pocuma traveling to the cities to sell their produce. While staying in Pocuma, I attended the biweekly meetings of ten microfinance groups in the valley, conducted twenty-four semi-structured interviews with women who had taken out microfinance loans as part of a group, and held two focus groups. However, the bulk of my time in Luribay was with Doña M. as she took on the various arduous tasks involved in reproductive labor in a context where the water supply is limited and there is no time-saving technology. I worked alongside her as she went through a schedule of cleaning, tending to land, pruning trees, looking after animals, preparing food, getting supplies, and tending to the shop, all alongside a delicate balancing of community relationships and trust. I also attended public meetings of the agrarian unions in Pocuma and the municipality in Luribay Town—the administrative center of the valley. Each community had an annual fiesta, the preparations for which involved months of practicing, forming troupes, and acquiring festive sponsorship. I was invited to dance in two of the *entradas* (festival parades)—one in the Town and one in a hamlet—and became part of the sensitive negotiations involved in allegiance to certain dance troupes, reconciling various debts of sponsorship owed over years, and the strain that the pressure to be in a couple in order to participate fully in the fiesta, and therefore be seen as a legitimate citizen of the area, placed on young people, particularly women.

My time in Luribay allowed me to experience the various tensions involved in cooperation and competition, reputation maintenance, community belonging, and entrepreneurial success, not only as an observer but because I was also being judged on those terms: my decisions about whom I associated with or bought bread from reflected on Doña M., who was quite insistent that I only talk to people *de confianza*—who were trusted. My conversations with Doña M. about this represented in microcosm the encounter of individualist assumptions about consumption and agency with community dynamics. I was familiar with these tensions on paper, and aware that they constituted a false dichotomy in the West as well, where the contradictions and denials involved in belonging to a community in which individualism is a cultural value are frequently underestimated. However, I would not have understood the enormous pressures that the introduction of individualist expectations of empowerment and entrepreneurialism that come with "development" and "modernity" created had I not had to negotiate them in a way that laid bare my own initial suppositions and reactions as out of place.

In 2010, I went back to La Paz to conduct the project on the trade in used clothes, mostly from the United States via Chile, that was occupying increasing space in both Bolivian markets and political commentary. Again, prominent political discourses and economic understandings of the trade seemed to overlook or misrepresent the way these issues were talked about among the people I had met over the course of my research. Before my first period of fieldwork for this project in 2010, I asked contacts in Luribay if they knew of anyone I could stay with in La Paz, and I was put in touch with Doña B. in the neighborhood of Kollasuyo to the north. The people I was lodged with in Kollasuyo were not directly involved in the market for used clothes, but Doña B. was a tailor who specialized in wedding gowns, and our conversations about how clothes and fashion had changed over the years, and how her livelihood had been affected, provided a view that was not represented in national level discussions. I went back to stay with Doña B. on every subsequent trip: in 2011 to finish the used-clothes project; in April 2014 when I first saw the signs of the huge rise in real estate prices in El Alto; again in July–August 2015, July–August 2016, and May 2017 to explore the urban changes related to the Aymara bourgeoisie; and in May 2019 when I co-convened a symposium at the Universidad Católica on urban methodologies. Each time I was a paying guest, but our relationship developed from my initial—exoticized—status as a visiting foreign researcher. Her adult granddaughter, Alicia, an accountancy student, was frequently able to give context to the confusions and cultural misunderstandings that came up in our conversations at home, often in reference to the soaps we watched in the evenings and the family, community, and gendered pressures and expectations they portrayed. Both Alicia and I had lived in Barcelona, although under very different circumstances—I was teaching English for three years, and she was a care worker for an elderly couple. Crucially, as a European Union citizen at the time, I did not have to deal with the formal and informal exclusions and racism faced by a South American whose immigration status was far more complicated to regularize. Nevertheless, Alicia and I developed a relationship that went beyond the divides those structures put in place, and we have shared—often over beer—the various dramas life throws at you.

Both Luribay and Kollasuyo fall through the cracks of national discourses of identity and territory. The MAS discourse on indigenous identity, as we will see in chapter 2, is dominated by organizations from the Altiplano and the coca unions, particularly of the Chapare, where Morales is from. By contrast, Luribay is not strongly unionized and was more penetrated by colonial authorities—many of whom had property there, where the climate is akin to the Mediterranean as compared to the harsh Altiplano extremes. I rarely heard the terms that framed decolonization in Bolivia—*ayllu, chachawarmi, suma kamaña*—in Luribay, although the cooperative, relational cosmovision they represent was embedded in the rituals and traditions of community celebrations and work.

Similarly, the area of Kollasuyo does not feature in political discourse, and many of my interviewees in La Paz found it hard to place. It neighbors the area of Gran Poder, which is associated with the power of the fiesta economy, and Cementerio, one of the largest markets for fruits and vegetables in the city, and one that is also known for criminal activity and violence. Kollasuyo lies just below the crest of the hill that borders El Alto—and specifically La Feria 16 de Julio—the Sixteenth July market fair. It is a residential area where people are of indigenous descent but do not necessarily have the enduring quotidian interactions with people in the countryside that define El Alto. The area developed as one of the main thoroughfares between La Paz and the countryside, and two main, wide arteries converge there—Avenida Entre Ríos and Avenida Kollasuyo. There are multiple mechanics workshops along both of these roads where large trucks can be serviced en route to and from the city. Houses in Kollasuyo are mostly self-built, and many are occupied by lodgers. Contrary to assumptions made about neighborhood communities, people living in these streets do not necessarily know each other. Many were in favor of the Morales government, motivated not least by concerns about the horrors that could return if the far right got back into power, as they remembered the military curfews of the 1980s during which people in this area were shot at if out after a given time. However, Kollasuyo residents have also been caught on the wrong side of the polarizatión that was generated between popular indigenous movements and the elites—for instance, Doña B. was once jeered at by people in a queue for a municipal office because she was not *de pollera*. Staying in these areas also meant that when I talked to political activists and government ministers I did not quite conform to their expectations. I was not an activist, was not staying in any of the university neighborhoods, and was not working with an NGO. I was hence difficult to characterize, and the curiosity about how I had arrived in Kollasuyo may have brought more openness to our conversations.

My mobility around the city, however, was markedly different from Doña B.'s or Alicia's, as my whiteness and general out-of-placeness allowed me to go into spaces that had historically been off-limits to people who were indigenous or mestizo. As an international academic, I was invited to give talks at elite institutions, embassies, and private universities. Although these were welcoming and engaging opportunities, they were littered with moments in which my own class background was given away—table manners, quality of clothes, nerves, family background, accent in English—and created a flicker of surprise among my interlocutors, who had perhaps assumed that a white European academic would feel comfortable in elite environments. These encounters, and my slight unease and shame in reaction to them, were a world away from the level of discomfort felt by Doña B. in similar places and from the racism that she and others from Luribay, El Alto, and Kollasuyo would meet as she traversed cultural barriers—some of which were invisible, but others quite direct and explicit.

My main field sites for the project on the used-clothes trade were the markets of La Paz and El Alto, and particularly La Feria 16 de Julio, which is held every Thursday and Sunday (see Figure 1). The vast periurban expanse of the Sixteenth July market fair was generated from the patterns of rapid urban growth that took place in Latin America in the 1960s and 1970s. While being typically Latin American, it is also quintessentially Bolivian. Similar markets in other countries—for example, La Salada in Buenos Aires or Feirinha in São Paulo—are also dominated by Bolivians (see Dürr and Müller 2019 for overview). El Dieciseis—The Sixteenth, as the market is known colloquially—is estimated to take up about two hundred city blocks and is famed locally as the place where you can buy anything—from used cars, to ground lizards, to handmade

FIGURE 1. *The used-clothes section of the Sixteenth July market fair, El Alto, 2010. Author's photograph.*

furniture. It is classified in the United States as one of Latin America's largest "notorious" markets (USTR 2022)—a term that betrays the persistent naïveté in policy circles about the difference between illegal and informal, and what these terms can mean in a context where a state with its roots in colonialism lacks extension.

I researched the used-clothes trade in this market over two month-long periods of fieldwork in August 2010 and August 2011. I went to The Sixteenth twice a week over both periods of time and became a *casera*—a regular—at various juice and fruit stalls, and it was gratifying when a couple of stall owners recognized me the following year as well. I was often accompanied by Doña B. and Alicia, whose critical eyes were far more effective in finding the best deals and the best food, while my aim in talking to people was to extend the conversation—opening up a quite different dynamic. I was not perhaps the incongruous sight here that I had been in other parts of El Alto and the north of La Paz. Even at that time, before The Sixteenth had become a tourist attraction, it was not unusual to see people from traditional middle-class, predominantly white areas in the market, particularly in the used-clothes trade area where you could acquire the designer bargains that were valued in those circles. I might therefore be seen as one of the women who had come up for the day from the south of the city—dressed down in jeans, T-shirt, and a backpack, looking for quality U.S. brands. It would be a few minutes into the exchange before my accent in Spanish would provoke a question about where I was from, and then the conversation would tend to turn to concern for my safety.

Over those two months of fieldwork I conducted forty recorded interviews with people involved in the used-clothes trade: three with couples who brought goods from Chile and sold wholesale in the cities of Oruro and El Alto, four with couples who ran market associations, twenty-eight with people who ran their own stalls, and five with people who were employed to work on others' stalls. Six "key informants," including active and former government ministers and executives in Bolivia's garment industry, were also interviewed. These interviews provided focus for the project, but the analysis was rooted in the multiple discussions I had had with people working and shopping while I wandered around the market.

From 2015 to 2018 my research turned to the Aymara bourgeoisie and what this rise in wealth among indigenous people living and working in El Alto and the north of La Paz had meant for the city. My curiosity started when I was browsing the real estate section of the newspaper while staying with Doña B. and saw houses on the main commercial thoroughfare of El Alto—Avenida 6 de marzo—that were worth over a million U.S. dollars. This price disrupted many assumptions about the excluded, peri-urban, "informal" city that had supported Morales's socialist agenda. There were several periods of fieldwork involved in this project of one month in August 2016, July 2017, and May 2018. The way the city had changed was a talking point locally, as the dramatic *cholet*-style buildings—brightly colored mini-mansions incorporating Andean symbols (Walker 2014)—were changing the Paceña skyline. The contacts, research participants, and acquaintances with whom I met in my first week back in the country were keen to give me their views and to show me how these socioeconomic changes had affected their areas. One politician from Luribay took me on a drive to the south of La Paz to show me how the city was extending, as residents of the wealthy Zona Sur area were moving away from traditional middle-class neighborhoods

where housing was being bought by those from El Alto and the north of
La Paz. Similarly, people in Kollasuyo showed me the dramatic increase
in the number of people building extra stories on their houses. In both
areas, how light, and therefore warmth, was being blocked by these investments was a key issue.

This study became a neighborhood study, and I focused on two contrasting areas with which I was already familiar, Kollasuyo and San Miguel, the latter a commercial area of the Zona Sur. I conducted a total
of forty-seven interviews with residents and business owners in each
place, as well as those involved in real estate and construction, including estate agents and urban development firms. I also held focus groups
in each location, and with the help of a videographer from Kollasuyo I
made a short essay film—*¿Mientras más alto vives, más pobre eres?* I had a
research assistant from each place who helped to organize interviews we
conducted together. We also went on frequent walks around the neighborhoods during which we would discuss their own story and analysis of
how the neighborhood had changed and talked informally with friends,
acquaintances, and business owners about the transforming built environment and social makeup of the area.

One distinctive element of this project was the extent to which the
rise in the wealth of the Aymara bourgeoisie had become a phenomenon
in popular culture. The film *Zona Sur*—which features exactly the issue
of wealthy Aymara people coming to the area of the same name—was
frequently referenced, and I was able to interview the director, Juan
Carlos Valdivia. *Pollera* fashions had taken off, and I attended a fashion show dedicated to *la moda de la chola paceña* at the residence of the
Brazilian ambassador in the center of La Paz, where I learned that one
of the most prominent designers, Eliana Paco Paredes, had had her first
studio in Avenida Kollasuyo. Changes in fashion became a further focus
of the project, and my research assistants and I conducted eighteen interviews with those involved in the fashion industry (Maclean 2019).
Bolivia's new architecture, associated with the indigenous bourgeoisie,
had garnered international attention, and I was also able to visit the
exhibition of architect Freddy Mamani's work in Paris at the Fondation
Cartier pour l'Art Contemporain in February 2019.

Overall, the empirical work behind this book constitutes eighteen
months of fieldwork over twelve years, and while the semi-structured
interviews and focus groups provided structure and rigor to each of

these projects, the analysis presented here is based on reflections that would not have occurred had I not also had sustained periods in Bolivia. Living in Luribay and Kollasuyo gave me a sense of the inadequacy of prominent political discourses and identity categories—although used intersectionally—to describe those places or the experiences of Doña M., Doña B, and their families. It has also given me a sense of what it is to be perceived as a woman in those contexts—the fears, hopes, and pressures that constitute the affective landscape in which to develop a sense of self. These gendered expectations have been evident in the moments that have demonstrated my otherness in this context—the surprise that I live and travel alone, the particular shock that I do not have children— but they have also been demonstrated in the conversations that have crossed these boundaries and generated empathy and understanding. The stories, quotations, and pen portraits I present in this volume illustrate just how far removed the construction of mainstream economic values is from the way women in rural and peri-urban areas of Bolivia earn a living, but they have been generated by moments of connection and motivated by the aim to illustrate multiple ways of seeing the world.

Chapter Overview

Chapter 1 explores the theoretical development of pluri-economy in the work of the Grupo Comuna (GC; Comuna Group), which brought together Marxist and Indianist thinkers to reexamine critical theory in light of Bolivian political activism and to develop counterhegemonic strategies. The GC included Álvaro García Linera and others who would go on to have prominent roles in the MAS administration. I first place work on the pluriverse and pluri-economy in theoretical context to bring out the distinctiveness of the ontology and logic of identity adopted, as compared to liberal and critical—Marxist, feminist, and postcolonial— positions. I focus in particular on the dialogue between literature on economic diversity (e.g., J. K. Gibson-Graham) and the modernity/ coloniality/decoloniality school (e.g., Walter Mignolo, Arturo Escobar). The GC sought to bring together Indianist and Marxist thinking and resolve the theoretical and political "creative tensions" (García Linera 2011) to form a counterhegemonic discourse that could reflect the articulations of class and ethnicity that mobilized in Bolivia at the turn of the century. Criticism from within the Bolivian academy, however, made clear that the imbrications of gender, indigeneity, and urbanity were being overlooked. These omissions demonstrate the need for critique from the grounded perspective of the livelihoods of indigenous women, who find themselves excluded, conceptually and politically, from the naming of the categories of plurality and related policies.

Chapter 2, "The Political Space for Pluri-economy" looks at the historical conjuncture that enabled the rise of Morales and the "pink tide" governments in Latin America and the political articulations that formed the MAS. The contention of this chapter is that the processes and power relations developed during this period shaped the development of MAS policy, including theories of plurality. The MAS was not a political party but rather the "political instrument" of social movements, and as such it was committed to government by social movements to transform the colonial state apparatus from within. The discursive hegemony it formed was built on mass protest and opposition to a colonial, neoliberal elite. However, the fault lines between the articulations of indigenous, class-based, feminist, women's, and environmental movements swiftly began to show when the MAS came to power, as analyses of the negotiations in the Asamblea Constituyente (Constituent Assembly) have demonstrated. After surveying this political context, I analyze the construction of "pluri-economy" in the text of the 2009 Constitution to expose the theoretical and political priorities and exclusions. I particularly focus on the tropes of economic femininity that are recognized and recreated in the document. The way femininity is constructed in the text situates women firmly in the reproductive sphere, and the way the concepts of value, scale, nation, and production are constructed also betray masculinist assumptions. Indigeneity is associated with rurality, and while this counters the urban biases of orthodox economics, it excludes urban indigeneity.

The analysis in the first two chapters establishes the need for a grounded consideration of how Andean women working in rural, subsistence production and peri-urban informal markets earn a living in a political-economic context that has changed dramatically under the MAS but still places them in alterity. Chapter 3, "Andean Economic Femininities," takes women's livelihoods in the Andes as its starting point and looks at the history of markets in this area, which are famed for cooperative, reciprocal structures, community economies, and the powerful economic role women have there. Markets in the Andes are dominated by women, both buying and selling, and the stereotype of an Aymara woman is one who knows how to negotiate and bargain. It is clear, however, that myriad cultural, political, and material flows—from traditional ideals of household and femininity to material goods from around the world—create the economic and political dynamics of Andean markets. Via iterative, performative processes, the strategization of market spaces has both reaffirmed and transformed the notion of indigenous "traditions" and so reconstructed gendered meanings and gendered subjectivities. The MAS government reasserted indigenous culture and institutions and used indigenous women as iconic symbols of the Bolivian nation. However, the national production strategy and approach to modernization that the MAS adopted betrayed a masculinist notion of value, underpinned by a gendered construction of the economic terms of scale, nation, and production and of the dichotomy between tradition and modernity. Nevertheless, these apparent gendered contradictions created a space in which women who are negotiating the economic roles of rural producers, *comerciantes*, workers, and consumers could challenge both the MAS's and orthodox interpretations of these terms. The landowning *campesina de pollera* in charge of organizing agricultural production and the wealthy *chola* of the Aymara bourgeoisie are the pinnacles of Andean economic femininity, and they have ascended at a historical conjuncture that has allowed them to overturn assumptions about the political and economic roles of indigenous women.

The exploration of cash in chapter 4 examines the attempts to manage and channel capital in service of the pluri-economy while recognizing that capital is also a grounded, physical object serving a symbolic and cultural role. The chapter aims to ground abstract theorizations of capital in the complex cultural, institutional, and material realities that shape how capital flows. Cash—as opposed to money deposited in a bank account—is definitive of the informal economy, which in Bolivia and around the world is dominated by women. This chapter outlines debates on regulation of capital in Bolivia and the changes implemented by the MAS, including the Financial Services Law (Ley de Servicios Financieros) of 2013, dedollarization, Bolivia's participation in the regional currency (the SUCRE), and the institutionalization of the national development bank—the Banco de Desarrollo Productivo. Terms that are fundamental to the "natural" laws of capital, such as risk value, and corruption, as well as the institutions through which capital flows, are then deconstructed on the basis of empirical work in popular markets and rural areas. The contention of this chapter is that the symbolic changes the MAS decolonial policy has enabled, together with the boom in natural resources and concentration of wealth in peri-urban, popular markets, has enabled financial subjects that defy the way the laws of capital have been theorized.

The subject of chapter 5 is clothes, and while clothes and fashion might not always be deemed central to questions of power and economy, these most everyday of items are intimately connected with political identity. Nowhere is this more visible than in Bolivia, where the nomenclature of cultural and ethnic identity comes from clothes—*de pollera, de vestido, de corbata,* and so forth. Clothes are also a touchpoint between the personal and the everyday, on the one hand, and the worldwide production chains of the global textiles industry, in which Bolivian manufacturing has historically played a significant role, on the other. Since 2006 there have been major developments in the Bolivian textiles industry. The closure of the Bolivian luxury textiles manufacturer Enatex in 2016 illustrates the difficulties of policies oriented to vertical integration and internal consumption, particularly given the significant global pressures under which this industry finds itself. National production in Bolivia and elsewhere had been threatened since the 1990s by cheap imported clothing from East Asia and used clothes predominantly from the United States. The contrast between the flourishing of markets for imported and contraband clothes and the closure of Enatex highlights the attenuated power of the Bolivian nation-state in a globalized world. Over this same period, however, *la moda de la chola paceña*—luxury fashion brands selling the traditional *pollera* pleated skirt, blouse, and derby hat—have taken off both nationally and internationally. Aymara designers who started their careers in the popular markets of La Paz now have their own international labels. The feminine economic subject they represent—the successful, modern, and fashionable indigenous woman—is not predicted in the theoretical formulations of pluri-economy.

Chapter 6, "Construction: Aesthetics, Recognition, and Urban Mobilities," explores the economic conditions behind the astonishing boom in this industry in Bolivia as well as the effects it has had on mobility and inclusion in La Paz. There was a surge in construction and in real estate prices worldwide after the financial crisis of 2008, due to quantitative easing and low rates of interest. In Bolivia, the overvalued currency and extensive labor regulations have created incentives to invest in land and real estate rather than export-oriented industries. The explosion of real estate prices in peri-urban and informal areas of La Paz and El Alto, which has enabled this phenomenon, was not the intent behind the production focus of MAS policy. Nevertheless, this construction boom has had dramatic effects on architectural aesthetics, and as wealth has accumulated in informal markets, an urban environment has developed that appeals to the tastes, traditions, aspirations, and livelihood strategies of this emerging Aymara bourgeoisie, coinciding with the decolonial aims of the ruling party. The brightly colored *cholets,* from Aymara architect Freddy Mamani, provide the clearest illustration of a decolonized city and of an indigenous political subject who is recognized for modernity and art.

The Conclusion synthesizes the conceptual critique that can be drawn from these case studies and also offers final reflections on the future of MAS rule in Bolivia in light of the 2019 elections and the party's reelection in October 2020. The terms that are central to both heterodox and orthodox understandings of political economy—scale, exchange, value, production, capital, formality, and nation—are deconstructed on the basis of this inquiry, and the gendered and colonial constructions of those terms are exposed. The potential for creating a pluri-economy has been found not in the explicit policies of the MAS but rather in the livelihood strategies of women who are negotiating myriad cultural, financial, and economic flows and interpreting, recreating, and challenging tropes of economic femininity that consistently place them in alterity. The historical conjuncture that enabled the MAS to gain power by uniting movements for decolonialism, plurality, and post-neoliberalism, and the political landscape created by the alliance and articulations that brought them to power, is more indicative of the possibilities of economic diversity than the explicit theorizations of the idea of pluri-economy. The undeniable value of symbolic and cultural changes transformed the affective economic landscape, and the economic subjects that emerged defy the femininities that are permitted even in critical debate on inclusion and diversity.

1

The Vision of Pluri-economy

The aim of this chapter is to situate the development of pluri-economy in Bolivia in its theoretical context and explore the potential of this formulation of the economic to recognize diverse forms of exchange and recast ideas regarding which feminine economic subjects are permitted. I first look at the relationship between economic theory and the assumptions made about the economic subject, identity, and value. There is substantial confluence between decolonial theories of plurality and feminist theories of economic diversity, but there are also conceptual and political divergences. I then look at the specific development of the idea of pluri-economy among intellectuals and activists in Bolivia and examine commentaries at the time that were concerned about lacunae around femininity and urban indigeneity in this emerging body of thought.

Economic plurality is the pivot that brought together the Marxist and Indianist theoretical strands that defined the MAS agenda, and it was inspired by the civil unrest and activism of social movements in Bolivia at the turn of the century. The confluences and tensions between these two revolutionary schools had a history in Bolivia. The 1952 Movimiento Nacionalista Revolucionario (MNR; Revolutionary Nationalist Movement) party had focused on class-based struggles and land reform, which had alleviated the suffering of the rural poor by ending the feudal *pongueaje* system, which obliged indigenous people to provide free domestic labor, and implementing land reform. However, the MNR's modernization program cast rural, indigenous people as feudal peasants and so overlooked the exclusions and oppressions of colonialism along the lines of race and ethnicity. The inadequacies of this approach led indigenous movements to break away and develop a movement that focused on the extractions, damages, and humiliations of colonialism. The Indian Party of Bolivia and the Katarista movement of the 1970s sought to recover a specifically Aymara political identity, following dissatisfaction with the MNR's modernization approach (Albro 1998), and emphasized the importance of autonomy and recognition of indigenous identity and the trauma and loss of colonialism. The inadequacies of

Marxist theory to capture the complex diversity of Bolivian society and the demands of indigenous peoples for autonomy were placed in sharp relief by the protests led by indigenous social movements against multinational corporations' exploitation of natural resources, which led to the expulsion of those corporations (Shultz 2003). These demonstrations were led not by syndicalists or anti-globalization protesters but by indigenous social movements and communities, who construed multinationals' actions in terms of the continued colonization of indigenous territory. Indigenous organizations and popular social movements had succeeded in creating a popular uprising that would result in the expulsion of the multinationals attempting to privatize natural resources on the grounds of colonialism and identity rather than class-based revolution.

The theory of the *pluriversal* vision behind MAS strategy was developed by the Grupo Comuna (GC; Comuna Group), a collective of Marxist and Indianist intellectuals who recognized the potential but also the limits of Marxist theory to understanding Bolivian politics during this period. Members of the GC included Álvaro García Linera, who would go on to become vice president of Bolivia from 2006 to 2019, as well as Luís Tapia and Oscar Vega Camacho, who would both be involved in the Constituent Assembly that produced the text of the 2009 Constitution. The aim of the GC was to reread Marxist theory in relation to the popular uprisings of the gas and water wars and to unite the theoretical perspectives of Marxism and Indianism. Their agenda-setting publication *El Fantasma Insomne: Pensando el Presente desde El Manifiesto Comunista* [The unsleeping specter: Thinking the present from the *Communist Manifesto*] (García Linera et al. 1999)—an allusion to Marx's quotation on the "specter" of communism haunting Europe—reengaged with Marxist and Indianist theorists in light of contemporary struggles in Bolivia. A series of works emerged that showed some meetings of Marxist and Indianist thought while also addressing the frictions between the two movements, which had historical roots in the Marxist, state-led modernism of the 1950s and 1960s, which had undervalued indigenous cultural identity, sovereignty, and autonomy. The fundamental theoretical tension addressed was between the Indianist rejection of Marxism as generated from a Western, and therefore colonial, epistemological, and ontological tradition, and Marxist claims that dialectical logic and material issues of class were fundamental.

The GC's work paralleled the modernity/coloniality/decoloniality (MCD) movement of academics (e.g., Escobar 1992; Mignolo 2000; Mignolo and Escobar 2013), which sought to develop a specifically Latin American engagement with Marxist theory, reimagine modernity on the basis of the "pluriverse," and reject the universalizing tendencies of Western thought. The GC's theories in the Bolivian context highlighted the uniqueness of the pluriversal vision, which was to go on to inspire MAS electoral victories and policies. There were, however, criticisms from within the group and from other Bolivian intellectuals that the GC's theories and praxis created significant exclusions, particularly along the lines of gender and urban indigeneity, which continued to be placed in alterity by the taxonomy of identities that framed "plurality" (Rivera Cusicanqui 2010, 2012).

Thinking through the unification of Indianism and Marxism gives rise to what García Linera would later label "creative tensions" (2011) and which others would call, more critically, "aporias" (Moreiras 2015, 281). These tensions include some of the most polemic debates in social theory: the relationship of the cultural to the materialist project of Marxism (Alexander 1995; Butler 1998), postmodernity (Harvey 1989; Morris 1992), the tensions between recognition and redistribution (Fraser, Honneth, and Golb 2003), and the role of the state (Jessop 2008). These debates, however, had been rooted in the political realities of the industrialized North, and the development of the theory of pluri-economy on the basis of the Bolivian experience and Andean cosmovisions and logics recast the conceptual framing of these issues. The pluriversal logic of identity espoused underpins a notion of value and interdependence that challenges both the liberal assumption of an individual subject and Marxian ideas of subjectivity as generated by conflictual alienation. The valorization of reciprocity in the conceptual framing of pluri-economy also has the potential to recognize the economic relevance of activities associated with femininity, such as care and the recreation of community traditions, and the distinctive logic of plurality potentially captures and values work that is mischaracterized by the dichotomies of tradition/modernity, culture/economy, and rurality/urbanity.

However, despite this conceptual potential, feminist and indigenous intellectuals involved in these debates expressed concern that femininity was essentialized and that the everyday struggles, in particular, of women of indigenous descent working in informal, urban settings were overlooked. A particular point of conflict in both theory and practice was the role of the state in ensuring the socioeconomic conditions for inclusion and social justice, while also ensuring plurality and indigenous autonomy (Regalsky 2010; Mamani Ramírez 2017). There was a lack of reflexivity upon the identity categories that were being constructed and the political and economic subjects that were being assumed. In particular, the imbrications of indigeneity, gender, urbanity, and informality were overlooked in the categories that framed postulated notions of plurality (Rivera Cusicanqui 2010). The construction of the identity categories via which plurality is understood in the GC's theory and later MAS policy would come under critique in Bolivia from feminist and indigenous intellectuals and internationally from postcolonial theorists, who emphasize the importance of deconstructive process rather than a reconstruction of precolonial institutions (Vuola 2003; Rivera Cusicanqui 2010, 2012; Asher 2013).

Tacit assumptions regarding femininity and indigeneity were present in the theorizations that brought together Marxist and Indianist thinking, and these assumptions created exclusions in the envisioned pluri-economy. The framework the GC and the MAS used to bring together these two perspectives drew in particular on the work of Bolivian theorist and former MNR minister of mines and petroleum René Zavaleta Mercado's idea of the "motley society," which recognized the need to problematize the abstracted "mestizo" citizen, and that of Fausto Reinaga, whose *La Revolución India* rejected Marxism as a form of colonialism and argued for the need to recover Indian identity and create an anticolonial, anti-occidental order. For Zavaleta the prime motor of identity was capital; for Reinaga it was colonialism. The GC used a Gramscian framework that recognized the importance of cultural and symbolic hegemony as well as the movements of capital to unite these Marxist and Indianist philosophies and reimagine political institutions and configurations of state and civil society (Webber 2016; McNelly 2017). The aim of this chapter is to look at the discourses and identities which that theorizing produced, and how in particular the economic subjects that were permitted informed the values and exchanges that would be recognized in the vision of pluri-economy.

It has been a criticism of the modernity/coloniality/decoloniality body of scholarship overall that, despite significant political and theoretical confluence, gender has been all but omitted (Vuola 2003; Escobar

2007b). Arturo Escobar acknowledges, following Elina Vuola, that among theorists in this area there has been an "inability to identify the race and gender position of their theorizing" (2007b, 192). Nevertheless, theories of the pluriverse and feminist theories of economic diversity have the shared aim to uncover multiple economic worlds and rethink the economy. It is acknowledged that there are "many points of actual or potential convergence between feminism and the theory of Modernity/ Coloniality" (Escobar 2007b, 193) and that Latin American decolonial scholarship has pushed feminist theories of economic diversity, which have their genus in the "developed" world, to "go beyond the genealogical and deconstructive . . . [to] make the non-credible, [and] the non-existent present as 'alternatives to hegemonic experience'" (Gibson-Graham 2005, 5, quoting Boaventura de Sousa Santos). Feminist post-Marxist and postcolonial work that explores the labors, exchanges, and values obscured by a sole, even if critical, focus on capital can then in turn be used to elucidate the potentials and exclusions of pluri-economy.

The following section situates the pluri-economic approach within the landscape of theoretical debates on the liberal economic subject, which was the main target of the critique of both Marxist and Indianist intellectuals in the GC. The conceptualization of the neutral, abstract individual underpins value in the liberal economy as well as the ortho-dox adjustment policies that had caused such decimation of Bolivia's social fabric in the 1980s, and consequently high levels of inequality and exclusion. The false neutrality of the abstract individual at the heart of liberalism implicitly favored colonial, white culture, omitted the social, and obscured and compounded class exploitation. Marxist and decolo-nial perspectives coincide with feminist theories in their criticism of liberalism as the competitive, rational values underpinned by the ab-stract liberal individual also marginalize care work, reproductive labor, and reciprocity, which are typically coded feminine. Despite having the liberal economic subject as a common object of critique, these different critical perspectives espouse distinct assumptions about how the sub-ject is formed and the values accorded to different exchanges.

The Feminine Economic Subject and the Logics of Identity

The economic subject is the personification of the motives, needs, and desires of political economic actors to be found at the heart of political and economic theory. The *Homo economicus* of liberalism is motivated by the maximization of one's own profit and happiness, and while this is intended as a heuristic device, that construction of the economic subject has created exclusions and iniquities in liberal institutions and values. The alienated subject of Marxism is predicated on a conflictual logic of identity that, while capable of capturing the exploitation that liberal theory can render invisible, can shore away the relevance of the cultural and the feminine with an economistic focus on labor and class. The pluriversal logic upon which pluri-economy is based is a rejection of the universalism that is at the center of Western metaphysics, and specifically the false neutrality of abstract universals and the binary law of noncontradiction upon which orthodox liberalism and Marxism both rely (Dussel 2003; Grosfoguel 2007). The problematization of the dialectical movement in which the particular is subsumed by the universal is at the heart of Latin America's decolonial thinking and is what differentiates it from other schools of critical theory. This logical position is inspired by the original languages of the continent, including Aymara and Quechua, which are trivalent, meaning that, whereas bivalent statements only have one truth value, true or false, trivalent languages allow for the existence of both at once. This provides the linguistic tools for understanding the pluriverse as a "parallel coexistence of difference" (Rivera Cusicanqui 2012, 105).

The aim of pluri-economy is to recognize multiple forms of economic subject and forms of exchange, but there is nevertheless a specific metaphysics that underpins the vision. The pluri-economic subject, which is defined as embodying the values of community, complementarity, and reciprocity (2009 Constitution, Article 306) is an inherently relational being, one who cannot be thought of as existing without community, family, or environment, in stark contrast to the liberal *Homo economicus*. This relationality is underpinned by a logic which holds that diverse identities are generated from interdependence and cooperation rather than conflict and alienation, as in Marxist theories. There is an ecology of distinct but interdependent beings, rather than an inherently conflictive identity that can only be defined by its other. This reciprocal, interdependent logic of identity makes the model of pluri-economy well placed to valorize the social and therefore reproductive and care labor, which can be shorn away from both liberal and reductionist Marxist models of economic behavior. By recognizing that the subject is always socially and culturally situated, individual and group rights are not opposed, as they can be, for example, in liberal multiculturalism. The construction of scale that pits local against universal is also disrupted, and hence emotional life and particularist community exchanges are not erased from a supposedly neutral, rational public sphere. The change in values that stems from the recognition of the particular, the emotional, and the communal has the potential to valorize activities that have been constructed as feminine and marginalized in both liberal and Marxist models of the economy.

The rational, utility-maximizing individual at the heart of liberal ideas of democracy and equality has its roots in the colonial encounter. The genealogy of the liberal subject is—quite explicitly—male, upper class, and white. This construction provided a rationale for hierarchies on gender, race, and class grounds, and hence on the assumed European superiority that justified the brutalities and violences of colonialism. Silvia Wynter (2003, 261) calls the ostensibly neutral, abstract individual at the heart of liberalism "central ethnoclass Man" whose particularity is denied and who is allowed to claim the status of the universal human. The heuristic device of the state of nature, which gave man no choice but to secure his own security in a context where life was "nasty, brutish, and short," also created the rationale for the exploitations of empire, "a script, therefore, whose macro-origin story calcifies the *hero figure of homo oeconomicus* who practices, indeed normalizes, accumulation in the name of (economic) freedom" (Wynter and McKittrick 2015, 10, emphasis in original). This "hero figure" entrenched racialized dichotomies between rational and subrational, and hence established the colonized as the "Human Other . . . to correlated postulates of power, truth, freedom" (Wynter 2003, 282). The construction of *Homo economicus* effectively rendered alternative ways of being impossible and "other" epistemologies unthinkable. Uncovering alternative scripts of ways of being human is hence central to decolonization.

Colonial capitalism also brought with it the gendered binary of masculinity and femininity that liberalism assumes and in effect imposes. In its classical formulation, the liberal subject is divided between a public sphere governed by ideals of toleration, equality, and universal rights, and a private sphere in which personal characteristics, including cultural identity, can be expressed (Calhoun 1992). This division into public and private spheres creates a gendered division of paid productive

labor in the public sphere and unpaid reproductive and care labor conducted in the private sphere. This formulation is ideological in that it
is based on ideas of how the family and the household *should* operate,
rather than empirical examination of how they do. In the industrialized North, families and households that do not conform to this ideal
are hence pathologized, even by assistance programs, such as maternity
care and child support, which seek to offer support but are themselves
formulated on this norm (Lister 1997; Wright 2010). In a colonial context however, gender was imposed as part of a civilizing mission. As
Maria Lugones asserts, "'colonized woman' is an empty category: no
women are colonized, because no colonized females are women" (2010,
745)—to the colonizers, the colonized lacked humanity and therefore
gender. Given this history, which violently erased myriad conceptions
of personhood, "other" notions of gender are prone to be exoticized and
mistranslated into a binary man/woman distinction (Lugones 2010;
Spivak 1994). A decolonial feminist reading focuses on the processes
of subjectivization and resistance to these gendering processes in the
context of the multiple fragmentations and hierarchies of colonialism
(Lugones 2010).

As capitalist modernity proliferated, the liberal division between
public and private generated gendered economic values and ideals that
would assume and impose certain gendered divisions of labor, hence at
once creating and undervaluing the feminine and the communal. The
public/private divide creates correlate binaries that define what can
be valued in a liberal economy and structure the economic landscape to
be negotiated. As opposed to the rational public sphere, the household is
postulated as the space where relationships are based on specific bonds
of care and where emotions can therefore be expressed. Activities in the
public sphere are supposedly based on "reason" and hence defined and
valued in contrast to exchanges within the family. The characteristics
of exchanges within the household are particularist, and preferential
treatment from family members at home is expected, whereas in the
liberal public sphere, which is supposedly governed by ideals of equality,
reason, and competition, particularism is considered corrupt. Skills that
are deemed natural, such as care, are not as valued as those that are seen
as cultural and requiring expertise and certification. Achievements that
have been won competitively are more valued than those that have resulted from cooperation, and activities that involve risk gain more profit

than those that require care (Cameron and Gibson-Graham 2003). These binaries underpin the exchanges that are deemed valuable in market liberalism and neoliberal orders, hence creating a world in which care labor is undervalued while competitive, risk-taking exchanges make a profit, which has colonial and gendered implications (Maclean 2016).

There is, however, a recognition among liberal theorists of the false neutrality of the abstract individual and the public sphere (Phillips 1993). The dilemma at the institutional level for the liberal is how to create a polity in which equality across difference can be imagined and measured, as the abstracted, "neutral" individual provides the basis for equal rights. The liberal response is the postulation of multiple, counter-public spheres to maintain the advantages of a liberal order, in terms of Rawlsian principles of justice and equality, while recognizing the gendered, classed, and racialized structures framing these spaces, subjects, and values (Fraser 1990, 2009). The tensions between group and individual rights are resolved in liberalism by seeing identity as a free, individual choice, and so groups are reducible ontologically to their constituent individuals. Liberal multiculturalism and decentralization, which were seen in Bolivia in the 1990s, are examples of a liberal approach to diversity (Kohl 2003), and it has been suggested that the effect of the MAS's approach to plurality, despite theorizations and intentions to the contrary, has been to create a multiplicity of public spheres (Schilling-Vacaflor 2011). However, the formulation of plurality at the heart of the GC's and later the MAS's ideas of pluri-economy presented a far more penetrating critique of the values and structures of liberalism by recognizing forms of exchange other than liberal competition and choice (Walsh 2009).

In contrast to the liberal model of the subject, for whom the competitive drive for security and profit is the motivating force, alienation is pivotal in the formation of the economic subject of Marxism (Ollman 1976). This sense of estrangement is produced primarily by alienation from the fruits of one's labor, as subsistence labor becomes a coerced and regulated activity to produce for commerce and profit, rather than for use, which also gives rise to an inability to express oneself through creation and see oneself reflected in one's surroundings (Chatterton and Pusey 2020). The value of what is produced is not dictated by the labor that has been invested but rather by supply and demand and the "fetishism" of the commodity, which values, to use Adam Smith's famous example, the diamond over fresh water. Alienation results from the decline of community cooperation, as a consequence of the development of social relationships that weaken to be commensurate with competitive, capitalist exchange (Musto 2010), and the angst that is produced at not feeling fulfilled or recognized in one's surroundings is to be eased by consumption (Castree 2003).

The conflictual logic of identity renders liberal deliberative democracy unworkable, as, in seeking consensus, it in effect denies the inherently political and exclusionary nature of its own terms of debate (Mouffe 2005). It may follow that any notion of "the public" or plural democracy will necessarily be based on antagonism and conflict, as any process will necessarily produce an "other." Group identities that could underpin representation are therefore by definition in conflict with power. Conflict is hence an inherent, but not desirable, fundament of the political. This raises the question of which political institutions can sustain diversity without dissolving into either conflict or an exclusionary consensus. The theory of agonism postulates a polity in which groups relate to each other as adversaries rather than enemies, and as such the necessity and indeed benefits of political conflict are maintained rather than denied, or, conversely, inflamed (Honig 1993; Mouffe 1999). As conflict does not disappear, there will always be a hegemonic order, and the aim is not to dissolve that order but rather to produce a counterhegemonic strategy. The GC's theorizings successfully developed such a strategy by bringing together those disenfranchised by both neoliberalism and colonialism to the same side of a conflict framed as being between "the people" and "the elite," recalling Chantal Mouffe's analysis "with and against" Carl Schmitt (Tambakaki 2014). This was successful electorally, but from the outset the fault line between an Indianist communitarian approach, with its emphasis on autonomies, and the leftist vision, which required a powerful redistributive nation-state, albeit temporarily, was apparent.

Cultural interpretive and narrative accounts can be seen as epiphenomena of the economic conflicts that drive processes of identity formation or be themselves attributed to the neoliberal fragmentation of class structures (Harvey 1989). Postcolonial and post-Marxist feminist accounts of identity formation aim to bring in a cultural critique without losing sight of the structural, material processes that shape social relations (Spivak 1994; Rivera Cusicanqui 2010; Asher 2013). Grand narrative accounts of class, race, and gender that have the effect of erasing difference are destabilized and deconstructed in order to avoid recreating terms on which identity and therefore exclusion are created. Conflictive accounts of identity overlook the way that people understand and define themselves, hence, in effect, perpetuating a silencing oppression; the scripts themselves need to be rewritten. In terms of analyzing gendered exclusion from the economy, this has taken the form of starting not with the postulation of unremunerated, reproductive labor, which in effect continues the focus on capital and production, but in looking at the plethora of exchanges and values that are rendered invisible by this language (Gibson-Graham 2006, 2008). Care, family, community, nature, and markets can therefore be explored empirically to reimagine capitalism rather than to illustrate its exclusions.

Indigenous and feminist communitarian praxis in Bolivia adopts a critical, pedagogical approach that facilitates a reflexive attitude to deconstructing the concepts that underpin power and the economy. Bolivian feminist group Mujeres Creando works with communities and activists to draw out the distinct histories of indigeneity and femininity and form an identity that is discursively disruptive and also anti-state. Julieta Paredes describes their epistemological praxis thus:

> In colonial and colonizing practices, the West had the pretense
> of wanting to name the planet from its Eurocentric perspective.
> This is nothing more than a claim that is constantly answered by
> the different peoples that we have thought and named our reality
> from ourselves. Centers of power wanted to reduce us to the reach
> of their understandings, and ridiculous, mediocre, cynical and
> self-sufficient actions. The way to sustain this belief of omnipotence is from a theoretical epistemology. In other words, creating
> theories of theories, with little or no support in real practice. . . .
> [We need to] name our practices and feelings ourselves without
> being afraid of the sound of our own voice, not being afraid to
> create theories, concepts and explanations, not hesitating to interpret what happens to us, not being afraid to project our desires,
> our dreams and our utopias. Recover the right to exist differently
> in the world. (Paredes 2010, 119)

This epistemological praxis gives voice to the silences described by Boaventura de Sousa Santos (2004) as a "sociology of absences" and pushes
poststructuralist feminism based in the developed North to go further
in its deconstruction of assumptions (Gibson-Graham 2005)—and "unlearning of learning" in order to not recreate meanings and values that
erase the "other" (Spivak 1994). Concepts of scale, production, nationhood, household, family, territory, environment, and care need to be
fundamentally reimagined in order to hear, let alone valorize, the voices
of those who have been excluded by the politics of colonialism, gender,
class, and rurality.

Mujeres Creando's antiauthoritarian vision of governance was to create what they called a "Community of Communities" rather than a state
that will unavoidably be a "remnant of the Republican bourgeoisie"
(Paredes 2010, 120). The Community of Communities is the pluriversal
alternative to the liberal public sphere, and the indigenous reciprocal
logic provides a framing for diversity and justice within the community, rather than the inherently conflictual notion of identity indicated
by the dynamic of alienation. Paredes also indicates that a process of
"auto-critique" which reflects on the identities and exclusions that were
being created is necessary to achieve a Community of Communities that
does not become itself dominant and exclusionary. As the MAS period
in power progressed, feminist, indigenous, and environmental groups
in Bolivia would criticize the lack of reflection on the identity categories underpinning plurality and the powers that were being reinforced
as the state became more powerful (Oporto 2013; *Página Siete* 2014b;
Soliz Rada 2014).

This trajectory from the vision of plurality and revolution was in part
due to a gradual fragmentation of the alliances that formed within the
MAS and the compromises that had to be reached with other powerful
actors, particularly elites in the economically dominant eastern prov-
ince of Santa Cruz. However, it also indicates a theoretical divergence
between the reflective approach of autonomous feminism and the MCD
imperative to reconstitute identities in order to overturn colonial domination, which takes on a further dimension when scaled up to the level
of the state. The MCD school holds that deconstructive critiques of modernity are not sufficient, either theoretically or politically, to overturn
colonial domination (Mignolo 2000). Their argument is that critical the-

ory, including postcolonial and cultural theory, as developed in Europe and North America, maintains modernity as the point of reference. By contrast, decolonial theorists argue for transmodernity—"the positivity rooted in a tradition distinct from the Modern" (Dussel 2012, 50). Concepts, categories, and theories should be reconstructed on the basis of precolonial Latin American epistemologies and the lived experience of colonialism (Mignolo 2000). However, in adopting a positive reconstruction of categories rather than a constant process of auto-reflection, the exclusions and power dynamics behind the identities postulated as comprising the pluriverse at state level may be hidden from view.

The debate over whose vision of plurality was to count, and fears about the increasing authority of the state, particularly in the second term of the MAS government (Uharte Pozas 2017), resulted from the tension between the relationality and cooperation of community and the redistributive role of the state, which requires set identity categories— women, children, indigenous—in order to redistribute. As we will see below, the conceptual framing for the GC's unification of Marxist and Indianist theories was developed using Gramscian ideas of hegemony, civil society, and the integral state. It is not clear, however, that a Gramscian framing was capable of addressing the complexities and messiness of the myriad effects that the hegemonic projects of neoliberalism and colonialism have had on subject formation, contestation, and resistance (Barnett 2005; Larner 2003).

The next section explores the specific development of the idea of pluri-economy in the discussions of the GC that went on to form the MAS agenda. The success of social movements in fighting the private exploitation of natural resources in Bolivia in the early 2000s served as an example of the strength of this politics of scale in that local, self-organized groups overthrew global corporations (Escobar 2010; Grosfoguel 2011; Zibechi 2005). The signifiers that enabled this were "indigeneity" and the "nation," both of which underpinned the drive for sovereignty over territory, which went on to frame the vision of plurality espoused in the 2009 Constitution. The challenge the GC set themselves was to bring indigenous activism and worldviews into dialogue with a Marxist analysis of neoliberalism and so form the agenda that would lead the MAS to victory in 2005. Already visible in this process, however, were the potential exclusions along the lines of gender,

indigenous urbanity, and informality, and the tensions between Marxist and Indianist views of the state, which would prove huge challenges
to the MAS over the course of its rule.

Grupo Comuna and the Intellectual Vision of Pluri-economy

The scholarship of the GC framed both the vision and implementation
of pluri-economy. Its members represented various theoretical positions: political philosopher Luis Tapia, Deleuzian Raúl Prada Alcoreza,
mathematician and Marxist activist Álvaro García Linera, sociologist
and militant intellectual Raquel Gutiérrez Aguilar, and political scien-
tist Oscar Vega Camacho (Kanahuaty 2015). Their work brought Bolivian social theory into dialogue with a Gramscian framework that would
enable the recognition of plurality of identity. The tension between a
vision of communitarian autonomy from Indianist thinkers and indigenous leaders, on the one hand, and the perceived need particularly on
the part of García Linera for a nation-state, albeit transitory, to redress
the inequalities and injustices of neoliberalism, on the other, was resolved by proposing a plurinational state that recognized autonomy but
had sufficient power to redistribute and confront transnational capital. The result of the unification of the two "revolutionary rationales"
of Indianism and Marxism (García Linera 2014) was to be a theoretical
framework that had the potential to valorize theoretically, politically,
and institutionally a plurality of economic exchanges. The vision of
pluri-economy in which the state had such a powerful role was, however,
criticized subsequently by feminists who had initially been involved and
by indigenous leaders who saw that the provisions for autonomy were
inadequate. Although the way pluri-economy was theorized opened new
avenues by which to reimagine the economy, dynamics of gender and
informal economic activity were occluded by some of the starting theoretical assumptions.

The GC drew on the work of Bolivian scholars René Zavaleta and
Fausto Reinaga, both of whom wrote in the decades following the MNR
revolution of 1952 and addressed the inadequacies of class-based revolution to incorporate indigenous demands for territory, recognition,
and autonomy. Zavaleta is best known for the development of the
idea of the *sociedad abigarrada*—the motley society (Zavaleta Mercado
2002)—which describes the plebeian masses in a way that recognized

the different modes of production and governance that constitute Bolivia (Freeland 2019b). Zavaleta's definitional framework constructed difference in terms of historical economic categories and modes of production. Applied more broadly, the motley society also allows for an understanding of the remarkable cultural multiplicity in Bolivia without appealing to homogenizing notions of *mestizaje* or multiculturalism within a liberal market (Hale 2002; Wade 2005). It is a recognition of the different logics of diversity to be found in the multiple modes of production, accumulation, and dispossession and involves, in Luis Tapia's words, "different historical times, different modes of the production of subjectivity, of sociality, and especially different forms of structures of authority or self-government" (Tapia quoted in Gago 2017, 63).

Zavaleta's work was structured in terms of capitalist production and contrasts distinct feudal (precapitalist) and Andean communitarian dynamics with the capitalist nation-state (Freeland 2019b). His idea of the motley described diversity in Marxist terms, rather than deconstructing those categories, as postcolonial theorists later did. He spoke to debates on dependency theory and focused on logics of production, but he also recognized the importance of the historical, social, cultural, and linguistic, drawing on Gramsci to incorporate the relevance of culture and history to processes of subjectivation. He recognized the need for recognition of the subaltern gaze for the legitimacy of the state, and for state institutions to reflect heterogeneous social dynamics and patterns (Thomson 2019). Scholars of Zavaleta's work, notably Luis Tapia and Silvia Rivera Cusicanqui, extended Zavaleta's insights to speak to subaltern studies and the reconstitution of the postcolonial subject on their own terms (Freeland 2019b). Gender, however, is absent from Zavaleta's analysis, despite the prominent place of women activists in miners' unions and the MNR itself (Thomson 2019). The omission of gender from Zavaleta's theorizing, and the formulation of "the motley" economy in terms of different forms of capital exchange, also occludes the exchanges that are associated with the feminine, and the logics of care, subsistence, social reproduction, and gift exchange that cannot entirely be reduced to a material analysis.

The notion of "motley" was still Marxist and economistic at root, as opposed to Indianist visions of plurality that emphasized the primacy of ethnicity and colonialism in oppression, and relied on an ecological rather than a dialectical logic. Reinaga's work, by contrast, emphatically distinguished Indianism from Marxism, defining it as the anti-occidental vision of indigenous writers, rather than the *indigenista* interpretation of this position, which incorporates indigenous identity into a Marxist class analysis. Both Morales and García Linera cite Reinaga as a key influence. "More than any politician . . . I admired a writer, Fausto Reinaga, and his works like *La revolución india*. . . . He allowed me to understand who we are as Quechuas and Aymaras" (Morales quoted in Lucero 2008, 13). Reinaga himself was a descendant of the indigenous leader Tomás Katari, and due to his heritage he was trained as a leader. He was greatly influenced by Franz Fanon, whose work he cites at length in his own, and this is shown in the emphasis he places on the lost dignity and humiliation that the Indian (a term he reclaimed) had experienced and the need to reconstitute that which had been destroyed by colonialism. Disillusioned with the MNR and the homogenizing ideas of the mestizo citizen, Reinaga called for revolution based on Indian identity rather than class, for "Christ and Marx to be removed from the head of the Indian" (Reinaga 1969, 397), and for an Indian identity and philosophy to be reclaimed and developed.

While Zavaleta's theorizings omit gender, Reinaga's openly disparage the status of indigenous women, and it has been argued that his vision was one of the emancipation of the Indian man who had been feminized and humiliated by colonialism (Canessa 2010). His reassertion of indigenous identity and culture, despite the potential of indigenous cosmologies to frame a communitarianism that is consistent with feminist praxis, was openly disparaging toward women. Reinaga's work positions femininity as motherhood with reference to the Pachamama—the Andean earth goddess—but his portrayal of femininity suggests the toil of labor rather than power: "She procreates and works, works and procreates. That is the Indian woman" (Reinaga quoted in Canessa 2010, 181–82). Reinaga holds the Indian woman responsible for the creation of the mestizo race, but due to her submission and passivity rather than agency. Reinaga's disrespect for the treachery of Indian women for being raped by *q'ara* (white) men is dehumanizing.

When she was still a girl she was deflowered by the white sacristan or priest of the village. Virginity has no value for her; she lost it before she ever had any sense of what it was. And if she is impreg-

nated she gives birth in just the same way as a ewe. (Reinaga
quoted in Canessa 2010, 182)

Nevertheless, Reinaga's theorizing of Indian identity, nation, and revolution had a significant influence on the development of the GC and
later the MAS. Reinaga's contrast between the two Bolivian nations—
"the Indian is of an oppressed nation. The cholo is of an oppressor nation" (quoted in Lucero 2008, 18)—is echoed in Morales's decolonial
discourse. However, the MAS distanced itself from the explicit essen-
tialism of Reinaga's position in uniting Indianism with classed oppression (Lucero 2008).

The GC's rereading of Reinaga united Indianism with proletarian
struggles by recognizing that the roots of colonialism, race, and the very
category of the "indigenous" is part of the "othering" produced by the
expansion of capital (Feldman 2015). Societal forms are "grounded in an
understanding of the social as a productive process closely tied to political economy" (Baker 2015, para. 10), the reproductive labor that maintains the system of reciprocal community exchanges. The recognition
of the importance of the social and cultural to bourgeois hegemony is
essential to understanding how indigenous social movements, based on
identity rather than class, are able to "contest the territorial, ideological and symbolic control of society" (Webber 2015, para. 13). The GC's—
and particularly García Linera's—response to this was to reengage the
Gramscian debate on culture as being closely related to systems of production and the maintenance of bourgeois hegemony and recognizing
the role of the cultural construction of knowledge and technology as
forms of colonial alienation and exploitation (Feldman 2015). However,
this position received criticism from indigenous academics and activists who concluded that the MAS was in danger of co-opting Indianist
discourse by maintaining in this formulation the primacy of economy
and class, rather than ethnicity and colonialism, and that potentially
radical ideas were being used by, in the words of Rivera Cusicanqui,
"middle-class intellectuals and mestizos, many of whom have historically carried out ideological pirouettes of all kinds in order to achieve or
maintain power" (quoted in Farthing 2007, 4).

A crucial point of contention in the unification of Indianist and Marxist thinking was the role of the state. Zavaleta's work as it was originally

formulated used the conception of Bolivia's "motley society" and the Katarista demands for autonomy to outline a limit on the formation of a nation-state, whereas García Linera in particular uses it as the basis of a nation-state. García Linera's theoretical move was to turn this plurality into the "fictive ethnicity . . . of the new Bolivia" and to postulate the plurination—the "disarticulated coexistence of society of diverse modes of production, historical times, symbolic horizons and political systems, which constitutes the insurmountable limit to the hegemonic articulation that would enable the fulfilment of a nation-state project" (Cerrato 2015, 337). In terms of political institutions, one of the main challenges for the GC was to imagine a state form that could appropriately reflect heterogeneous social dynamics. This was to be achieved by an "integral state," which would integrate civil society and the state to better reflect the motley diversity of social reality. However, despite the constitutional recognition of the importance of civil society, and an economy that would encompass public, private, cooperative, and community institutions, the state would be chief among political institutions (García Linera 2008b). The autonomous organization of communities and social movements that constitute Bolivian civil society into a "semi-state configuration" (Freeland 2019a, 103) would then lead toward the abolition of the state entirely. Autonomy was crucial to the theoretical and political settlement between Marxist and Indianist thinkers and leaders. The concept of plurinationality was intended to resolve this, but the risk cited by Bolivian theorists at the time was that the plurination would not sustain that level of heterogeneity and would resolve into a singular entity (Lucero 2008). Concerns were raised that this vision of the state was a cosmetic recasting of the modernizing nation-state and that the postulation of plurinationality, rather than transforming state-society relations, would reinforce the state while disabling criticism (Lucero 2008).

Recognizing diverse forms of exploitation and alienation opens the historical possibility of multiple forms of resistance, which can, theoretically, be brought together if the appropriate signifiers and forms are found. The challenge for the GC, and later the MAS, was to scale up the autonomous, identity-based, communitarian critique they had developed to the national level without relying on the false neutrality of the "public" or of a mestizo identity (Moreiras 2015). Their counterhegemonic strategy involved a search for appropriate signifiers to designate heterogeneity, while bringing resistance to global capitalism and colonialism together. The main signifiers to achieve this were "indigeneity" and "national sovereignty," and a particular construction of indigeneity that imbricates with rurality and community traditions. Other identity categories were built into this by implication/interpellation—for example, the characterization of the working class, informal market traders, the urban, the mestizo, and various characterizations of legitimate and illegitimate femininity. The relational ontology espoused in Latin American decolonial approaches has the potential to allow for a recognition of the fluidity of identity categories, but this potential had to, inevitably, be simplified in developing a counterhegemonic strategy. However, the distinct power relations involved within groups, and the importance of people's own interpretive accounts, were underestimated in order to stay wedded to a Marxist cultural vision and the decolonial commitment to reconstruction rather than a reflexive process of deconstruction.

The plurinational formulation of an integral state that recognized civil society was intended to respond to the autonomous organization of indigenous communities and also to bring local community dynamics to the national scale. To achieve this, the GC adopted the idea of a "universalized *ayllu*" to imagine the state. This move "overcomes localism and constitutes itself as a community nation" (Cerrato 2015, 338), and hence the dialectical tension between local communities and the nation-state is not resolved by the particular being subsumed under a universal notion of a public or a nation, exemplifying pluriversal logic. This is a clear instance of the power of indigenous relational ontology to reimagine state institutions in a way that can address the reductionism of an ideal typical characterization of Marxist and liberal theory. This dialectical shift, which prioritizes the communal in the synthesis between local and national, also problematizes the mercantile value that comes with liberal capitalist development. Making the communal the point of reference means that use value, which motivates reciprocal, cooperative exchanges, is the value that guides nation-state decisions, rather than exchanges for profit. There are notions of the public and the state in liberal theory which would recognize that state investments and decisions are guided by a different logic than the utility and profit maximization that guides decisions in the market. This idea, as elaborated in *Forma Valor, Forma Comunidad* (Value form, community form), involves the community in all its dimensions, "materially-subjectively-culturally-religiously" (García Linera 2009, 366) sublating into the universal form. The use value of community exchanges extends to the cultural and symbolic realms, not just the economic, and hence the political subject and the culture of public space are reimagined. This framework has the potential to valorize the local and the community, responding to feminist and postcolonial critiques of scale, and hence address the masculinist biases in the construction of public and state. It does, however, maintain that the economy is fundamental, and the question remains whether this potential is realized, given the continued emphasis on a nation-state both theoretically and politically during the MAS administration.

The GC's work created a framework to valorize community exchanges and social reproduction and to recognize the importance of colonialism and ethnic identity. Although absent from Zavaleta's formulation, the economic diversity represented by the idea of the "motley" also had the potential to recognize informal markets and the plurality of exchanges therein. But understanding the role of peri-urban markets represented a challenge for the Marxist-oriented GC to theorize, as the petty *comerciantes* (market traders) and micro-entrepreneurs who populate these areas also represented a fragmentation of class identity and union organization.

> A new form of vast proletarianization is emerging, but deterritorialized and without organizational roots, traversed by a deep internal distrust, and nomadic young workers with a precarious, short-term mentality as they have to combine small businesses, smuggling, wage labor, and agricultural work, depending on the seasons and needs. (García Linera 2008a, 350)

The above description dovetails significantly with comments by Michael Hardt on the postindustrial West, where "there is no longer just one form of work, like the miners or the industry workers, who can decentralize the world of work. Today there exists a kind of plurality, of heterogeneity in the forms of work" (Hardt 2008, 42).

However, the movement against the privatization of water in Cochabamba that brought together indigenous social movements, neighborhood associations, rural syndicates, and factory workers under the umbrella of La Coordinadora de Defensa del Agua y de la Vida (The Coalition in Defense of Water and Life) was a counterexample to the assumption that this fragmentation would disable active resistance. To understand the power of these coalitions, the GC postulated a difference between the "multitude" and the *muchedumbre*—the crowd. The "multitude" was the energy behind these protests as it brought together distinct segments of the subaltern classes, and in particular the dynamism between rural and urban constituencies, who had inherited the traditions of labor and community organization. It was a "block of collective action that articulates the autonomous organized structures of the subaltern classes, workers and non-workers, around different discursive and symbolic constructions, which have the particularity of varying in their origin among different segments of subaltern classes" (García Linera 2003, 163). This definition built on Zavaleta's ideas to explain the particular dynamics behind the rise of social action in Bolivia at the turn of the century, and hence the GC's "multitude" represents a different genealogy to that of Negri and Hardt's (2004) use of the same term.

The multitude as an organized political force was distinguished from "the crowd"—*la muchedumbre*—which is the term García Linera uses to refer to the indignation of the masses whose power is to "say no . . . to resist, to oppose, to destroy" (2003, 59). While the *muchedumbre* retreats and "withdraws and dissolves back in to the anonymity of its own self-interests," the multitude seeks resolution and has the organizational bases to achieve it. In García Linera's formulation, those working informally in peri-urban markets, particularly those involved in petty trade and commerce, are cast, in their absence, as the *muchedumbre* and themselves become the other of the active resistance of the multitude. This leaves the social dynamics which perhaps force those working in these conditions back into "the anonymity of their own self-interests" unexplored, as well as the multiple interpretations, aspirations, and strategies via which they understand the exploitative forces of global capital and colonialism with which they are dealing every day.

The theoretical tools to better understand the political agency and radicalism of those engaged in informal livelihoods were nonetheless present in the GC's discussions. For example, Verónica Gago (2017) took inspiration from Bolivian theorizations of the motley to explore the political agency of those—mostly Bolivian—working in the "illegal" La Salada market in Buenos Aires. She analyzed the pragmatic strategization of the forces of global capital evident in La Salada, and the interplay of resistance and capitulation to neoliberalism that subjectivizes those working in Latin America's expansive informal markets, in a way "that opposes seeing the popular sectors as victims" (Gago 2017, 18). Those working in La Salada are hence seen to resist neoliberalism while also recreating it, and their pragmatism is a complex assemblage characterized by the union of opposites represented by the Andean concept *ch'ixi*. The economic subjects apparent in popular markets, who to the neoliberal can exemplify the drive to make a profit and maximize their own self-interests, are rather producing value in the broader sense of a striving to persevere and survive, but in a way that disrupts the dichotomy between the individual and the community (Gago 2017, 13). Gago's formulation does justice to the way that "illegal," "informal," or "notorious" markets, far from representing unbridled neoliberal capitalism, have inherited the structures of Andean collective organization and cooperative forms of market organization. The fiestas that underpin community cooperation play a vital role in the maintenance of community ties and the regulation of market activity in these areas. The continued ties that most households in peri-urban areas with links to the countryside maintain ensure the importance of reciprocity and community ties, which guide market dynamics.

Both the GC's and Negri and Hardt's (2004) accounts of the fragmentation of labor under neoliberalism have been criticized for overlooking gender. In looking at the processes of subjectivation involved, the cultural, symbolic, and affective are taken into account, and both formulations have in common a multiplicity of possible forms of resistance. Nevertheless, both formulations remain based on the categories of capital—whether Andean feudalism or the precariat—rather than allowing that culture could also be a basic organizing principle (Hall 1980; Featherstone 1995; McRobbie 2011). Neither formulation engages with gender or the feminine directly. Despite the fragmentation of identity, and multiple forms of symbolic subjectivation and of "baroque" economies being recognized, the imaginary of the feminine is still associated with domestic labor and reproduction (Rivera Cusicanqui 2010; McRobbie 2011, 65). This omission means that feminine economic subjectivity, which has always involved a multiplicity of livelihood strategies—including reproductive but also commercial activity, rural production, wage labor, community gift exchange, natural resource management, subsistence agriculture, and so forth—is overlooked. Furthermore, the categories that describe these economic activities are based on masculine experience, and the omission of gender from the formulations of the motley and the multitude means that gendered terms which produce this othering remain intact. The definitions of labor, the focus on union organizing, and the terms on which scale is constructed and production is defined all remain coded masculine.

The Permitted Subjects of Plurality

The GC's theorizations were shaped by the political developments in Bolivia of the time. The construction of plurality evident in their publications reflected assumptions that were generated from a particular historical conjuncture, which implied a particular imaginary of the subject positions that were to be permitted in a pluri-economy. The focus on community and indigeneity was a reaction to the multiculturalism of the 1990s that aligned with decentralization and the extension of a consumer market (Hale 2002). This "neoliberal multicultural" model allowed for diversity of language and judicial systems, but devolved administrations still had to work within an orthodox economic, market-led logic. The cooperative, reciprocal, economic dynamics that defined indigenous communities were overlooked. Across Latin America social interventions targeting indigenous people and aiming for "inclusion" sought to "capitalize" the community relations, which were constitutive of the identity and trust that underpin economic production (Maclean 2010). Neoliberal multiculturalism accepted a specific economic role for indigeneity; in Rivera Cusicanqui's words, the "permitted Indian" of neoliberal multicultural Bolivia was "an exporter of handicrafts or values or medicines, but all under a scheme of subordination to the transnational corporations" (quoted in Farthing 2007, 7–8; see also Hale 2004). The only form of economic subject permitted was that of the consumer and producer in a neoliberal market. The imposition of such a restricted notion of legitimate economic exchanges was itself a cultural rather than merely technical imposition, and while cultural products were valued, cooperative traditions, which are definitive of community, were not.

The GC's, and later the MAS's, focus on indigeneity reflected a discursive shift from the classed, feudal signifier of "peasants" to the cultural signifier "indigenous" (Albó 2004). This shift coincided with the decline of leftist discourse after 1989 and the events of 1992 marking the five hundredth anniversary of the colonization of the Americas, which brought colonialism and indigeneity to the fore of the political agenda. Politically, in promoting the idea of the resistance of indigenous peoples as the main counterhegemonic strategy, the GC distinguished its approach from that of the "old left," which aimed for a national-popular hegemony based on a mestizo idea of the citizen (Moreiras 2015). By the early 2000s the MNR had become very much part of the political establishment. The party had been in government in the 1980s and had implemented the world's harshest structural adjustment program under President Víctor Paz Estenssoro in 1985. They had twice brought Gonzalo Sánchez de Lozada, who had been the minister of planning under Estenssoro and was generally seen as the architect of the structural reforms of 1985, to the presidency. It was hence politically effective to construct this party as conservative, and the MAS as a genuine break with the MNR's view of citizenship as *mestizaje*.

The economy and structures of the labor market had also changed dramatically since the period of the MNR revolution, notably with the rapid urbanization of the 1970s. The discourse of *mestizaje* produced a discursive double bind for migrants to cities from rural areas as indigenous people working in industry or urban contexts were obliged—formally, informally, or by inculcating those norms themselves—to adopt the mimetic character of the *mestizo* in order to be recognized as a citizen, despite this incurring the pejorative characterization of *cholo*. This dynamic of strategic mimesis is what indigenous leaders Fausto Reinaga and Félix Patzi objected to so clearly in their characterization of the Marxist left, which they claimed did not capture the elimination of cultural recognition and the sense of shame that imperialism created. *Cholo* can be used as a racialized slur, but the term also brings out the complexities of indigeneity, urbanity, gender, and class. While the word's meaning varies across the Americas, in Bolivia, and specifically El Alto, a *cholo* can be defined as someone from a rural, indigenous background who "has come to live in the city and is somewhere between being an Indian and being a mestizo" (Lazar 2002, 35). By contrast, the feminine *chola* does not necessarily have pejorative implications, and refers to a successful market woman *de pollera*.

The term *cholo* reveals the false neutrality, normative, and exclusionary implications of mestizaje. However, *cholaje* also demonstrates the agency and power of popular markets to disrupt the political landscape.

There is a risk that, in adopting Reinaga's approach to Indianism and constructing the urban migrant as necessarily adopting mimetic strategies, there is an implicit notion of an authentic indigeneity that can further pathologize those who have moved away from that culture, and particularly women, who bear more responsibility for maintaining "traditional" identity (de la Cadena 1995; Yuval-Davis 1997). "Authentic" indigenous identity and traditions were associated with rurality and land, as Rivera Cusicanqui states in her critique of the way the notion of indigeneity had been constructed in the 2009 Constitution: "the localization of ethnicity in bounded rural territories leaves aside the political imprint of urban ethnicity and multi-ethnic lowland settlements" (2010, 44).

Inequality and exploitation within indigenous social movements that had inspired the GC were not addressed in their theorizations. Work being generated in Bolivia at the time, however, did shed light on the everyday resistance strategies, gender dynamics, and hierarchies within these groups. This included the work of the Taller de Historia Oral Andina (Rivera Cusicanqui 2008), Mujeres Creando (Galindo and Paredes 2000), and anthropological work on gender and social movements (Arnold and Spedding 2005). Although these writers and activists were involved politically with the rise of the MAS and crucially the Constituent Assembly, their lack of influence on the foundational texts meant that the revolutionary potential of the everyday had limited influence on the underpinning ideology of the GC and later the MAS. With the emphasis on traditional indigenous norms, women who took up the characteristics of urban modernity were not reflected in the images of femininity offered by this decolonial approach. Urban indigenous women are marginalized, as they are particularly pathologized by discourses emphasizing the importance of traditions that women are under unequal pressure to maintain (Rivera Cusicanqui 1996).

Hence a critical, reflective eye can still be cast on the constructions of femininity apparent in the Latin American decolonial project as embodied in the GC's theories and the de jure and political positions built thereupon. The permitted femininities implied, which have been discussed here, exclude the subject position of women working in peri-urban popular markets—the urban *chola* (Rivera Cusicanqui 2010). They may have had to adopt a mestizo *chola* identity and thus be criticized for leaving their indigenous identity behind. However, to overlook this position or dismiss it as conformity to colonial and neoliberal structures is to perpetuate exclusion and to disregard everyday strategies to resist the demands of capital and the strictures of colonialism and of gender.

Conclusion

Pluri-economy is rooted in Latin American decolonial scholarship and inspired by indigenous social movements and epistemologies. It combines a relational ontology and cultural critique with a Marxist analysis of injustice and inequality. The relational ontology at its heart has the potential to recognize the value, in an economic sense, of reciprocal and cooperative labor, typically the responsibility of women, and to culturally and socially situate economic actors while also valorizing care and maintenance of community and tradition. Challenging the notions of universality and scale has the potential to resolve some of the more difficult conceptual challenges of a gender-inclusive political and economic framework, and hence also to challenge gendered constructions of productivity and value. However, in the specific development of these ideas in the work of García Linera, the potential for pluri-economy to valorize various forms of exchange is curtailed by a continued emphasis on the power of a centralized state and the continued prioritization of economic over cultural dynamics. The GC's theoretical framing of pluri-economy failed to sufficiently take into account either the feminine economic subject or the intersections between femininity, urbanity, and indigeneity.

The development of the MAS platform and the vision of pluri-economy had a unique trajectory that was specific to struggles in Bolivia. The logic of identity espoused by the Indianist movement has specific roots in the relational epistemology of indigenous worldviews, as opposed to the deconstructive tradition of feminist and postcolonial thought. The resolution of these tensions found in the GC was built on Gramscian notions of hegemony and articulations, but it remained economically deterministic. In finding a hegemonic signifier— indigeneity—that could bind together the fragmented positions of social movements, a binary notion of power was adopted: the oppressor and the oppressed. As will be discussed further in the next chapter, in denying or abstracting away the complexities of power, and of different possible taxonomies of identity and narratives of oppression, the MAS agenda created a narrative that produced its own subjectivization and alterities. This criticism, particularly from feminist postcolonial critics such as Rivera Cusicanqui and Gayatri Spivak (Asher 2017), can throw light on the lacunae—in theory, policy, and practice—of the pluriverse, particularly in terms of gender, agency, informality, and the need for constant reflection and deconstruction of the categories created (Rivera Cusicanqui 2012; Asher 2013). The challenges involved in uniting the materially based claims of Marxists in a world where undeniably wealth is accumulating to specific groups of people demands a recognition of racialized exploitation on the grounds of colonialism and cultural identity, but "labels continue to obscure the details and complexity of the processes involved" (Larner 2003, 509).

By drawing on contemporary scholarship from Bolivia, we have seen that the vision of pluri-economy developed by the GC is itself culturally situated. The evocation of the signifier "indigenous" as a counter-hegemonic strategy was an observation on political activism as much as a theoretical proposal, and so was true to the commitments of the philosophy of liberation and the Zapatista approach to "bottom-up" political activism and theory. However, this notion is of necessity delimited by the contemporary discursive context. The political subject that is evoked is that of an indigenous community activist whose political priorities are territory and autonomy. Urban mestizo and non-syndicalized workers had also been marginalized by racialized discourses from both the urban criollo elite and those invoking an "authentic" indigeneity. The renewed discourse of indigeneity proposed by the work of the GC may provide a more effective discursive tool with which to negotiate inclusion, but this potential is attenuated by what is an essential, albeit strategic, identity. Nevertheless, as will be discussed in the following chapters, the economic power of popular markets was itself going to challenge this script.

While the recognition of community and use value has the potential to valorize feminized reproductive labor, the traditions underpinning community and cooperation imply an uneven gendered duty to maintain cooperative relations. Nevertheless, the construction of femininity offered here could be less limiting than the roles of marriage and motherhood offered by modernity and state-led development, or the romanticized visions of the indigenous woman entrepreneur offered by neoliberalism. Pluri-economy brings together these theorizations, and it is where the economic reductionism of orthodox Marxist positions and the claims for recognition and autonomy of indigenous movements meet. However, the array of potential subject positions that are absent from or diminished by the GC's particular formulation of plurality demonstrates the need for a continued reflexive and deconstructive approach, one that would allow a continued bottom-up approach to theorizing and politics.

The following chapter looks at the implementation of pluri-economy and how the political alliances that were formed and compromises that were struck as the MAS gained power shaped the way this highly theorized concept was put into practice. The political processes that led to the rise of the MAS and the negotiations involved in the Constituent Assembly indicate the discursive and material forces that shaped how pluri-economy was operationalized and instituted. The text of the constitution itself betrays culturally situated tropes of indigeneity and femininity that delimited the economic subjects that were permitted in the vision of pluri-economy.

2

The Political Space for Pluri-economy

This chapter looks at the social movements that formed the MAS and the historical conjuncture that enabled its rise. The processes and power relations that were salient in Bolivia at the turn of the century shaped the development of MAS discourse and policy on pluri-economy, framing the way diverse economic identities were constructed and valued. The MAS initially formed not as a political party but rather as the "political instrument" of social movements and was therefore aligned with the idea of government by social movements and transformation of the colonial state apparatus. The discursive hegemony that the MAS formed to win the 2005 election was built on mass protest and opposition to a colonial, neoliberal elite. However, the fault lines between the articulations of indigenous, class-based, feminist, women's, and environmental movements swiftly began to show when the MAS came to power, as analyses of the negotiations in the Constituent Assembly demonstrate. The construction of pluri-economy in the text of the 2009 Constitution reflects the priorities of the social movements involved and the Grupo Comuna's reconciliation of class-based revolution with indigenous movements' demands for decolonization. However, the text also reflects the multiple and complex compromises and commitments that the MAS had made to various bodies to gain power. Although women's, feminist, and indigenous women's social movements were involved in negotiations in the assembly, the tropes of economic femininity that are recognized and recreated in the 2009 Constitution situate women firmly in the reproductive sphere, and the way the concepts of value, scale, and production are constructed betray masculinist assumptions. The intersections of discourses of femininity and indigeneity in the text marginalize indigenous women working in popular markets who fall between the conceptual cracks of tradition, modernity, production, and reproduction. Nevertheless, although not the intended effect, the messy confluence of political influences on MAS discourse and policy, along with the strategies employed by the leadership to maintain power, enabled substantial growth in peri-urban popular markets and potentiated the wealthy, urban *chola*.

Both the strength and the weakness of the MAS was its ability to articulate various concerns and build support across a breadth of social movements, unions, and political parties. Critics from all sides have argued that the way the MAS handled negotiations after the election compromised its principles to both class-based revolution and indigenous empowerment, displaying the fault lines in the GC's theorizing. The nationalization of hydrocarbons in 2006 fell short for those seeking full state control of those industries (see Webber 2011), while the strength of the state buoyed by the wealth from natural resources revenue curtailed the potential for indigenous movements to control their territory (Regalsky 2010). The reliance on extractive industries was felt to be a betrayal of the ontological vision of relations with the environment held by many indigenous organizations (Rodriguez Fernandez 2020). The text of the 2009 Constitution encompasses these various tensions and influences as the language shifts back and forth between an idealized view of pre-Columbian indigeneity, class-based resistance to neoliberalism, and compromises with powerful economic actors about private property, rights to resources, and business. These divides would go on to underpin the main controversies of Evo Morales's presidency. Morales's leadership style was based on the horizontal structures of rural organizations and coca unions, but, despite a commitment to a horizontal approach to governance, MAS power was highly concentrated in the partnership between Morales and García Linera. The MAS oscillated between commitments to communities, social movements, and decolonization of the state, and amid that ambivalence its leaders relied on a highly personalized populism that at times could not be effectively held in check by civil society.

In tracing these various influences, my aim in this chapter is to stress that plurality is found not in the statements or policies of the MAS but in the processes that were created in its rise to power and administration. The political processes behind the new constitution and the policy instruments intended to enact the vision of pluri-economy shaped the economic identities that emerged and the way exchanges and networks were valued. The multiple influences on MAS power necessitated compromise and a strategic discursive fluidity around national populism, indigeneity, decolonization, and modernization. Although formal proclamations and categorizations tended to overlook the complex position of urban indigeneity and the dynamics of popular markets, Morales's government would be frequently accused of favoring those working in the popular markets of El Alto, as they did form a key constituency for the MAS. Indeed, the executive's approach to resolving the multiple, complex "creative tensions" they faced reflected the strategies of being an "intermediary" that Aymara markets, and particularly Aymara women, are famous for.

MAS Political Bases and Articulations

The MAS's election landslide in 2005 represented a victory for the social movements that had embodied, inspired, and created the political space for the GC's vision of pluri-economy. The MAS administration, which included members of the GC, had the opportunity to put into effect the highly theorized unification of Marxism and Indianism explored in the last chapter. Once the MAS was in power, it had the challenge of instituting the "creative tensions" that had been identified theoretically and maintaining power among the supportive movements with which it was articulated politically. The GC had established a balance between Indianist and Marxist visions of community, state, autonomy, and redistribution with reference to Gramscian cultural theory and the logic of the pluriverse, and these theorizations were developed based on a commitment to praxis and community engagement. However, the implementation of these ideas was a matter of politics and hence was shaped by power dynamics and processes within the MAS, the articulations it had made with other organizations, and political negotiations with other powerful actors. The articulations the MAS formed to gain power diluted its initial aims as it aligned itself with organizations that adopted economic dynamics, identities, and priorities different from those of the social movements that had created the MAS originally.

The MAS's transition to formal electoral politics was part of a trend across the region in the 1990s. Disillusioned with elite politics and spurred on by the mobilizations of 1992, indigenous social movements across Latin America decided to mount a political arm in response to widespread dissatisfaction with the political system (Van Cott 2005). Formal politics on the continent was dominated by traditional parties that represented only the interests of the elite and were seemingly inured to protest and unrest, despite ubiquitous inequality, exclusion, corruption, and clientelism. In Bolivia, the decision to establish a political wing to represent social movements and unions was made in the mid-1990s and driven by the coca unions, indigenous movements, miners' unions, and agrarian syndicates (Van Cott 2003). In 1995, the Central Obrera Boliviana (COB; Bolivian Workers' Center), in alliance with the coca unions and indigenous campesino unions, including the Confederación Sindical Única de Trabajadores del Campo de Bolivia (CSUTCB; Confederation of Peasant Workers of Bolivia), the Confederación Sindical de Colonizadores de Bolivia (CSCB; Union Confederation of Bolivian Settlers), and, as it was known at the time, the Federación Nacional de Mujeres Campesinas de Bolivia "Bartolina Sisa" (National Federation of Peasant Women of Bolivia "Bartolina Sisa"), generally referred to as Las Bartolinas, approved the formation of a "political instrument" that was initially named the Assembly for the Sovereignty of the Peoples. The following year the MAS was formed, with the full title of Movimiento al Socialism—Instrumento Político por la Soberanía de los Pueblos (Movement toward Socialism—Political Instrument for the Sovereignty of the Peoples) (Harten 2011). Participatory, consultative processes of social movements and unions were hence at the heart of the formation of the MAS; the MAS did not just *adopt* a horizontal, reciprocal approach—its power base was constituted thus.

The coca movement had initiated the development of a political instrument as a way to combat the coca-eradication policies demanded by the United States as part of its war on drugs (Potter and Zurita 2009). Coca cultivation is centered in the coca-growing area of Chapare, but the spread of its influence and power was enabled by the fact that many people had moved to Chapare over the 1980s as a result of job losses from the privatization of mining in the Altiplano. Those of the Chapare region hence tended to have connections throughout the country. The coca union is in effect the state in the area—taking on responsibility for deciding land disputes, distribution of resources, infrastructure, and tax (Grisaffi 2017). Morales's political career developed in the coca unions, and before leading the MAS he was the leader of the Comité de la Coordinación de las Seis Federaciones (CCSF; Coordination Committee of the Six Federations)—the highest-level federation of the coca unions, whom he represented on the COB.

Morales's leadership approach initially incorporated the deliberative, cooperative ideals of the coca and agrarian unions, albeit only symbolically. Unions' power and responsibility is mediated by communal norms of participatory assembly and rotation—*usos y costumbres*—and leaders are kept in check by the community itself (Harten 2011). Leadership within the constitutive social movements of the MAS and adopted by Morales was characterized as *mandar obedeciendo* (Harten 2011), recalling the pedagogic, "walking while asking questions" approach of the Zapatistas to establishing power. Community members themselves elect and rotate leaders, who are responsible for disseminating information, coordinating community justice, maintaining social control of coca, and distributing and coordinating communal land. Governance is via community forums, in which regular meetings are held and decisions deliberated at length. Community organizations are hence more responsible and more responsive to their local communities than mainstream, liberal institutions, which would be more alienating even if they may have better transparency and accountability (Wolff 2013).

In a local economy, particularly in rural areas where reciprocity and cooperation are essential to subsistence and production, the norms and customs that control behavior and safeguard cooperation are strong. Such community horizontal structures of power and governance also characterize El Alto. At first glance the preponderance of informal commerce makes it appear that *alteños* are in business for themselves, but a closer examination of the built environment and infrastructure of the city, its organizations, and its markets "reveals a type of community organization that in many ways reflects the traditional organizational patterns of rural Aymara and Quechua communities" (Zibechi 2005). El Alto is predominantly built by citizens themselves, as the boomtown adjacent to La Paz grew without central assistance due to migration from rural areas to the city. The organizational culture and sense of community self-reliance these migrants brought with them engender a particular sense of belonging and social engagement that Aymara sociologist Felix Patzi termed "obligatoriness." This "obligatoriness" underpins the consensual command that constitutes the power of neighborhood organizations in El Alto (Zibechi 2005).

It may be, however, that the vertical and potentially exploitative power involved in social and community governance is underestimated. While I was in Luribay I saw the disgruntlement caused by the agrarian union's demand that at least one person from each household should attend protests or else face a fine, and the genuine fear that the protests could turn violent. The protests and blockades deployed by social movements could also have a differential impact on women. Typically, it would be women traveling from rural to urban areas to sell, and the blockades—which could last weeks—meant that they could lose their perishable produce. Women also assumed the responsibility of providing food for their families and dealing with the scarcities caused by the protests (Arnold and Spedding 2005). It is also not clear that horizontal social dynamics are sufficient to hold executive power in check once the community is scaled up to the level of a nation-state, with its inherited colonial apparatus that does not rely on the social and economic obligatoriness that characterizes Andean communities. Nevertheless, the elevation of community and indigenous rituals to the national level that Morales's presidency represented was to change the cultural markers of expected behavior in political office and in power.

There were significant differences among the social movements making up the MAS originally, particularly around the issue of indigenous territorial control. The groups in the MAS arguing for territorial autonomy were the Aymara nationalist group the Kataristas and the indigenous movements of the eastern lowlands that led the water wars of 2003, the Confederación de Pueblos Indígenas de Bolivia (CIDOB; Confederation of Bolivian Indigenous Peoples) and the Coordinadora de Pueblos Étnicos de Santa Cruz (CPESC; Coordinator for Ethnic Peoples of Santa Cruz). There had been a split, however, within the Kataristas between the followers of Victor Hugo Cardénas, who worked with the central government during the 1990s, and Felipe Quispe, who emphasized autonomy from the state (Postero 2010). Leaders from Quispe's faction were prominent in the MAS, including the future vice president García Linera, who had been involved in the Katarista guerrilla organization Ejército Guerrillero Túpac Katari (EGTK; Túpac Katari Guerrilla Army) (Harten 2011, 46). The CIDOB and the CPESC also demanded official recognition of their communal territories and forms of government throughout the 1990s and early 2000s. This issue of recognition of territorial autonomy was to become one of the most controversial of the Constituent Assembly, and accusations would be leveled that the MAS was merely co-opting the ideas of those social movements rather than delivering meaningful autonomous authority (Regalsky 2010).

The major indigenous peasant women's organizations involved in the establishment of the MAS were Las Bartolinas and the Coordinadora de Mujeres Campesinas del Trópico de Cochabamba (COCAMTROP;

Coordinator for Peasant Women of the Tropics of Cochabamba). Las Bartolinas was founded in 1980 as a counterpart to the CSUTCB, and COCAMTROP developed as an organization within Las Bartolinas specifically of coca-growing women in the Chapare region. There were divisions within the movement between those who wanted more proximity to the male-dominated unions and those who wanted separate women's representation, but unity was found in the fight against the United States' war on drugs. From the outset, Las Bartolinas and COCAMTROP were aligned with indigenous movements on the issues of land, territorial autonomy, and corresponding rights over natural resources. However, they were consistently strongly critical of the male-dominated leadership of the unions (Arnold and Spedding 2005). They emphasized women's rights to education and literacy, political representation, and access to identity documents that would facilitate other rights— including voter registration, land ownership, and access to finance. As indigenous women, they argued that their relationship with the land and hence their priorities were different from men's and therefore not represented fully by male-dominated unions. Las Bartolinas emphasized food sovereignty and sustainability as "inextricably linked to their interests and rights as indigenous and peasant women, [whereas] male-dominated organisations argue[d] that there were 'more pressing' issues on the table" (Potter and Zurita 2009, 235). Their demands also included the unfair distribution of lands by agrarian unions, which, despite a tradition of equitable inheritance rights in the Andes, favored male ownership, and lands would be returned to the community rather than given to the wife after a man died or moved away (Deere and León 2002). Despite the "ever-present machismo" (Potter and Zurita 2009, 236) of the unions and indigenous social movements with which Las Bartolinas was affiliated, indigenous women's organizations decided in 2004 to "stay with [their] brothers in the struggle for decolonization" (Monasterios 2007), partly in response to the inadequacies of the technocratic, liberal approaches to gender equality represented by NGOs. The position of Las Bartolinas as a constitutive organization of the MAS also brought significant power to the indigenous women's movement, and gender equality on indigenous terms was a central plank in the MAS agenda.

The MAS, unlike other parties based on indigenous social movements in South America, managed to extend its reach beyond the social movements that formed it. It did so by building a "populist logic of articulation" (Harten 2011, 8), based on an idea of the people versus the elites, and by employing signifiers that could capture the widespread dissatisfaction with the status quo. While the MAS base in rural areas had developed organically from social movements, in urban areas it adopted the strategy of alliances with community organizations. Whereas rural and indigenous organizations constituted the MAS, alliances with movements outside this immediate constituency were formed by having the MAS place "their people" in the leadership of those organizations in return for promises of representation once in power (Anria 2013). This approach, while electorally successful, created a vertical and clientelist relationship between the MAS and certain social movements, many of whom felt that they had been co-opted rather than integrated into the state (McNelly 2020a).

A key site for MAS political mobilization in the early 2000s was El Alto. The population of El Alto is characterized as families from rural areas who maintain constant contact with their places of provenance in the countryside as they manage family and household production in rural areas as well as commercial income-generating activities in the city (Lazar 2007). Due to the history of its formation, El Alto is thought of as existing "in between" rurality and urbanity, as its population travels back and forth to the city frequently, and this connection was strategically important as the MAS extended its support. Market traders act as intermediaries between the city and the country, a role that has historically strengthened the power of indigenous communities (Tassi 2017), and El Alto was pivotal in the gas and water wars precisely because of its organic connections with rural areas (Lazar 2006). The MAS's approach to extending its base was inspired by this rural/urban in-betweenness that had been so successful in the protests of the early 2000s, but whereas its connections with coca unions and indigenous social movements were generated from the bottom up, the way the MAS incorporated urban organizations represented a vertical logic of articulation.

In El Alto, MAS leaders gained places in the Federación de Juntas Vecinales (FEJUVE; Federation of Neighborhood Boards), the Central Obrera Regional (COR; Regional Labor Federation), and the Federación de Trabajadores Gremiales (FTG; Federation of Street Traders) (Lazar 2006; Anria 2013). These organizations held substantial power in El Alto, which is home to vast areas of commerce and informal trade. Urban *comerciantes*—market traders—are organized in associations that feed up through the federations to the COR and the COB. Syndicates, trade guilds, and market associations, as well as communities themselves, regulate trade, administer market space, and lobby for their particular industries, often organizing protests. This range of organizations represents the complicated patchwork of economic exchanges in El Alto, underpinned by various cultural traditions that correspond to different racialized categorizations. Indigenous peasants whose agricultural production is based on community organization and gift exchange become competitive traders when they encounter their urban clientele, which can then perpetuate the stereotype of the Aymara trader as "miserly." The *cholas—cholaje* being itself a fluid "ethnocultural category somewhere between Indian and mestizo" (Lazar 2007, 239)—operate as intermediaries between the producers, wholesalers, retailers, and the *detallistas*—women who retail in small quantities—who sell on to other markets. They travel constantly to and from rural areas where they buy produce to the city where they sell, and in the process pass through various networks, perceptions, and imbrications of culture, community, and economy.

This fluidity was reflected in the way the MAS dealt with some of the key crises that sprang from the tensions among its commitments to indigenous territorial autonomy, social movements wishing to decolonize the state, and a modernization program based on extractivism. In the Territorio Indígena y Parque Nacional Isiboro Sécure (TIPNIS; Isiboro Sécure National Park and Indigenous Territory) dispute, for example, the proposed road through indigenous territory was justified in terms of class and modernization—that it was necessary for the development of the area and for inhabitants there to access social rights (Laing 2015). The protests were based on indigenous identity and territorial control, and leaders from the area emphasized that the MAS had reneged on its commitments to prior consultation (McKay 2018). The movement gained in strength internationally because of the potency of the signifier "indigenous" within the global environmental movement. García Linera, in response, was vociferous in his dismissal of the way international organizations were perpetuating stereotypes of indigenous people and their dependence:

These NGOs . . . by opposing, for example, the construction of
roads or technological investments claimed by indigenous organizations themselves, are in effect tenaciously opposed to the
satisfaction of basic needs of the working population. What they
want is "communities" frozen in deprivation . . . because of course,
their officials do not lack electricity or drinking water . . . they can
travel by plane, and earn wages in dollars. (García Linera 2013, 11)

The MAS, by contrast, claimed to be representing the contemporary, modern reality of the way indigenous people earn a living. This in turn was
characterized as Aymara and Quechua ideas of indigeneity trumping
those of lowland indigenous groups (Fabricant and Postero 2015). This
dispute indicates the complexities behind the signifier "indigenous"
and illustrates the way the MAS slipped between different rural and
urban identities, as is the reality for many people earning a living in
the vast popular markets of Bolivia's cities. This "tacking back and forth
between mass activism and parliamentary politics" was part of what
allowed them to build an "indigenous nationalism" (Postero 2010, 19),
albeit one centered on Aymara and Quechua practices. However, it also
demonstrates a shift in the dynamic within the MAS from horizontal, consultative processes to more vertical, authoritarian governance
(Geddes 2016).

El Alto was a key locus of rebellion in the run-up to the 2005 election, but there was also support for the MAS in the more traditional,
middle-class areas of La Paz such as the Zona Sur, and there was significant middle-class mobilization (Harten 2011, 126). Although in
the whiter, more urbane, and middle-class areas of La Paz traditional
parties still held sway and social movements did not have the purchase
or power they did in El Alto, one emerging party, the Movimiento sin
Miedo (MSM; Movement without Fear), had been building up strength
since the 1990s. This party was run by Juan del Granado, a former mayor
of La Paz, and was positioned on the center-left. The MAS formed alliances with the MSM to extend its reach. While the water wars of 2003
centered around indigenous identity, they also permitted the forging of
significant rural-urban alliances, including with the traditional urban
middle classes (Harten 2011, 126). The gas wars had a notable presence in urban areas as well and were largely a middle-class revolt. The

MAS was not directly involved in these protests and had supported President Carlos Mesa's proposed liberal, constitutional resolution of the crisis (Postero 2010). Nevertheless, the MAS was able to harness this middle-class unrest with the strategic decision to have politician and publisher José Antonio Quiroga as vice-presidential candidate in the 2002 elections, and García Linera in 2005, both of whom are white and middle class (Anria 2013).

This courting of the middle-class vote was a necessary electoral strategy—and is consistent with the characterization of the MAS as the "pragmatic left." However, from the outset it produced concerns that too many compromises were being made. The nationalization of natural resources was incomplete, to the dissatisfaction of commentators and critics from a range of perspectives, as contracts were renegotiated with companies to give the state a significantly larger role and proportion of the profits. Commentator Wilfredo Ramírez Terceros in the national paper *El Diario* succinctly summarized the complaint: "In practice this bombastic 'nationalization' was nothing more than an adaptation of oil contracts, subject to legal provisions in force, and with a significant tax increase for the General Treasury of the Nation" (Ramírez Terceros 2011). This meant that although the state did gain greater revenues, the neoliberal approach of the transnational corporations was left unchanged. For the political analyst Iván Arias, "despite the nationalization driven by the government, transnational companies still dominate the national production of gas and oil" (*El Diario* 2011).

Raúl Prada Alcoreza, who was directly involved in the GC and the Constituent Assembly, became very critical of the way the nationalization of natural resources had been managed:

Many of us knew that it was not a nationalization, but a process of nationalization. A nationalization means an expropriation implying a real recovery of technical control, of everything from exploration, exploitation, to industrialization. None of that has been done; the only thing that was done is to change the conditions of the distribution, the conditions of the contracts. We knew—I knew it and the people who were in the Government at the highest level knew that it was not nationalization, but we had to support it, we couldn't ruin the party. (*La Razón* 2011)

Prada's dissatisfaction with this fundamental issue grew, along with that of other social activists, as it became evident that the radical potential of the "government of social movements" was not being realized (Zibechi 2010). Social movements' ability to critique the state was in effect curtailed by the establishment of government bodies dedicated to social movements, which brought them into government without the more radical elements of their agendas being adopted (McNelly 2020a). Negotiations with the business powers of the Oriente meant that agrarian land reform and the socialization of property relations were not achieved (Webber 2015). In response to these criticisms, García Linera, in *Las Tensiones Creativas de la Revolución* (Creative tensions of the revolution) (2011), explains the various political balances that had to be struck after the election of Morales and argues that they were inevitable and that they enabled a more meaningful plurality within a new symbolic order, represented primarily by the election of an indigenous president, a radical change in the terms of inclusion of the national bloc, and the values and processes that could therefore be represented politically.

Nevertheless, there are examples of MAS policies that were central to pluri-economy that were able to be implemented because of these compromises and coalitions. Bolivia's conditional cash transfer (CCT) programs, introduced after 2006, are unique in the region in being universal rather than means-tested. All public school children are entitled to the Bono Juancito Pinto (2006)—200 bolivianos annually on the condition of school attendance. The Renta Dignidad (2007) is an unconditional universal program for all Bolivian citizens—a basic state pension. The Bono Juana Azurduy (2009) is for expectant and new mothers and offers payments on condition of health visits before and after birth. These programs can be seen as a policy instantiation of a post-neoliberal agenda and an institutional foundation to the idea of multiple forms of exchange being recognized, as they constitute investments in social infrastructure that recognize the importance of care and social rights.

The *bonos*—welfare vouchers—were funded with revenues from the newly nationalized hydrocarbons industry. They were emblematic of the MAS's central strategy of ensuring that the wealth of Bolivia's resources went to the Bolivian people. However, they were viewed unfavorably by the departments where the newly nationalized gas was found— specifically, Santa Cruz, Tarija, Beni, and Pando—the Media Luna provinces in Bolivia's Oriente, where the MAS had not been as electorally successful as in the rest of the country. These departments are home to the country's economic powers, and soon after the election victory of 2005 they formed a powerful bloc arguing for autonomy and objecting to the nationalization of hydrocarbons. They were also against the Renta Dignidad, which would be paid for by a direct tax on hydrocarbons (Anria and Niedzwiecki 2016). The fact that Renta Dignidad was achieved has been credited to the social movements that defended the policy against mobilizations from the Media Luna (Anria and Niedzwiecki 2016). It is notable, however, that there were precedents for similar targeted social programs from the neoliberal era, and the predecessor for Renta Dignidad was Bono Sol, a targeted pension scheme brought in by the MNR in 1997. Indeed, in the 2005 election such programs were in the MNR's manifesto but not in the MAS's (McGuire 2013), suggesting that the development of these policies was part of a populist electoral strategy rather than representing a shift in values away from a modernizing state.

The *bonos* also caused divisions between the social movements that had supported the MAS. The powerful COB —the chief trade union federation in Bolivia—initially objected to the Renta Dignidad as it did not recognize the greater contributions made by formal workers (Anria and Niedzwiecki 2016). Their objection brought out the fault lines between the various factions that the MAS had managed to unite—the "old," classed-based social movements, indigenous social movements, and those working informally. However, the main opposition came from the municipalities and governors of the Media Luna. These disputes formed part of the broader political crisis with the departments of the Oriente, which had the effect of binding the social movements of the MAS. Their strength enabled the potentially existential threat from those departments that they would secede to be quelled, but not without compromises by the MAS to business interests that were strongly criticized by the left (Webber 2015). Although these events showed the strength of the MAS and social movements, once compromise had been reached with the Media Luna the MAS was no longer as dependent on those social movements for support. There was therefore widespread concern that the original cooperative and horizontal structures of the MAS had changed to one of a governing political party that had co-opted social movements rather than integrating them (McNelly 2020a).

The political strategies used to establish these programs also demonstrated the personalized leadership that the MAS would be moving toward throughout its tenure as well as the constructions of femininity that would in effect reinforce Morales and García Linera's paternalist, rather than collaborative, authority. This is evident in the way the Bono Juana Azurduy was presented as a discussion between Morales and García Linera personally in which they concluded that "single mothers are the most vulnerable, neglected of all . . . and the state must help support these women" (quoted in McGuire 2013, 17). This stance reflects problematic maternalist assumptions about femininity behind CCTs across Latin America (Molyneux 2006). As María Galindo commented,

> When it comes to social policy, they are not getting away from welfare programs that . . . were part of the neoliberal package; welfare checks that gloss over the problem and nothing else. The most embarrassing, the cheapest and the least effective is undoubtedly the Juana Azurduy program. State social policy has not been reinvented. (*Otramérica* 2011)

Despite the potential for the MAS vision of pluri-economy to valorize women's role while not replicating stereotypes, the culture within the MAS led to the reaffirmation of essentialized, traditional views of femininity.

The Constituent Assembly and the Text of the 2009 Constitution

The concerns about the relationship between the state and social movements, and the compromises that had been made with the business elites of the Media Luna, became swiftly apparent in debates within the Constituent Assembly. The assembly was established in 2006 to draw up the document that would frame the establishment of the new plurinational state, and the new text would represent the institutionalization of the MAS decolonial, post-neoliberal, and plural vision of state and society. The Constituent Assembly was to include direct representatives of social movements and indigenous organizations to demonstrate the MAS's commitment to a horizontal, political approach to politics, the social movements that made up its base, and community governance at the national level. The values, concepts, and processes defined in the Constitution delineated how plurality would be instituted and provided the blueprint for the "pluri"-economic subject. The political space, processes, and dialogues of the assembly shaped the political expression and institutional instantiation of pluri-economy as much as the theoretical visions and assumptions about value, production, and nation.

From the outset, the Constituent Assembly was not as participatory as intended. The initial demand from social movements and those critical of the inherently colonial roots of the state was that civil society and not political parties should shape the new constitution. The MAS had agreed to grant sixteen seats to indigenous organizations in the assembly. However, as the opposition dominated congress, the MAS had to prioritize seats for its own party to get its agenda through the second house. Approximately 60 of the 137 seats allocated to the MAS were taken by representatives from indigenous organizations (Schilling Vacaflor 2011, 8), but they were there as MAS delegates, not as representatives from civil society per se. Social movements that were subsequently excluded from this process characterized it as a betrayal of the participatory commitments that had formed the MAS and constituted its power base. In the words of Julieta Paredes of Mujeres Creando, "now we have to go and look for padrinos in the political parties" (personal communication, May 2006). The MAS initially wanted 50 percent women's participation, but with the decision to maintain the primacy of political parties rather than civil society actors, this policy was changed. Instead, seats would be selected from party lists on which women were represented. Women finally received eighty-eight seats, or 33 percent, with the majority of them (sixty-four) from the MAS (Rousseau 2011, 12). Over the course of discussions, the divide widened between the indigenous organizations, with their strong focus on decentralized territorial autonomy, self-government, and control over natural resources, and the MAS leaders, who emphasized state hegemony. What's more, the compromises the MAS had made in negotiating with opposing forces was reinforcing the role of the state and related institutions rather than decolonizing government.

The 2009 Constitution demonstrated a turning point in Bolivia's history and set the parameters for the MAS post-neoliberal, pluricultural, and decolonial vision for political process and governance. However, the text was as much a product of the discussions, allegiances, conflicts,

and compromises that occurred over the process of the Constituent
Assembly as it was of the MAS vision, and it is a mosaic of different
concepts and commitments that had been filtered through an array of
political compromises. The unwieldy document, which comprises 411
articles divided into five sections, accommodates contradictory notions of property, process, territory, and state. It contains individual
and group rights, and the identity categories on which group rights are
based associate indigeneity with rurality and femininity with family,
reproductive labor, and tradition. As Regalsky (2010, 36) puts it, "it is a
patchwork of overlapping and often conflicting claims" that result from
the compromises that were made between powerful business elites and
social movements. This "patchwork" indicates the logical difficulties of
inclusion if liberal frames of neutrality are discarded, along with the
difficulties in maintaining that decolonial "world in which many worlds
fit" while using the mechanisms of the state and an inherently colonial
bureaucracy. The definitions of productivity, nation, exchange, and
risk create a gendered economic landscape that reproduces masculine
biases in what counts as value, despite the increased representation of
women in politics and constitutional recognition of the need for state-
subsidized social programs. The power of the state restricts territorial
autonomy and the power of social movements and implies a delineation
of the formal/informal divide, which does not fully take into account
the liminal status of popular urban markets and the sense of identity
of people working there. However, the Constitution also formalizes a
rejection of neoliberal multiculturalism, recognizes that the economic
subject is culturally situated, and accords value to community and cooperative exchange.

The State

The power of the state was the most controversial element of discussions
in the Constituent Assembly, both in terms of the process and of the
final text. The establishment of a Constituent Assembly had long been a
demand from social movements, as was clearly articulated in the Unity
Pact (Postero 2017). For political reasons, however, the MAS—in its role,
perhaps despite itself, as the executive of state authority—had to as-
sert itself in the processes of the Constituent Assembly more than had
been hoped by the social movements that saw the MAS as their political

instrument. As a result, the state bureaucracy was not as transformed by the process of the Constituent Assembly as had been envisaged, and the powers accorded to the state in the resulting text, particularly with regard to rights over natural resources and indigenous territorial autonomy, were, particularly from the point of view of indigenous groups, too powerful (Regalsky 2010).

The tensions around the constitutional role of the state were exacerbated in the 1990s, when a balance of state power and the authority of indigenous territories had been attempted via neoliberal decentralization and the Law of Popular Participation (Kohl 2002, 2003). This administrative decentralization, accompanied by the privatization of national companies via the 1994 Law of Capitalization, had fragmented protests, as they were directed at governors and municipalities rather than the national government. Decentralization hence in effect facilitated transnational companies' access to Bolivia's national resources (Kohl 2002). A key mission for the MAS in government was to reassert national sovereignty, protect the country's resources, and address inequality and poverty by investing Bolivia's wealth in its people. To do this, it needed a level of centralization that was challenging to reconcile with territorial autonomy.

The vision of the state as a post-neoliberal entity is clear in the preamble to the Constitution, which stipulates the state's redistributive role to ensure the "principles of sovereignty, dignity, interdependence, solidarity, harmony, and equity in the distribution and redistribution of the social wealth" (Preamble). The figure of the state is also described in ways that bring together the notions of community solidarity and harmony, which are central to indigenous demands for autonomy with a modernizing state capable of distributing social wealth. The state's role is to guarantee respect for "economic, social, juridical, political and cultural pluralism" (Preamble) and to ensure social rights—including work and housing—for all. However, the specific details of the state's role in the management of sovereign resources to enable redistribution highlight the tension between the MAS's position as a "political instrument" of social movements and the power it needed to centralize to fulfill its redistributive role. Article 30.II.6 makes it clear that there is a collective right to "ownership of land and territories," and Article 30.II.16 accords to nations and rural native indigenous peoples the rights to "participate in the benefits of" the exploitation of natural resources in their territory.

This right is reiterated in Article 403.I, which also stipulates the right to "prior and informed consultation." However, the phrase "participate in the benefits of" is vague and avoids the questions of how the state would distribute these benefits (Anthias 2018), and the right to consultation does not necessarily entail power over the subsequent decisions (Laing 2020). The tensions produced by the ill-defined relationship between the state and territorial authorities over redistribution of resources and modernization projects gave rise to numerous "battles for *de jure* and *de facto* territorial authority" (Gustafson 2011, 223) related to the benefits from natural resources and state-led modernization programs, most notably the TIPNIS dispute.

The power of the state to intervene in the economy was a predictable point of contention with business elites. The relationship between the state, community, market, and formal private sector was controversial during the assembly, and these tensions come through in the text. While private property is permitted in the Constitution, the state had an interventionist role in regulating the market, promoting cooperatives, and guaranteeing collective bargaining. Its right to intervene is based on the collective interest, as "Every person has the right to dedicate him or herself to business, industry or any other legal economic activity under conditions which do not harm the collective well-being" (Article 47.I). This article was developed with the history of multinationals extracting unreasonable profits from natural resources in mind, but the notion of "collective well-being" is open to broad interpretation that could then be used to justify state intervention. The notion of the collective is also drawn upon in Article 56, which guarantees the right to "private property" provided it "serves a social function" and "is not harmful to the collective interests" by, for example, overaccumulation or using private real estate for speculation rather than housing. In abstract terms, these limits produce a communal, socially responsible economic subject and valorize the social exchanges that maintain community and solidarity, but also grant the central state significant powers.

As we will see in subsequent chapters, the relationship between the MAS government and formal private enterprise was embittered from the outset and would be further complicated by the growing strength of those working in the informal economy who were important politically for the MAS. Formal businesses would argue that they were being regulated out of existence and could not react to market pressures, while those working informally would not be subject to the same regulation or receive the same benefits (CEDLA 2015). In effect, the level of state regulation of business would diminish the incentives to formalize and consequently add to the tax base. The state regulations of the formal sector were indeed extensive:

> The following shall be regulated by law: labor relations related to contracts and collective agreements; general sector minimum wages and salary increases; reincorporation; paid vacations and holidays; calculation of seniority, the workday, extra hours, night time overtime, Sunday work; Christmas bonuses, vouchers, bonuses and other systems of participation in the profits of the enterprise; indemnification and severance pay; maternity leave; professional training and formation; and other social rights. (Article 49.II)

Predictably, concerns were expressed at the time regarding the level of regulation and obligation by law on employers:

> It is defined that by law issues such as employment contracts, minimum wages, wage increases, reinstatement and others will be regulated. The problem with the above is that by law the financial sustainability of companies cannot be determined. By law you cannot maintain or increase your sales and generate enough income to cover these constitutionally established labor obligations. (Ferrufino Goitia 2009, 534)

Business leaders argued instead for the establishment of "regulations that force balanced negotiations to be carried out, where the parties have equal information, capacity to analyze and ability to determine room for maneuver" (Ferrufino 2009, 535). This response from the business community, however, underestimated the breakdown in trust between workers and employers stemming from the iniquities of structural adjustment and the depth of the power differential between employers and employees in this context. Nevertheless, these central regulations placed significant pressures on formal businesses—a minority of the Bolivian economy—and while the motivation for these regulations was to prevent excessive profits at workers' expense, not all would be able to comply without state subsidy (*El Deber* 2013).

Article 54.III also grants workers the right to "reactivate and reorganize enterprises that are in the process of bankruptcy, insolvency or liquidation, or closed or abandoned unjustifiably." These stipulations were the corrections demanded after decades of neoliberalism had corroded social rights and wages, which had themselves led to the expansion of informal livelihoods. There is a recognition of the importance of communitarian production, which Article 47 binds the state to "protect, promote and strengthen." The market guilds were represented in the assembly, and the Constitution grants them "special protection" by the state "through a policy of equitable commercial exchange and fair prices for their products, as well as a preferential allowance of financial economic resources to promote their production" (Article 47.II). However, these powers also represent an expanded role for the state as well as a structuralist approach to the informal sector which in effect reinforces the formal/informal divide by assuming a trajectory toward formalization, and by default it mischaracterizes the multiple dynamics at play in popular economies—many, but not all, of which are exploitative.

The economic priorities expressed in the constitutional powers accorded to the state are based on the values of redistribution, production, and solidarity, which would go on to form the basis of state intervention in business and the regulations it placed on the financial sector. The intention was to prioritize production over commerce and make production more profitable than the informal commerce that had come to dominate since the structural reforms of the 1980s, when national productive industries were dismantled and national production was undercut by cheaper imported goods. The reinstatement of Bolivia as a "productive" country is also stipulated in the preamble as part of the vision of Bolivia beyond the "colonial, republican and neo-liberal State" that it had been in the past. However, the operationalization of the distinction between production and commerce would prove complicated in a context in which informal commercial activity had become a vital livelihood strategy for many.

Identity and the Pluri-economic Subject

First stated in Article 1 of the Constitution, the notion of pluri-economy is elaborated in Part IV, "Economic Structure and the Organization of the State," which stipulates that the economy is "composed of forms of community, state, private and public cooperative economic organization" (Article 306.II). The text recognizes, in stark contrast to neoliberal multiculturalism, different forms of economic organization and exchange, "based on the principles of complementariness, reciprocity, solidarity, redistribution, equality, legal security, sustainability, equilibrium, justice and transparency" (Article 306.III). The recognition and promotion of community and cooperative organization has its roots in Andean *ayllu* associations and hence achieves the aims of uniting the decolonial with the anti-neoliberal by moving away from the rational, utility-maximizing individual.

The importance of cultural identity is foregrounded in the Constitution and runs throughout the document. The juxtaposition of the logics of complementarity and conflict is apparent in the opening paragraph of the preamble, where the plurality of identity is juxtaposed with a "we" who were created at the times of colonialism:

In ancient times mountains arose, rivers moved, and lakes were formed. Our Amazonia, our swamps, our highlands, and our plains and valleys were covered with greenery and flowers. We populated this sacred Mother Earth with different faces, and since that time we have understood the plurality that exists in all things and in our diversity as human beings and cultures. Thus, our peoples were formed, and we never knew racism until we were subjected to it during the terrible times of colonialism. (Preamble)

The preamble describes a pastoral time of peace and harmony that would not stand up to historical scrutiny but does evoke an underlying dynamic of difference and harmonious complementarity rather than conflict, before making the move to identify conflict with colonialism—the central theoretical point in uniting Marxism with Indianism—and moving to a conflictive definition of identity. The conflicts erased with the evocation of that pastoral ideal, however, have an influence beyond that of merely a rhetorical device. The segmentation within the groups designated "indigenous peoples" is overlooked, and gender, urban indigeneity, and identities emerging from indigenous people's engagement with modernity and capitalism are occluded.

The use of static identities in this way is arguably unavoidable in a written document. The ecological, complementary logic of identity underpinning decolonial theories of plurality requires a participatory process, rather than the written documents and structures of colonial rule. The importance of political process was stressed particularly by feminist community organizations and social movements, who saw discussion and reflection as critical in not allowing new powers to themselves become hegemonic (Paredes 2010; also see chapter 1). Although the Constitution refers to complementary, ecological logics of identity, it adopts what are in effect static categories of absence—identifying those who have been marginalized by neoliberal and colonial rule. The identity categories adopted—"women," "indigenous," "rural," "traditional"— frame how recognition, representation, and redistribution function, and underpin decisions around state support in terms of welfare and subsidy that were a necessary corrective to the biases of orthodox economic policy. However, they can also have the function of reaffirming the exclusionary script.

Nevertheless, the text also articulates the rejection of assimilationist notions of the mestizo nation espoused by both liberals and the MNR who led the state-centered modernization program post 1952. The text goes on in Article 21 to guarantee the rights "1. To cultural self-identification" and "2. To privacy, intimacy, honor, their self-image and dignity." The inclusion of self-image and dignity is testimony to the damaging affective consequences of colonial oppression and exclusion which had been continued with the false neutrality of governance post 1952. This sense of degradation had been produced in part by juridical exclusion of indigenous people and culture, but also by the more impalpable factor of consistently not feeling reflected in one's environment or recognized on one's own terms. The Constitution marks a dramatic reframing of the culture of governance, the nation, and the public and of which norms of behavior, traditions, and rituals are appropriate for government. In economic terms, these changes also affected employability in the public sector and altered the economically vital yet intangible factor of confidence.

Valuing communities as productive units is at the heart of the notion of pluri-economy. Beyond the institutions and exchanges listed in the text, GC member Raúl Prada commented during the processes in the Constituent Assembly that the "community" referred to in the Constitution is rural as well as urban and includes, "as well as the *ayllus*, the *tentas*, the *capitanias* . . . the migratory settlements, the fiestas, the market fairs, the *challas*, the rituals and the ceremonies, where the collective symbolism nests" (2008, 38). This inclusive list grounds the institutions and exchanges that are referred to in the Constitution; *tentas*, and *capitanias* are indigenous land-management systems, and *challas* are ritual libations to the Pachamama. By referencing specific institutions and practices Prada illustrates the everyday processes and logics involved in "communities" and their modern, changing nature. The focus in the written Constitution, however, is on a traditional, rural construction of indigeneity. For example, Article 307 defines community economic organization as the "productive and reproductive systems of public life, founded on the principles and visions of the nations and rural native indigenous peoples." However, Chapter IV of the Constitution extends the "Rights of the Nations and Rural Native Indigenous Peoples," to those who "share" in precolonial cultures, and thus opens a definition that could include urban indigeneity:

> A nation and rural native indigenous people consists of every human collective that shares a cultural identity, language, historic tradition, institutions, territory and world view, whose existence predates the Spanish colonial invasion. (Article 30.I)

In Article 30 the multiple elements that constitute identity also come through: "that their traditional teachings and knowledge, their traditional medicine, languages, rituals, symbols and dress be valued, respected and promoted" (Article 30.II.9). Nevertheless, these definitions are constructed in opposition to the urban and the modern.

Urban economic institutions are referenced in Article 334.II as "The guild sector, the self-employed, and retail commerce," which the state is committed to promoting with "credit and technical assistance." There is, however, limited recognition that these organizations could be indigenous or run or staffed by people of indigenous descent who self-identify as indigenous. There is one mention of "crafts with cultural identity" at 334.III as being a sectoral priority, but other than that there is no indication that urban economic organizations can be "indigenous." The implication is that people in urban areas have adopted commercial practices mimetically, but this assumes an essentialized view of rural indigenous community economies, which is circular and may not correspond with the way people working in the popular markets of urban areas self-define.

The 2009 Constitution explicitly recognizes reciprocal and cooperative exchanges as constitutive of identity and culture, and hence
moves away from the "permitted Indian" of neoliberal multiculturalism, whose cultural practices based on reciprocal exchange were being
eroded by the imposition of a commercial market model. Nevertheless,
these communities as constructed in the Constitution are identified
and bounded in ways that limit the legitimacy of certain identities and
subjectivities. Critics frequently cite the association between rurality
and indigeneity, and in particular highland and specifically Aymara indigeneity as being problematic, both in the text and surrounding political discourse that overlooked urban ethnicity (Rivera Cusicanqui 2010).
Andean *cholaje*—people of indigenous descent who are working in an
urban setting, generally as domestic servants or market traders, and
who have adopted a form of Western dress but remain subaltern—is
excluded from the indigenous community groups who frame de jure ex-
pressions of indigenous rights. Urban people identifying as indigenous,
particularly in El Alto, constituted a significant element of Morales's
electoral power base, and the invisibility of this political subject underpins many of the contradictions that the MAS was going to face in
maintaining this support.

Gender

Stéfanie Rousseau's intersectional review of indigenous women's organizations' participation in the Constituent Assembly highlights the diversity of claims represented by the notion of "indigenous" and the
distinctive perspective of indigenous women's social movements within
the "male dominated indigenous movement" and "*mestiza*-dominated
women's movement" (Rousseau 2011, 6). There was significant tension
between indigenous women's movements and their middle-class, urban
counterparts, which were perceived to function more on an international, individualist agenda and monopolize NGO funding (Rivera
Cusicanqui 2010). These frictions had their roots in different conceptions of gender, as indigenous women's organizations adopted a complementary approach to equality, rather than the individualist ideas of
empowerment that dominate international agendas. Indigenous wom-
en's movements were more likely to situate gender discrimination with
colonialism, and thus have an affinity with indigenous movements, but

they also recognized discrimination from male indigenous movements and unions (Potter and Zurita 2009). While this was hailed as a breakthrough in terms of women's political representation, there was a tense political struggle as the 50 percent quota for women was seen by some to be at the expense of the representation of indigenous groups. The leader of the Consejo Nacional de Ayllus y Markas del Qullasuyo (CONAMAQ National Council of Ayllus and Markas of Qullasyuo), Rafael Quispe, lamented the absence of the *pueblos originarios* from the cabinet, as had been promised by the MAS, but nevertheless emphasized that CONAMAQ respected the president's decision (*Los Tiempos* 2010). The political struggles involved in achieving gender parity were described as a "permanent battle with union leaders to incorporate women into the political fight in Bolivia" (Rojas 2010).

The Constitution explicitly recognizes gendered subjectivities. As Prada asserts:

> Gender is a crosscutting axis throughout the whole document. . . . Gendered subjects, especially feminine subjects, the diverse subjects and subjectivities of plurality, as well as collective subjects all emerge as new imaginaries and actors in the new scenarios of the new political horizon. (Prada Alcoreza 2008, 39)

Prada reminds us of the potential of pluriversal theory to radically reframe the relationship between subject and the state and to move away from the reductionist individualism of liberal theory. However, this potential does not come through as strongly in the text itself. There is a commitment to gender equality, listed among other forms of plurality and equality throughout the document, and a specific reference to gender-based violence (Article 15.III) and gender equality in the cabinet (Article 172.22). However, in Part IV, "Economic Structure and the Organization of the State," the word *gender* does not occur, and the only reference to women is a specification that women have the right to hold land titles in Article 395.I and Article 402.2. Part IV, Chapter III, "Economic Policies," makes no reference to gender or women.

The gendered political subject Prada is referring to is one that, following Andean traditions, has equal rights to participate politically, but aside from that the provisions specific to women associate the feminine with motherhood, marriage, and victimhood. Under neoliberal structural adjustment policies, provision for reproductive and sexual rights, including women's crisis centers, was cut from the public budget, and gender issues became the domain of NGOs. Enshrining these rights in the Constitution was something that feminist organizations fought for (Rousseau 2011), and public provision of these rights was a recognition that they were fundamental rather than a "sticking plaster" on mainstream orthodox economic policies that would increase women's vulnerability and in effect erode their ability to access these rights. However, there is little evidence, at least in the way gender and women have been specifically evoked, that the construction of femininity implied in the Constitution has moved on from that of the modernizing state, which situated women as wives and mothers in heterosexual partnerships (Article 63).

The articles that specifically address women's issues fall in sections on social and family rights and violence and abuse. "Woman" is specified with reference to victims of violence (Article 15.II); equality in political participation and representation (26.I; 147.I; 210.II); and marriage, maternity, childbirth, and sexual and reproductive rights (45.V; 63.I; 66). The categories of activity that are recognized, however, do suggest that liberal economic concepts that have rendered women's work invisible have been reformulated and revised. Article 338, for example, stipulates that "the State recognizes the economic value of housework as a source of wealth, and it shall be quantified in public accounts." The value of reproduction is explicitly referenced in the definition of community in Article 307: "community economic organization includes productive and reproductive systems of public life, founded on the principles and visions of the nations and rural native indigenous peoples." These reproductive systems of public life would include social and cultural reproductive labor: housework, child care, community labor, and cultural work that tends to be women's responsibility and is systematically overlooked in public accounting. There is a sense, then, that the economic agent in Part IV does include the feminine reproductive labor that is generally rendered invisible.

These stipulations do not, however, reflect the decolonial critique of gender or the history of Andean women's participation in economic activities. Despite the recognition elsewhere in MAS policy that gender is a colonial imposition, the text of the Constitution recalls the construction of gender adopted by the MNR, with its focus on workers and the peasantry, which recast indigenous women as wives and mothers, sub-ordinate to a male "household head." It is also apparent in the text that indigenous movements involved in the negotiations were preoccupied by masculinist concerns and that urban indigenous women fell between the conceptual cracks of the postulated identity categories. Women, as bearers of cultural reproduction, are on the front line of negotiating cul-tural identity in a political and economic context in which colonialism and neoliberal capitalism conspire against them. Urban indigenous and mestiza women can be villainized by those who discriminate against the indigenous in the cities and by those who in response are advocating a reaffirmation of indigenous traditions. As Rivera Cusicanqui comments with regard to the constructions of indigenous femininity apparent in the 2009 Constitution, while

> migrant women's (cholas' or birlochas') construction as a de-graded space of "mestizaje" within the structure of the urban labor market constitutes a prime example of the phenomenon [of mimesis] . . . none of the indigenous rights discussed [in the Constitution] actually addresses the specific problems these women face: labor discrimination, the lack of educational oppor-tunities, and the frustrations of citizenship that affects precisely these emergent and upward-climbing middle rungs of the socio-economic ladder. (2010, 46–47)

The economic strategies of the *chola paceña*, despite being marshaled as an image of the triumph of indigenous people under Morales and an icon of La Paz, disrupt the framing of economic activity provided by the 2009 Constitution.

Conclusion

The 2009 Constitution is remarkable in its level of detail and demon-strates the struggles to enact the theoretical tensions between plurality and a strong state as well as the vision to bring community dynamics to the national level. It also demonstrates the political tensions in main-taining the relationship with the indigenous social movements that had created the MAS as a political instrument and whom the MAS had nego-tiated with to broaden its appeal, while also dealing with the pressures of the wider political landscape. The Constitution is hence as interesting for its declarative juridical content as for the map it provides of the political space that the MAS was working within.

The construction of identity in the text of the Constitution is a blueprint for the permitted subjectivities in the MAS's pluri-economic vision. The intellectual work of the GC is apparent both in the text of the Constitution itself and in the processes behind it, which demonstrate a commitment to participatory pluralism and process. The conceptualization of pluri-economy is central to the attempt to cast a new, transitory role for the modernizing state, unite anti-neoliberal and decolonial policies by recognizing a plurality of legitimate economic institutions and forms of exchange, and make a reality of the distinction between surplus value and use value. There is, inevitably, however, a limited range of permitted economic subjectivities, forms of exchange, and notions of value, and those adopted in the text overlook women's multiple economic strategies, the position of urban indigenous people, and the informal economy. However, the contradictions and fluidities of the text, which are in part a result of what Nancy Postero called the "tacking back and forth" between class and decolonial concerns, created an economic framing that, while marginalizing indigenous women on the grounds of the masculinist definitions of production, nation, and value, did create a space in which informal commerce in popular markets—traditionally the terrain of Aymara women—could flourish.

One of the more complex tenets of the pluriverse and the unification of cultural plurality with a strong state is the scaling up of community dynamics to the level of the nation-state. The MAS was well placed to achieve this because of the way it was formed and the institutional processes that were at its heart. The fact that the MAS was a political instrument of social movements rather than a party, along with its adoption of community dynamics in its leadership, was itself an instantiation of some of the theoretical commitments of pluri-economy. The most significant impact of the drive to bring community dynamics to the national scale in the Constitution and over its period of governance was symbolic, which in itself was to have a powerful economic impact. The false neutrality of the liberal assimilationist state was replaced by the language, symbols, and rituals of indigenous nations, and rights to cultural identity and self-image were enshrined in law. These elements of the Constitution have been dismissed as folkloric, but these affective factors were to create confidence and, as we will see, enable economic subjectivities that were absent in the spectrum of economic plurality imagined in the Constitution.

The discursive strategies the MAS used to gain power—plurality, post-neoliberalism, and sovereignty over natural resources—lent it an appeal that extended beyond its rural roots. The MAS also had power bases among the urban and the middle class, and, crucially, among the *comerciantes* in the popular markets of El Alto. However, its negotiations and alliances with a range of organizations meant that it owed allegiance to a range of actors with different economic visions and ideals. Once it was in power, the MAS had to negotiate these multiple divisions both within its own party and in the broader political landscape. The political difficulties of its position were quickly apparent in the debates surrounding the Constituent Assembly, and the conflictive points of the process of developing a new constitution show up the underpinning theoretical contradictions that had not been resolved. While the false neutrality of the assimilationist, liberal view of government had been replaced, the conundrum of equality and difference had not been resolved, and the community style of government would quickly be identified as predominantly Aymara and Quechua, with a limited role for the other nations.

The language around women and gender reflects the traditional form of household associated with indigenous Andean traditions, and this was used as a platform to guarantee women's representation. The construction of femininity elsewhere in the document, however, identifies women with the family role, as recipients of welfare, or as victims of violence. These measures were needed to redress the gender biases of previous economic restructuring, but nevertheless they echo the gender biases of the modernizing state, and the powerful economic role that indigenous Andean women are famed for was absent in the language of the Constitution. Nevertheless, there are conceptual developments in the Constitution that could open the discursive space for the recognition of feminine economic subjectivity, the valorization of the social and communal, and the explicit interplay of different scales. The state-backed support of community and employment rights, led by a focus on cultural identity rather than redistribution, values social reproduction. However, the most remarkable characteristic of the Constitution is its contradictions, which were themselves a product of political negotiations. In this way, the melee of different forms of ownership, community, and competitive dynamics and contradictory notions of identity is reflective of the "motley" character of the Bolivian economy. The various institutions and myriad cultural and material flows characteristic of economic activities that have defied formalization are in a sense present in the contradictions of the document. It is hence perhaps not surprising that the economic subjects to emerge and gain power during the initial MAS administrations were the Aymara women who had for so long been placed in alterity or liminality by predominant economic policies.

3

Andean Economic Femininities

The activities and values that express economic femininity in rural communities in the Andes and the informal markets of La Paz and El Alto break through the tropes of indigeneity and femininity that tend to be assumed in political economic theory. They also disrupt the assumptions underpinning these terms in the discourses of the Grupo Comuna and in the Constitution of 2009. Exploring the experiences of women who are negotiating the economic roles of rural producers, *comerciantes, minoristas,* workers, and consumers demonstrates the gendered inadequacies of the economic terms of scale, nation, and production and the dichotomy of tradition and modernity. Cultural tropes emerge from the characterizations by which people are perceived and perceive themselves and social ideals of how a person should be and behave. These characteristics and ideals are generated within a discursive, material, and institutional architecture that makes them attributable to a certain community (Swinehart 2018). They are crystallized via the intersubjective dynamics of shame and approval that are indicative of values—both economic and cultural—that are inherently social. "Economic femininities" are the tropes by which economic exchanges are categorized and judged in terms of effectiveness, gendered propriety, and cultural belonging. The typology of economic femininities I present here is not a static gallery of personalities but rather the images distilled from a hall of mirrors that reflect self-identity, the perception of others' perceptions, one's sense of self in the world, and what one is recognized to be. The landowning *campesina de pollera* in charge of organizing agricultural production and the wealthy *chola* of the new Aymara bourgeoisie are the pinnacles of Andean economic femininity, and they have ascended at a historical conjuncture that has allowed them to overturn assumptions about the political and economic roles of indigenous women. These ideals frame the perception of "other" femininities—the informal traders and market laborers—who may be excluded from wealth, land ownership, and community status, but not on the terms via which this exclusion is understood by the development industry, orthodox economists, or the Marxist and Indianist intellectuals behind the Constitution.

Political discourses of gender and indigeneity changed dramatically over the time of Morales's presidency, as women *de pollera* attained political office and, in some cases, great levels of wealth. Gender had a prominent place in the MAS decolonial *procesos de cambio* (processes of change), and the principle of complementary but equal gender roles drove the *"chachawarmi* cabinet" of 50 percent women in 2010 (Vaca 2010), including *ministras* in key economic positions. The appointment of *ministras de pollera* challenged the colonial images of indigenous femininity as situated solely in family and community. However, their experiences demonstrated the continued inequalities inherent in the way this discourse has been marshaled. In what follows I will first explore the tropes of indigenous femininity used by indigenous women's social movements in their resistance against colonial and gendered oppression. The historical figure of Bartolina Sisa, after whom the country's most prominent indigenous women's social movement is named, demonstrates how political and economic power entwine with indigenous femininity in ways that are overlooked or mischaracterized. I then analyze economic femininity in the rapidly changing political economic context of peri-urban and informal markets, where the values and community exchanges that underpin traditional ideals are being renegotiated. The vision of complementary but equal gender roles is only one influence among the myriad cultural, political, and material flows that form the economic and political landscape of Andean markets. Women working in agricultural production in the Andes and urban informal markets negotiate dichotomous divides between tradition and modernity, cooperation and competition, gift and commerce. Via iterative, performative processes, the strategization of market spaces has both reaffirmed and transformed gendered economic roles, identities, meanings, and subjectivities. The tropes of Andean femininity that emerge demonstrate a radical deconstruction of ideas of scale, nation, productivity, and value, and break through the conceptual borders that had consistently associated indigenous femininity with economic "in-betweenness."

Las Ministras

In January 2010, following the ratification of the Constitution of 2009, President Morales appointed a cabinet consisting of 50 percent women. In announcing the new cabinet, he stressed that this was achieved in the name of *chachawarmi*—the Andean notion of gender complementarity, "or, as the *mestizos* say, gender equality" (Rojas 2010). The inclusion of indigenous women *de pollera* in the MAS administration was part of the decolonial project that recognized gender as a colonial imposition, and was a result of the power of indigenous women's social movements within the MAS. As activist Martha Lanza from Colectivo Cabildeo stated, "There is no possible decolonization without fighting patriarchy and vice versa. We must decolonize the social, economic and political relationships in order to emancipate our peoples and break the patriarchal power relations that subjugate women" (AWID 2011).

The significance of these appointments reaches beyond the individual power of the ministers themselves and creates a trope of indigenous femininity that allows a reimagining of what gender, indigeneity, and power can be. With the appointment of a Quechua woman, Casimira Rodríguez, to the Ministry of Justice, one newspaper ran the headline "De Empleada a Ministra"—From maid to minister (Díaz Carrasco 2013)—and documented the effect this had on the aspirations of other indigenous women who could now see themselves in powerful roles. *Ministras de pollera* in power at the state level represented a challenge to internalized colonialism and extended the permissible "horizons of possibilities" for indigenous women (Díaz Carrasco 2013, 76). This opened a space to renegotiate both power and femininity, and hence performatively rework ideas of value that underappreciate feminine labor.

The political acceptance that patriarchy was a colonial imposition was a result of the activism of indigenous women in the MAS and in particular the strength of Las Bartolinas. Their eponymous hero, Bartolina Sisa, was an indigenous woman commander who fought against the Spanish in the eighteenth century. Alongside her husband, Túpac Katari, to whom she was fiercely loyal, she personifies the anticolonial struggles of indigenous people. She is featured across popular culture in Bolivia and in public art. The respect she had as a military commander, particularly after her husband had been captured, remains the symbol of the power of indigenous women. Her vicious public execution at the hands of the invading Spanish army in the center of La Paz, where she was raped, hung, and dismembered as a warning to others, underscores the potency of the resistance she posed to the colonizers. As such she remains a powerful symbol of the decolonization movement, and specifically for women *de pollera*.

The icon of Bartolina Sisa as a warrior stands in stark contrast to other national feminine symbols on the continent, whose agency had to be reclaimed from dominant representations of complicity with colonial forces and treachery—for instance, La Malinche in Mexico (Melhuus and Stølen 1996; Romero and Nolacea Harris 2005). Nevertheless, the notion of the indigenous woman as "intermediary" is ubiquitous and has also characterized the role of the *chola* in Bolivian national politics. Robert Albro observes the way local mestizo politicians cultivate relationships with women *de pollera* to heighten their popularity: "Authorities initiate token economic exchanges with *cholas*, both to participate intimately in the popular cultural milieu, and to solidify their claims to personal roots in this world" (2000, 30). The notions of femininity being drawn on in these interactions are motherhood, community, and the connection the *chola* has between rural areas and urban markets as a trader. Rather than recognizing the power and the agency of the *chola* in politics, these roles cast indigenous women as the acceptable face of relations between colonizers and indigenous people and as "important political cultural capital for men" (Albro 2000, 31). In contrast, the heroic icon of indigenous women's social movements is known for her role in military planning alongside her husband and his sister, Gregoria Apaza, and is remembered as a *caudilla*—a commander—of the movement. The Bartolina Sisa Confederation describes her as "a historical milestone which broke with the traditional paradigms [of femininity] which the colonial state brought with it" and draws on her image to reimagine politics and the economy. They contrast the image of the Aymara warrior with that of the central figure of femininity in Christianity—Eve—who represents a paradigm of femininity that is "submissive . . . emerging from the ribs of man . . . a model of woman only to satisfy the functions of familiar reproduction . . . who can only be liberated via individual rights" (Bartolina Sisa n.d.).

There have, however, been multiple transformations in gender relations since the time of Bartolina Sisa, and indigenous feminist organizations also point out that "'in Aymara communities where they supposedly apply *chachawarmi*, there isn't a correlation between this idea and the reality,' and that Andean machismo is still present 'in every area'" (Julieta Ojeda quoted in Butters 2012, 16). The machismo referred to by Ojeda is compounded by colonial and capitalist influences that not only situate women in the reproductive sphere but at once both laud and devalue women's contribution as a natural, and therefore unpaid, duty. The warrior image of Bartolina Sisa contrasts with the high rates of violence against women, particularly in rural communities in Bolivia (Camargo 2019), which can be compounded by the pressure to be in a partnership in order to be allowed to participate in community politics and social life—a norm that is also reinforced by Bartolina Sisa's loyalty to Túpac Katari. The *marianismo* for which colonial Latin America is known also compounds the strictures around women's reproductive role and the villainization of women who do not conform to the expectations of motherhood and community.

Nevertheless, the power of indigenous women's social movements led indigenous women activists to direct ministerial power under the MAS. Antonia Rodríguez Medrano, a Quechua woman, *de pollera,* from Potosí, served as minister of productive development and plural economy from 2010 to 2011. She had moved to El Alto in the 1980s having worked as a land laborer and as a domestic servant. In response to the economic hardships of that time which she experienced firsthand, she established an artisanal knitting cooperative—Asociación Artesanal Boliviana Señor de Mayo (ASARBOLSEM; Association of Bolivian Artisans Señor de Mayo) and became an activist for women's rights and equality (WFTO n.d.). The *ministra* recounts that a number of women would arrive at the workshops bruised from incidents of violence at home, and in response she decided to directly address the problems of gender-based violence, in addition to supporting women's livelihoods, by running self-esteem workshops and raising awareness of women's rights (Escudero Pérez, Heras, and Campaignolle 2018). ASARBOLSEM was an exemplary social cooperative "with cultural identity" as per the Constitution of 2009, and in itself demonstrates the interplay of local and international scales that were to be at the heart of Rodríguez's economic strategy.

The experience of running a cooperative was central to her approach as *ministra* to the country's economic strategy. I interviewed Rodríguez in 2010 in an imposingly formal government building on El Prado, the main thoroughfare in the center of La Paz, and was surprised when she greeted me with an invitation to also visit her knitting cooperative in El Alto. My surprise indicated my own assumptions about the scale at which government should be operating and about how that national scale would be recreated in a personal interaction with a minister of state. In continuing to work with her cooperative while also minister for productive development and plural economy, Rodríguez was breaking through economic boundaries of scale, and in proffering the invitation she was disrupting the expected cultural performance of scaled power at the national level. Reflecting that approach, when I visited the co-operative, the members, all local to El Alto, were hand-knitting alpaca garments that would be exported around the world.

The focus of the interview was the textiles sector in Bolivia, and the *ministra* highlighted her achievements in managing to persuade large, medium, and small businesses to work together. She observed that the fights tended to be between the large companies and the small and medium-size ones, who thought that the larger ones would take an ever increasing share of the market. These battles had been exacerbated by previous ministers who had taken one side or the other, but she had been determined to work across scales:

> So I said, "Mr. President, I'm going to work with both sides." So I asked for a meeting with the representatives of CAINCO, the federation of the big companies, CONAMIC, representing the small and medium ones, and COCEDAL, representing microenterprises: all three administrative levels. And I put together a working group for the agenda—what criteria shall we have this month? And next month? We've got to think about how to go into parliament with something that will satisfy all three levels. We can all support each other. (Interview with Antonia Rodríguez, August 2010)

She went on to explain how her strategy had been to use the state to regulate the export market share for each administrative level, which would prevent large companies from hoarding while also opening doors for those companies to negotiate new deals. The economic difficulties of this approach will be discussed in chapter 5, but in holding discussions and negotiations across all three levels in this way, Rodríguez was demonstrating a new approach to the scales of both economics and politics:

> At the beginning the big companies wanted to eat me alive, but I said to them, "Just a minute, let me negotiate with all three administrative levels, and I tell you that we'll do it without strikes or marches." We gave ourselves three months and we got an agree-

ment in three months. And then they said to me, "Ah, Antonia, you're all right as a minister."

Rodríguez had worked with the MAS as an activist, and when she was called in 2010 to take up the post as minister she commented that she wasn't of the MAS, the MAS was of her—a phrase that brought out the importance of interdependence and horizontal power to the construction of the MAS (Escudero Pérez, Heras, and Campaignolle 2018). Her vision of pluri-economy and her experience as a leader of social movements brought the economic strategies of indigenous women to center stage. As a minister she prioritized the development of small social enterprises by opening up international markets, particularly with Venezuela and later China, and had a vision of forging accords between small, medium, and large enterprises "like brothers" in a way that would flatten the dynamics of scale. She was also responsible for the development of nine state-run enterprises that had been beset by problems at the time she took them on due to the incommensurability of the pressures of community participation and political patronage, as well as the unforgiving practicalities of international markets (Gil 2010). She left her post at the end of 2011, after only two years, due to the difficulties suffered by the envisioned state-led enterprises.

Also appointed to Morales's *chachawarmi* cabinet was Nemesia Achacollo, a rural union leader and former national leader of Las Bartolinas, who took on the role of minister of rural development and land. Achacollo had a presence on the international stage, promoted Bolivian quinoa on international markets (FAO 2013), and oversaw investment from China to industrialize its production. She was referred to as one of Morales's "untouchables" (*Latin News* 2015) but was nevertheless forced to resign in 2015 over her role in the misallocation of funds from the Fondo Indígena scheme—FONDIOC. The scheme was intended as a fund dedicated to the development of indigenous communities. The distribution was determined by a board of representatives of the main indigenous organizations including Las Bartolinas. The fund was established in 2010, and in 2013 concerns were raised that much of the money had disappeared or gone into fantasy or incomplete projects. Morales's critics viewed the ensuing scandal as confirming what they had said from the outset, that a lack of institutionality and relevant administrative experience would lead to misallocation of funds (Herrera and

Leonardo 2018). The workings of the board were placed under scrutiny, and it became apparent that the funds were rotated between key organizations in a way that was intended to reflect the reciprocity of communities but was open to abuse and a lack of oversight. Released in 2015, the report into this affair led to multiple arrests and scandals, but only one ministerial resignation—that of Nemesia Achacollo.

The resignation of Achacollo, one of Morales's closest allies and one of the most prominent indigenous women activists, was seen as the MAS wishing to draw a line under the affair (*Latin News* 2015). However, because Achacolla was the only minister to resign, her treatment brings out various other aspects to the iconic image of the *chola* in Bolivian politics and society: she was easily associated with avarice and corruption and was villainized in the press. Achacollo was seen to have transgressed the other tropes that had originally helped to get her to power—the maternalism, the savvy but wholesome market woman, and the diplomatic intermediary. It is notable, however, that despite the fact that Achacollo was the only minister to resign, Morales, while inaugurating the replacement in her post, referred to her as "poor comrade Nemesia" who was incapable of stopping the other eight members of the board of FONDIOC from mishandling the funds (*Página Siete* 2015). Despite the fact that the party had made her accountable for the scandal, her agency was not recognized.

The *Campesina*

The presence of *ministras* in Morales's *chachawarmi* cabinet was enabled by the importance of partnership to leadership in rural areas, which diminishes the tension between femininity and power that can exist in colonial patriarchal systems where headship, power, and leadership are coded masculine. However, the experiences of Rodríguez and Achacollo illustrate the limits of the discourse of gender complementarity that brought them to power. The traditional reading of gender complementarity is also inadequate to describe the realities of kin and community networks in rural areas as well as the complexities of the economic subject represented by indigenous women in rural production—the *campesina*.

The *campesina* can be a powerful economic figure (Figure 2). She manages agricultural production and weekly transport to markets in local towns or peri-urban areas, organizes and pays wage laborers, tends to animals, and is a mother and godmother to various families. Managing land involves finding, contracting, and organizing labor, providing a good lunch, and arranging transport to the city. She is involved in the policing of community trust and maintenance of reputation, often chastising with the phrase *¿Qué va a decir la gente?*—"What will people say?"

FIGURE 2. *Aymara woman from Luribay looking over her land, 2006. Author's photograph.*

She holds a prominent place in community events and takes on sponsorship of fiestas thanks to her reputation for reliability and her wealth.

The power of the *campesina* is founded on the gendered division of labor of rural production, which valorizes both masculine and feminine roles, and in the bilateral inheritance rights dictating that women inherit from their mother and men from their father. However, as social relations are increasingly capitalized, the developing gendered inequality between reproduction and production is exacerbated, as commercial exchange becomes more valuable than community exchange. While the conceptualization of gender in rural areas and the activities of the women involved in rural production can represent a radical reconfiguration of gendered values and activities, the notion of complementarity can compound hierarchies within rural communities and the iniquitous impacts of the global capital economy. Although the traditional reading of gender complementarity reinforces the strictures around acceptable femininity, there is nevertheless radical potential in conceptualizations of gender in the rural Andes to reimagine femininity and economic subjectivity.

Gender in the Andes is understood in terms of activities, labors, and tasks (Choque Quispe 2007). Traditionally feminine tasks include reproductive labor, tending to animals, and weaving, while tasks associated with masculinity include tilling the soil, driving vehicles, and operating machinery. Both men and women work on the land, but they have distinct tasks, symbolizing the unity of opposites exemplified by *chachawarmi* with, for example, the man digging and the woman sewing the seed. This symbolic division between masculine and feminine activities is not constituted by the bodies involved but by the activities themselves (Choque Quispe 2007). During my fieldwork in Luribay, it rapidly became clear that the discourse of *chachawarmi* was not as frequently used as political speeches and policies implied, but the values, ontology, and social relations this term represented came through in the way that masculinity and femininity were discussed. At the same time, there were multiple complex influences on gender relations that were being negotiated, including land ownership, inheritance, migration, and capital in the form of access to paid work and credit, as the following examples from my fieldwork in Luribay show.

Doña Sofia, an Aymara-speaking woman *de pollera* from the valley of Luribay, is divorced with six children. When her father died, she returned to Luribay from Brazil to look after her mother and the mother's small plot of land. "I work the land alone," she said. "I'm both a woman and a man. I plow and everything, even though that's a man's job. . . . There's just me working on my own, no one helps me" (interview, Hamlet, Luribay, August 2006). In terms of feminist critiques of economics, situating gender in the activity rather than the body is a penetrating starting point that could lead to a conclusion that any *body* can perform those gendered tasks. However, a gendered lens creates a kaleidoscopic effect that includes the sense of how one is being perceived and how one is situated and treated in a given community. Doña Sonia does not find her ability to do men's work empowering, and she felt teased when people would see her plowing the field and shout over, "What are you, a man?"

According to Andean bilateral inheritance rights, women can inherit and own land. This tradition has its roots in the system of vertical farming in which marriage would ideally be between families of different altitudes. In this system, the woman moves to the man's land but retains rights on her own, providing the family with access to different kinds of crop (Bastien 1979). However, even when women do own the land, it does not necessarily imply household headship, or even conformity with the notion of equal partnership. Doña Lucia is an Aymara woman *de pollera* who inherited a large amount of land, and her husband lives with her.

> My husband's from the Town but he had to come here, to the community where I was born. Most of the time the man takes his wife away with him, but it wasn't like that with me. My mother had died, my sister lives in Cochabamba, my other sister lives on the Altiplano. So, I was the only one living on the land. So, my husband had to be present here with me. But I'm the owner of the land. (Interview, Hamlet, Luribay, 2006)

Despite owning land, Doña Lucia felt that she was limited in her participation in the community because she was a woman. She was known locally for being particularly outspoken and for participating in public meetings, but she expressed frustration at not being given as much right to speak in meetings as men. She explained that it was difficult to be taken seriously if you had not done military service, which discounted not only the participation of women but of certain men (see also Gill 1997). People in the community would admire Doña Lucia and recognize her wealth and power, but they would also feel sorry for her, as she did all the work while her husband would spend his days drinking with cash earned from wage labor and trying to hit birds with a catapult.

Despite the history of bilateral inheritance, land ownership in the Andes is predominantly male (Deere and León 2001b). Traditional systems of inheritance have changed with the *hacienda* system, land reform, commercialization of agriculture, and out-migration, and overall there is "heterogeneity in inheritance patterns nationally" (Deere and León 2001a, 22). The case of Doña Celia, also from Luribay, shows the vulnerability of women who do not own their land and the specific way that a move from a subsistence to a capital labor economy can render women dependent.

> I do all the work. I work on the land, I raised eight children, I go to La Paz every week to sell my tomatoes. My husband's terrible. He just sits around drinking all day and when I complain he just says, "This is my land, you, you don't have anything, and you better remember that." He won't work for me, on our land. He leaves me to do everything. He'll go and work on other people's land, because they'll pay him money and then he can buy spirits and get drunk. (Interview, Hamlet, Luribay, June 2006)

Doña Celia's words indicate the effect of the development of capital on the value and valorization of household activities. The development of a labor market will favor the time and flexibility of men who do not have the social expectation to do household and care work and who will often be paid more for the same labor. While Doña Lucia does own her land, she had the same complaints about her husband, and specified the problems that came with him having cash and buying alcohol. In this way, in a rural, subsistence context, the division between subsistence, production, and a labor market is established, and with it the othering, gendering, and devaluing of reproduction that comes with capital.

Rates of domestic violence in the Andes are extremely high, with over 80 percent of women in rural and peri-urban areas reporting having experienced violence from an intimate partner or family member (Camargo 2019). Gender-based domestic violence is enabled by economic control and dependency, and so it is on those terms surprising that Andean women who own land and property and are engaged in production and income-generation activities should suffer such high rates. However, there is a powerful moral economy that means women's—and particularly a mother's—earnings have to be for the family. This does not apply, as we see from Doña Celia's words, to the labor earnings of men, who are more able to access cash in the labor market. Both the shame associated with not being in a partnership and the attenuated ability to participate in community politics and festivals without being in a *chachawarmi* household exacerbate women's vulnerability to abusive relationships.

Reputation is extremely valuable in highly interdependent rural communities—not only in terms of the economic goods and services accessed via gift exchange but also in terms of a sense of identity and ontological security. It is a feminine duty to maintain reputation and nurture community relationships, which are vital to the maintenance of extended networks of kin and fictive kin. The gendered scrutiny placed on women and girls centers around sexual propriety, and a familiar double standard is put to the test in the numerous festivals that punctuate the agricultural calendar. The borders of community, and of who counts as a person *de confianza,* are policed by gossip—engaged in by both men and women; as the popular saying in Bolivia goes, *pueblo pequeño, infierno grande*—small town, big hell. Gossip, although it can be used to voice concerns that are silenced by dominant discourses (Adkins 2002), also has the social function of recreating moral notions of acceptability and demarcating belonging. Particularly in communities where social networks are highly interdependent, these notions of acceptability carry economic weight, and the moral codes that delineate gossip in the Andes are "grounded in an ontology of reciprocal exchange" (Van Vleet 2003, 494). Failing to return favors owed via *ayni* or to perform the public works labor mandated by the agrarian union can result in exclusion from those reciprocal networks and a loss of a sense of belonging and group identity. Exclusion from the community was historically the worst punishment, and a comment frequently made in response to an experience of shame is that people would "disappear."

The feminine power that the indigenous *campesina* can attain emerges from a rural context renowned for cooperation and the intensity of social networks, where livelihood, community, and reputation are entwined.

Community valorization of feminized reproductive labor is a corrective to the oversights of orthodox economic policies, and related appeals to gender complementarity reinforced the MAS post-neoliberal aims to value the community. However, despite the radical potential of Andean ideas of gender, femininity is constrained by the social obligations to be in a household and by the importance of reputation. The economic subject of the *campesina*, however, who either has or aspires to own her own land and have the wealth and influence to lead fiestas, can bring together notions of femininity, gift exchange, wealth, and value in ways that defy the gendered construction of capitalist divisions between reproduction and production, value and wealth.

The *Chola*

The icon of the Bolivian nation, who ascended to the status of "elite" over the period of MAS rule, is the urban Aymara *chola*. The *chola* is an urban woman of Aymara origin, *de pollera*, who sells in Bolivia's urban markets, where the gendered division of labor reflects that of rural production: the woman organizes the purchases, workers, and sales, and the men handle transport and logistics. The reputation of rural Aymara women in the city is that they drive a hard bargain. Women who will strictly obey and enforce the unwritten rules of livelihoods in rural communities—that everyone should make a living, that no one should get too far ahead of themselves, and that it is absolutely forbidden to enter into competition with a fellow member of the community—are famed for their ruthlessness and business savvy in urban markets and are proud of their reputation. This apparent contradiction is resolved geographically, as the women who are responsible for community cooperation in rural areas are also responsible for competitive sales in urban markets. While this has led to the construction of the *chola* as "intermediary," they are creating a consistent economic subject that resolves the dialectical tensions between cooperation and competition. Traversing the economic worlds of rural community and urban markets involves passing through a prism of racialized and gendered tropes via which they are perceived, recognized, and evaluated. These women may go from being admired as effective marketeers in their rural communities to being villainized and treated with suspicion for their wealth in the city.

Mobility between rural areas and the cities is part of everyday life that fosters linguistic and cultural bilingualism. Mobility is a source of power in the community as well as in politics, and it recalls the recognition of Bartolina Sisa's ability to gain political support across communities, which is attributed to her travels as a trader. While this very mobility is part of everyday life, when viewed and categorized in these spaces severally there are continued strictures and double binds in terms of the conceptual framing of economic activity that construct rural economies and specifically the role of the *chola* as peripheral to theorized economic worlds. "Across the many descriptions of *cholas* as intermediaries . . . perhaps more than any other social category, the *chola* has been thought to connect up the different parts of mixed Andean economies" (Albro 2000, 32). Albro summarizes, citing Linda Seligman, Silvia Rivera Cusicanqui, and Florence Babb, the various ways in which these "different parts" of Andean economies have been analyzed from the point of view of the *chola*: nonmonetized peasant economies versus capitalist production and markets; production versus consumption; informal versus formal. These different spheres have been united via the extension of the *chola*'s household role "dispersed across space and types of social relations" (Albro 2000, 32, citing Babb 1989 and Paulson 1996). These categorizations demonstrate the economic plurality of feminine livelihood strategies, which involves a diverse range of exchanges—including gift exchanges in the community, cash exchanges in the market, and care exchanges in the household, all of which follow different logics of reciprocity and accrue different kinds and degrees of value. However, casting *cholas* as intermediaries also denotes a framing of their everyday lives as being "between" the generally accepted discourses and boundaries of economic life rather than recognizing the holistic way their economic activities are experienced.

The language used to categorize and judge women indicates their worth vis-à-vis the exchanges that take place in these respective cultural spaces and indicates how the presentation and recognition of femininity is itself an exchange that creates value and esteem. To be an indigenous woman *de pollera* or *de vestido* is a question of cultural identification, and one that can involve transgression if the wrong clothing is worn in the wrong place. Racial discrimination against women *de pollera* in formal settings remains, and being *de pollera* in certain places is a challenge, a transgression, or uncomfortably inappropriate (Casanovas 2018). Similarly, to wear Western dress—to be *de vestido*—can be stigmatized as an abdication of the feminine responsibility to uphold and recreate cultural identity. The indigenous woman working in peri-urban markets and wearing Western clothes, which are often a far more affordable alternative, will incur the derogative epithet *chota*. These exchanges form the gendered economic geography of esteem that shapes performances of femininity and accords value to place and a person's presence there. Gender, value, and identity are all hence intertwined—the exchanges that create value also come coded with a gendered identity and are part of the performance of gender.

The cash that is carried from rural to urban areas transforms in meaning from a status symbol in the community to a marker of suspicion of illicit activity in the city. Market women are frequently the subject of muggings and drug attacks on coaches as it is known that *tienen plata*—they carry money. A frequent topic of conversation is different ways to hide the cash while traveling, such as sewing an extra lining into clothing or hiding it in swaddling clothes as if it were a baby. The fear this engenders reinforces community groupings, as it is safer to travel with people *de confianza,* and transport is organized on that basis rather than according to a commercial timetable. Once in the city, the fact that peri-urban markets trade in cash is associated with contraband and even narcotraffic, as informality is erroneously elided with illegality. The long history of Andean markets is forgotten and perceived by those in the "formal" mainstream simply as a way to avoid tax (Sheild Johansson 2020).

Commerce in El Alto and the north of La Paz began historically as markets for agricultural produce, but their recent rapid expansion has been due to the growth in all manner of imported goods. In the twenty-first century, fueled by the overvalued boliviano, families who own transport have dedicated themselves to bringing new and used goods across Bolivia's ample borders, including white goods via Brazil and car parts and clothes from Europe and the United States that arrive via the free port of Iquique in Chile. The importance of commerce has long been recognized in informal areas of La Paz: the Avenida de Uyustus is synonymous with the trade in white goods and electronics and with the wealth of the "Aymara bourgeoisie"—a phrase first coined in relation to that area in the early 1990s (Toranzo 1991). This neighborhood rapidly breaks down any proposed dichotomy between indigeneity and modernity, as store owners and workers, many *de pollera,* sell the latest technology, detailing the innovations and providing information on how to crack pirated software. The vast expanse that is the biweekly market fair in the Sixteenth July district of El Alto is similarly crammed with imported used electronics, car parts, white goods, and used clothes. Although commerce has always been important to these markets, the recent boom in imports to be sold informally has changed the economic geography of La Paz and El Alto. The wealth generated by the Sixteenth July market has made this the most expensive area to buy real estate in the metropolitan area, and the Aymara bourgeoisie has generated its own unique architectural style—the *cholets*.

The MAS's national economic strategy focused on resource extraction—a predominantly male occupation—while evoking an ideal of nationhood based on indigeneity. Although Aymara communities have always been involved in cross-border trade, the importers of commercial goods are nevertheless a threat to Bolivian productive industries, particularly textiles, leather, and food, as the scale of Bolivian production cannot compete with cheap imports from overseas or neighboring Peru (IBCE 2005). Certain trades were banned multiple times by the MAS over its first fourteen years in power in order to protect Bolivian production, but the importation of used clothes and cheap white goods grew exponentially over this time. The "national" production strategy, of which the iconic *chola* is a symbol, characterized the indigenous women involved in cross-border commerce either once more as intermediaries or, particularly in the case of imported used clothes, as traitors to Bolivian national identity. However, these markets in which imported goods are sold in effect challenge gendered and racialized constructions of scale. Allowing the local to become the national is a centerpiece of MAS pluri-economic strategy—"hegemony plus community" in García Linera's formulation. However, invoking a romanticized idea of the "local" that does not reflect the realities of traders who have constantly crossed these boundaries created inherent conflicts for the way indigenous women involved in cross-border commerce were perceived.

There are families who have made successful commercial businesses trading in traditional artifacts and rituals. One example is *las chifleras*— the traditional healers who sell products for Andean spiritual and medicinal remedies. They have their stores in the Ceja in El Alto and Calle Linares in La Paz—also known as Calle de las Brujas—the witches' street (see also Justo-Chipana and Moraes 2015). They sell the elements needed for ritual offerings, including coca leaves, incense, and llama fetuses, as well as potions, candles, and soaps manufactured and imported from Peru and Brazil that can cure everything from warts to jealousy. People from across the city and from a range of backgrounds will have their favored *chiflera*—their *casera* or regular, whom they trust to have *las buenas manos*, to assemble their ritual offering—*la mesa*—to the Pachamama. The *mesa* is also an example of how cash is incorporated into the traditional symbolic system and how capital and tradition have long coincided in Andean markets—the relationship is one of syncretism rather than opposition. The *mesa* is made up of coca leaves, cotton wool, sugar, and incense, which are assembled in a circle on a flat piece of paper and then burned with alcohol and buried as a ritual offering to the Pachamama. Included in the *mesa* are small, brightly colored tablets representing what you wish for in the future—for example, a house, or a good job in an office (represented by a computer). Fake dollar bills are also offered—and *plata* is what is most frequently desired. While commerce can corrode social networks, cash—the unit of exchange of commerce—is also reincorporated symbolically to strengthen them.

Despite being excluded from the explicit conceptualizations of decolonization and gender equality espoused by the MAS, the *chola* has achieved the aim of uniting a plurality of economic worlds with economic strategies that synthesize the apparent opposites of gift and commercial exchange, thereby destabilizing the gendered, colonial construction of the local, national, and global.

Petty Traders

Informal markets are populated by *mayoristas*—wholesalers who bring in merchandise from abroad or buy in bulk in the markets of Oruro near the border with Chile; *minoristas*—retailers who own and manage their own stalls; laborers working for others; and petty traders selling on the streets. The hierarchies are marked: those with means and transport have influence over the market associations, which gives them substantial power and control over the petty traders. The dramatic increase in wealth that accumulated in the informal economy is clear in the real estate value around the Sixteenth July market, but the lavish architecture stands in stark contrast to the poverty and precarity of the laborers and petty traders in surrounding stalls. It has been argued that community reciprocal networks function to redistribute this wealth (Tassi 2017), which can be a corrective to orthodox assumptions that wealth will trickle down via market mechanisms, or indeed structuralist accounts that emphasize poverty and exploitation in informal markets but overlook informal wealth and institutions. However, poverty in informal trade undoubtedly persists, and the majority of those affected are women (World Bank 2015). Although official gender-disaggregated data on employment in informal markets in Bolivia are limited, market association leaders estimate that the vast majority of petty traders and employees of stall owners are women and single mothers, for whom informal activities are part of a portfolio of livelihood strategies that are typical of the "entrepreneurial poor," or in GC terms, the *muchedumbre*. Both of these categorizations, from development economics and Marxist theory, respectively, underestimate the agency and skill required to survive while dealing with the multiple gendered contradictions at the nexus between community, capitalism, colonialism, and globalization.

The *comerciantes* and *mayoristas* who managed to increase their wealth—in some cases vastly—over the period of MAS rule work in extended kinship and community networks. Women whose families do not have land or transport, or who are single mothers, have limited income-generating options and tend to adopt a portfolio of activities (Moser 2010), including domestic work, informal petty commerce, various multilevel marketing schemes (such as Herbalife, which sells dietary supplements), and the entrepreneurial activities encouraged and temporarily supported by NGOs (Wanderley 2008). For the poorer members of indigenous communities, the possibilities for generating direct income are secondary to the strategies of nurturing relationships with wealthy members of the community who can be enlisted into *compadrazgo* networks and festive sponsorship. These community relationships, although vertical and potentially exploitative, are somewhat controllable within the community via gossip and the politics of reputation, and hence represent long-term financial stability compared to the whims of the informal market.

The women I got to know in Luribay and El Alto who work in "petty trade" have complex portfolios of income-generation activities. This can be read as evidence of the exploitative precarity of neoliberal globalization, but their strategies also demonstrate how the history of the area informs gendered aspirations, as they manage diverse economic dynamics in the hope of attaining community belonging, the security of the land ownership, wealth, and partnership. Below are portraits of three individuals with whom I have maintained contact since my time in Luribay in 2006 (in the case of Noelia) and since interviewing them in La Paz as part of my project on the used-clothes trade in 2010 (in the case of Alejandra and Charo). Their stories, and the role of petty commerce within them, demonstrate the various instantiations of global capital and modernity in local context as well as the complexities of resistance on their own terms, which disrupt assumptions around indigeneity, femininity, nation, production, and scale.

Noelia is an Aymara-speaking woman who grew up in Luribay, wears Western clothes, and earns her living in petty commerce in Cochabamba and El Alto. She had a child with a partner when she was young, and although they did not get married, they initially stayed together. Both of their families had modest plots of land, but Noelia would need more in order to be able to establish her own household. To this end, she moved to Spain—alone and without the appropriate papers—where she worked as a domestic worker for three years and coordinated the export of used-car parts from Europe for her brother's business in El Alto. Her partner remained in Bolivia to look after their child, but the relationship broke down when she returned. She then took up various commercial activities, including selling artisanal crafts and registering with an NGO program that would teach her how to dress hair. She still has the equipment they gave her—the branded apron and scissors—but never took it up as a business, as the market was already saturated. She does, however, value the skills she acquired to dress her daughter's hair for festivals and school parades. She tried Herbalife, without success, and quickly realized that it would potentially strain valuable social relationships. She had the most "luck," as she put it, with a stall selling deep-fried chicken and fries in the Sixteenth July market in El Alto, and she was known locally for being a particularly good cook. She was able to combine this work with caring for her elderly mother and daughter, which involved traveling from the city to her home in the country on a weekly basis. Her aim was to buy land and so acquire the community status and belonging that represents long-term financial sustainability and success as a woman who is savvy in business and can manage the demands of family, community agricultural production, and commerce.

Alejandra is a grandmother who sells used children's toys in the Sixteenth July market. She did have a stall selling cooked food, but when she fell ill and her arthritis developed she could no longer perform the arduous labor that involved, and turned to petty trade. She lives with her daughter and grandchildren and continues to sell so that she can contribute to the construction of their house in the neighborhood of Villa Pabón, one of the poorest in La Paz. Alejandra is an elderly woman who wants to continue to sell in the market, even though her daughter and son-in-law earn enough to get by and the income generated by the occasional sale of her toys is minimal. She demonstrates a drive to work and earn that is a defining characteristic of Bolivian women and a transparent source of pride. However, the hardship she faced and the lack of choice she had in working informally are an inseparable element of her story:

> My dad was a drunk . . . and he died when I was young. So, we had almost no resources to study—my parents didn't have anything. Many of us were illiterate, but on my own I studied a bit, I learned, I went to school. While I was working I went to school. . . . I worked as a domestic worker, and I worked because I had nowhere to live. My uncle lived in a house in La Portada [north of La Paz]. And my uncle left me with a Señora and I worked for her as a little girl and slept on the floor, it made me cold and that Señora enslaved me and I didn't know how to leave. . . . And so that's how I grew up, and the uncle who left me there never did come either. But at one moment my uncle appeared and I clung to my uncle. "Take me, I don't want to be here! They abuse me a lot, they make me wash, they make me do all the work." And grabbing my uncle I left, because the boss kept wanting me to stay but I didn't want to. After that I worked with my cousins and brothers and sisters, and sold in the market. (Interview, La Paz, 2010)

Noelia and Alejandra would be seen as members of García Linera's *muchedumbre* and would be viewed by structuralist approaches to informality as victims of neoliberal capitalism. Such informal work is vulnerable and exploited, but assumptions of victimhood erase agency and the remarkable strategizing and organization of women who are proud of their work and their ability to manage the substantial risks involved. These livelihoods do not fit into the discursive framework provided by neoliberal economists, international NGOs, feminist organizations, Indianist or Marxist thinkers, and hence the radical potential of these income-generation strategies that erase boundaries between work and family, rural and urban, or indeed victim and agent, is overlooked.

Charo, who has a stall in the north of La Paz, buys bed linen in Brazil and smuggles it through the forests along the border with Argentina to sell in Buenos Aires and La Paz. She exemplifies the particularly Bolivian phenomenon of *contrabando hormiga*, "ant smuggling," in which petty traders take small amounts of merchandise across borders to sell at a profit. She revels in stories of outwitting border officials and drinking *mate* with Argentinian gauchos who were impressed by her Bolivian ingenuity. Although *contrabando hormiga* is decried for undermining Bolivian national production, Charo believes it is a quintessentially Bolivian skill and a source of national pride. As she recounts:

> I used to work in Argentina and I have relatives there who still do a fair amount of trade too. We used to bring in merchandise from Brazil to Argentina, and then on to La Paz. But in Buenos Aires we would sell in the Bolivian markets. There are a few—La Salada, la "Cancha Urcupiña" in Buenos Aires. Those markets are just like in Bolivia—Argentineans love them but it's Bolivian people who made them. That is why we say with great pride there in Argentina, thanks to us [Bolivians] they have little stalls there like this. Because before they didn't have markets like that. They had stores, yes, but humble people there also wanted to earn money, and now they can. (Interview, La Paz, 2011)

The importance of informal, petty commerce to "humble" people who want to earn a living is obscured by both structuralist and neoliberal approaches to informality. The petty traders selling what they can in the street lack not only income but also the family and connections to benefit from community distributive networks such as fictive kin and cooperative exchange. Throughout the fourteen years of MAS rule, these are the workers who have fallen between the categories of pluri-economy, both in theory and policy. The combination of a structuralist approach to informality that belies the connections between informal and formal economic activity, on the one hand, and the political dependence on the communitarian formation of Andean markets, on the other, has created a situation where workers in informal areas find themselves outside the protections of the state, both in terms of material benefits and discursive identity. Agency and ingenuity are at the heart of the economic subject of the informal trader who strategizes the multiple contradictory dynamics of the global economy and the colonial state while meeting the expectations of femininity in family and community. They epitomize what it is to maintain the contradiction of binary political and economic opposites.

The Consumer

Although it has long been recognized that there is wealth in indigenous communities (Toranzo 1991; Lagos 1994), the association of indigenous culture with conspicuous consumption has been a feature of the recent rise of the "indigenous bourgeoisie" (Schipani 2014; Maclean 2019). The notion of the Aymara woman as consumer is a dramatic divergence from the image of indigenous economic femininity exhibited in both the 2009 Constitution and the imaginary of international development organizations. The conspicuous consumption of the indigenous bourgeoisie also stands in stark contrast with the Bolivian stereotype that Aymara people are miserly. There have long been tales of the *campesino* who will not spend a peso for a lightbulb but has thousands of dollars under his bed, and an oft-cited stereotype of Aymara women among the city's traditionally dominant classes is that they "hide" their wealth in order to convince the NGO community that they are the most in need. The example of the rich *chola* sitting on the stoop of a bare-brick house in El Alto, selling cheese, was frequently evoked—"But you know, she will be the owner of that house" (interview with civil servant, La Paz, February 2006).

These evocations of "miserly" Aymara culture tend to be accompanied with accusations of clandestine activity that reinforce racialized stereotypes, and the reluctance to show wealth is interpreted as avaricious, duplicitous, and a way to avoid tax. However, seen from within the community, these patterns of expenditure and saving indicate the relative importance of social networks and capital in terms of access to resources and the lack of extension of the central, colonial state. Community economies can constitute a "competition to remain equal" (Bailey 1971, 19), in which signs of personal advancement or conspicuous shows of success trigger the mechanisms to reinvest that wealth into the community, with requests to be godparents and sponsor festivals, or the threat of malicious gossip and accusations of selfishness if those requests are refused. There is hence an incentive to disguise wealth, and therefore to limit conspicuous consumption. Status is acquired rather by ownership of land, and in urban areas any surplus wealth is reinvested in property with extra floors that can be rented out, rather than spending money on, for example, an inside bathroom or heating.

Fiestas, however, mark an exception to the austere impression given by Aymara thrift; here, extravagant amounts are spent on costumes, food, and alcohol. Fiestas mark the agricultural calendar, and each hamlet, town, or city neighborhood will have its own annual fiesta, involving traditional dances performed in groups—*bloques*. These dances involve months of rehearsal and significant expense to hire the costumes, contract the band, and provide food and drink. These costs are made affordable by the practice of festive sponsorship, in which people are designated godmother or godfather of the costumes, food, or drink on the understanding that in future years this favor will be returned to them by the principle of *ayni*. Expenditure at fiestas is given as an example of peasants' lack of rationality by people who do not understand the social and economic motivations behind these investments.

There are signs that the community dynamics of fiestas are changing, and many older people in rural Aymara- or Quechua-speaking areas look to local towns and city neighborhoods and bemoan that fiestas never used to be so commercial: they used to be entirely based on communal reciprocity and mutual sponsorship. Nevertheless, social relations recreated in fiestas guide patterns of consumption in rural areas and similarly influence the market in city neighborhoods. In rural hamlets, where the main economic activity is work on the land, there are small stores that sell dried goods and beer, and small restaurants. Custom in these areas conforms to local loyalties and allegiance to family and kin. To enter into competition on price would meet with disapproval on the grounds that everyone needs to earn a living, and the high levels of interdependence mean that undercutting a neighbor would be economically irrational. This dynamic is replicated to some extent in the city and indicates the continued importance of traditions associated with rural-based social networks. For example, the frequently heard term *casera* or *casero* denotes a regular customer or stall owner, and cultivating these relationships can mean a better deal or an extra *augmento*.

Since 2006 conspicuous consumption has been growing, but it is explained as an increase in confidence rather than in disposable income. As Freddy Mamani, the celebrated Aymara architect whose work can be seen throughout El Alto, said, "Aymaras have always had money. What's changed now is they have the confidence to show it" (interview, La Paz, August 2017). The tastes that are now on display are indeed conspicuous and driven by the brightly colored aesthetics of the fiesta. Since Bolivia's economic boom, the spectacular architecture, dance halls, and fashions of the Aymara bourgeoisie have made the international press (see Schipani 2014), and rumors abound of the levels of wealth that are to be found inside those houses: tennis courts, saunas, and even private petrol pumps. The Sixteenth July market has expanded exponentially over this time and has become known, somewhat condescendingly, as "the mall of El Alto." Informal markets that are defined by their continuous connection to rural areas and the dominance of community dynamics represent different economic and financial worlds from the Western-style shopping malls—the MegaCenter, the Las Torres Mall, Plaza Real—that have been constructed in wealthy areas of La Paz and represent the vision of commercial development encouraged by international financial institutions and constructed by international consortiums.

As an illustration of this clash, in the middle of the Sixteenth July plaza in El Alto there is a billboard from shoemakers Manaco showing a classically posed model *de pollera* wearing the ballet pumps associated with the outfit (Figure 3). This image stands in stark contrast to the working women *de pollera* who pass by and who do not relate or aspire to the passivity of the woman-as-consumer represented in the advertisement. Billboards are themselves a new addition to the urban landscape of El Alto, and the fact that international companies now manufacture accessories designed for the *pollera* indicates the growing consumption base among indigenous women. The implicit assumption that the advertisers have adopted is that increasing wealth gives rise to the economic subject of the middle-class woman as consumer. This assumption is defied, however, by the women *de pollera* who continue to have an active economic role and manage complex livelihood portfolios, transport

FIGURE 3. *Manaco billboard in El Alto, 2015. Photograph: David X Green,*
www.davidxgreen.com.

from rural areas to the city, import businesses and retail, while also
maintaining complex social relationships and traditions that have always entwined with wealth. The indigenous woman *de pollera* as consumer has created an economic femininity that crosses the conceptual
boundaries of how gender, finance, and economy have been imagined.

Conclusion

Feminine Andean economic subjects are discursively homeless. They
are erased by *Homo economicus*, which renders reproductive labor, social reproduction, and cooperation unvalorized, and their maternal
and community role is ossified and romanticized in the political discourse of *chachawarmi*. The construction of indigenous women as "intermediaries" means that the map of the borders they are crossing is
not drawn from their perspective. The *chachawarmi* household has its
roots in the land ownership and labor patterns of the agricultural economy, but the current use of the discourse takes into account neither
the way household divisions and values have changed with the development of capitalist markets nor the shame produced by the pressure

to be in a partnership. As indigenous women's status changed over the fourteen years of Morales's rule, tropes that frame the understanding of women's economic behavior—for example, the middle-class consumer, exploited informal worker, or NGO beneficiary—have also proven inadequate. There is a distinct confluence of agency, wealth, cooperation, and competition that frames the way feminine economic personae are performed, portrayed, and perceived in the Andes. This configuration defies the assumptions about gendered behavior that underpin orthodox and heterodox economic theories, and even some feminist critiques of both.

The livelihood strategies of women *de pollera* and women of indigenous descent working in informal markets demonstrate the diversity of economic exchanges that have been overlooked by neoliberalism, and also synthesize opposites in a way true to the ontology of the pluriverse. The MAS vision of pluri-economy is based on the rejection of the person at the center of neoliberal economic thinking—the competitive, individualist *Homo economicus*. The MAS's dual focus on decolonization and post-neoliberalism dovetails with Latin American feminism's assertion that there is no decolonization without depatriarchalization, as well as the experience of indigenous women activists, who find that Western, individualist ideas recreate colonial dynamics. The presence of women *de pollera* with executive power at the national level was enabled by the political discourse of *chachawarmi*. However, the experiences of the *ministras* in economic roles illustrate the continued gendered economic contours of pluri-economy. The controversy for which Nemesia Achacollo resigned from Fondo Indígena shows the need for neutrality in public decision making and resource allocation that is in tension with the community dynamics of reciprocity. Her expulsion also demonstrates the continuation of machismo within the MAS. Antonia Rodríguez's vision of the local and national sitting together "like brothers" is crucial to the MAS's vision of community hegemony and the valorization of gendered "local" activities. However, this aim was stymied—as will be discussed in further chapters—by the global economic structures within which national and local enterprises have to function.

As the economic and social context developed since 2006, with marked changes in wealth, property, and mobility among indigenous people, a new discursive context emerged. The strategization of material and cultural flows of goods, capital, and ideas in informal markets produced new feminine economic subjectivities, with accompanying tropes and images that allow them to be categorized and understood via the prisms of value generated in different economic "worlds." The portraits that I have used here to illustrate the diversity of economic femininity in the Andes paint a complex picture of identity and value and of the social, economic, and cultural prism via which identity is sensed and perceived and value is established. These portraits show that there are a range of pressures on femininity, and different ways in which feminine work is valued. The *campesina* unites community gift exchange and the politics of reputation with the competitiveness of urban markets; the *chola* collapses the gendered construction of scale as she imports merchandise from around the world to invest her wealth in community festivals and relations of *compadrazgo*. Informal workers, contrary to their construction in the MAS vision of pluri-economy, are fully aware of the structural discrimination they face, but they foreground their agency as they describe a portfolio of activities that have their roots in the Andean use of markets to maintain autonomy from a colonial state. The *contrabandistas hormigas,* frequently accused of undermining national production, are also discursively reshaping the nation to place Bolivian identity in an international context and build on their cosmopolitan experiences of migration and globalization from below.

The MAS implemented radical reforms across the economy that are exemplified by the transformations and controversies in the sectors under consideration in the following chapters. These reforms were based on the central ideas of pluri-economy: prioritizing cooperation and reciprocity and bringing community dynamics to the management of the economy at national level. However, the unintended effects of the policies, as well as Bolivia's continued dependence on natural resources, the pressures of global trade, and masculinist leadership, curtailed the potential of these policies fully to valorize feminine economic activity. The prominence of tropes of indigenous femininity in the debates that ensued is testament to the power of the gendered and racialized values that were being challenged in some cases but reinforced in others. The livelihood strategies described above invite a rethinking of production, nation, and scale, and of the boundaries between rural/urban, formal/informal, and community/competition, which can help reimagine economic values in a way that does not position indigeneity or femininity as lacking or transgressive.

4

Cash

The Culture of Capital and the Value of Symbols

The reconfiguration of state and capital after the election of Evo Morales changed the way money in its various forms flowed in Bolivia, as the state took on a redistributive role and employed various measures to regulate finance, to dedollarize and guide banks to value production over commerce and social over private goods, and to counter urban biases in lending. These regulations targeted the formal banking sector, but their effect cannot be understood without engaging with the meanings, social relations, and rituals that guide how cash flows and accumulates. At the regional level, the MAS was involved in the creation of the SUCRE—a clearing currency adopted by the regional trading bloc ALBA (Alternativa Bolivariana para los Pueblos de Nuestra América; Bolivarian Alliance for the Peoples of Our America) that was intended to enable cooperative transactions of solidarity between these countries, rather than relying on the U.S. dollar. Bolivia's Financial Services Law (FSL; Ley de Servicios Financieros) of 2013 imposed interest rate ceilings and targeted credit quotas on Bolivia's varied banking system with the aim of valorizing the social mission of finance. However, state management of the Bolivian currency in effect favored commerce, contrary to politics and policy that aimed to focus on national production, and the alternative approaches to finance instituted were largely funded and sustained by extractive state capitalism (Svampa 2019).

The reforms instituted by the MAS reached formal capital and the institutions that regulate it. Over this period of time, however, wealth accumulated in the informal sectors of the economy, which are by definition beyond the reach of those regulations and are characterized by the use of cash. The synergies and dynamics between cash flow and the institutions of gift exchange and community reciprocity that exist in the markets of La Paz and El Alto demonstrate the gendered inadequacies of "capital-centric" approaches to explaining the spectacular rise in wealth of the Aymara bourgeoisie, and in particular of the women who dominate these markets. Analysis of the movements of capital is incomplete without appreciating the cultural interpretations that its instantiations—coins and banknotes—have as they are saved, transferred, and traded. The culturally situated meaning of money places for-profit exchange within the complex of values, identities, and relationships that constitute community. To shore away these meanings and relations as mere epiphenomena of capital is to *assume* a division between for-profit and community gift exchange that exists only in the abstract. Cash, the material expression of the abstract values of capital, has a symbolic place within community relations, which frame the way capital flows as much as capital in turn generates social relations. In the popular markets of Bolivia, community belonging and profit are entwined in ways that defy reductionist economic theories across the political spectrum.

This chapter maps out developments in Bolivia's financial landscape over the MAS period of rule and explores the Morales government's attempts to bring the importance of cooperative exchange to bear on the way capital creates value. The contention of MCD scholarship is that modernity started in Latin America with the colonial extraction of wealth which underpinned European capitalism. The history of capital in the Americas demonstrates how colonialism and capitalism intertwined to create racialized and gendered biases in the way that capital flows and value are constructed. The example of the development of formal and informal financial institutions in Luribay, however, brings out the complexity of Andean communities' engagement with capital and of the markets and financial subjects that emerged as the contradictions among community, gender, capital, and colonial modernity have been interpreted and grounded in community exchanges. The messiness of popular markets' engagement with capital is obscured by both the orthodox approaches the MAS was railing against and the heterodox solutions they applied. The tensions between the political and economic power of Aymara popular markets, on the one hand, and the government's aims to decolonize finance by creating a regulatory framework that could force capital to valorize the social, on the other, throw into sharp relief the biases of orthodox and structuralist approaches to both capital and informality. These contradictions, imposed on a notably variegated financial landscape, created a space in which the indigenous *chola*—who benefited from both the cultural and economic outcomes of these policies—became a powerful market force, and so rewrote the rules of financial femininity.

Colonialism and Debt Relations

The colonial history of capitalism in Latin America is succinctly expressed by the word *plata,* which literally translates as "silver" but is used to mean "money." Referring to cash as "silver" highlights the colonial roots, and routes, of capitalism, as extractivism in Latin America created the wealth, and specifically the silver coins, in circulation in sixteenth-century Spain upon which colonialism and modernity were built. On the Iberian Peninsula, the phrase *Vale un Potosí*—It's worth a fortune—was coined by Cervantes after the name of the famous Bolivian mining town where the Casa de la Moneda minted the vast majority of silver that flowed from the Americas to Spain in colonial times (Kehoe, Machicado, and Peres-Cajías 2019). The currencies that instantiate capital in the twenty-first century are multiple times removed from any relation to valuable minerals, but capital flows, whether as physical cash or digital transfers, still follow colonial pathways.

The entanglements of indigenous, rural reciprocal communities with European markets and the consequent introduction of money has been argued to have had a deleterious effect on indigenous communities in Bolivia, and historians have concurred that "the introduction of money did not transform the native economy into a monetary economy: it played only a destructive and negative role" (Corcoran-Tadd 2016, 49, citing Nathan Wachtel). The Andean Altiplano was the location of the extractive mining that the MCD group defines as the genus of modernity. The colonizers extracted minerals and the labor of the people of the Altiplano, who thereafter became "indigenous." The introduction of private land tenure and colonial institutions of governance were intended to dismantle *ayllu* cooperation and society and had devastating effects. However, despite the destructive forces of both colonialism and capitalism, the *ayllu* survived and the Aymara and Quechua market networks expanded on the basis of those traditions to extend to urban centers and beyond Bolivia's borders, producing the "motley" racialized geography and configuration of capitalist relations referred to by Zavaleta. The configuration of ethnicity, class, gender, and markets in the Andes hence produced a complex of relations, ethnic identities, and gendered financial subjects (Larson and Harris 1995) that show not only the oppressions of colonialism but also the endurance of values and community relations on which the expansion of capital depends.

The finance that was generated by colonialism in South America recast the community economy of the *ayllu* as "agricultural production" while simultaneously favoring the rhythms of urban commerce. The urban, colonial bias in finance can be seen in microcosm in Andean communities, which are characterized as having a central town, which historically was the base of feudal authorities and landowners, surrounded by hamlets dedicated to subsistence and agricultural production, farmed by "peasants." The urban, commercial economy of the towns created credit relations that were constitutive of race and racialized hierarchies. Town inhabitants may refer to themselves as white by dint of their commercial economy and status as "neighbors" rather than the community relations of the "peasants" in rural hamlets. As capital markets developed, the need for credit increased to pay for wage labor and fertilizer, although reciprocal labor relations remained. Credit relations were grafted onto community exchanges, as festive sponsorship involved loans as much as exchange of goods, godparents were sought who would be able to be called upon for a loan, and dollars became more prominent—both symbolically and concretely—in celebrations, rituals, and ceremonies (Lagos 1994).

Financial institutions in Luribay, where I conducted my fieldwork on rural finance in 2006, bring out the complexity of the interactions between capital and community exchanges and the social relations and financial subjects that are generated. Historically, the inter-Andean valley was a location of choice for colonial authorities to build their residences, and one of Luribay's claims to fame is that President Pérez de Urdininea was born there. Today, large hacienda-style houses—some in ruins—can be spotted in the landscape, and those descended from colonial families are referred to by the specifically Andean term *blancón*—white. Most inhabitants of Luribay Town would be characterized as mestizo in the city but identify as "white" in the valley because of the racialized implications of commercial relations between business owners and *vecinos* rather than the communal relations of reciprocity that characterize the surrounding hamlets, where agricultural production is the main activity, the women are mostly *de pollera,* and Aymara is the predominant language. Resentments from the colonial era remain. The Town, for example, where people would think of themselves as more urban and modern, had bathroom and kitchen facilities but only an intermittent supply of running water. In the hamlets, by contrast, there was ample water supply but the facilities were lacking. While I was there in 2006, a topographer from Save the Children was taking measurements to install a water pipe from the hamlet, to which the source of the water belonged, to the Town. He was quite pessimistic about the chances of the pipe being built and explained that the issues were not technical but political. The feudal exploitation of the hacienda period before the 1952 revolution was in living memory, and racism and discrimination remained. Those living in hamlets could recount multiple incidents of their parents being humiliated at the hands of those of colonial descent in the Town. For those reasons, the community authorities who controlled the source of the water would not grant access to those living in the Town.

The historical presence of criollo, colonial elites resident in Luribay, the links between this area and the cities that developed as a result, and the ties of kinship and fictive kin between families highlight the messiness of capital's colonization of the Andes. The complexity of the relationship between class, ethnicity, and urbanity was evident in the credit relations between the rural, peasant hamlets and the more commercial Town. For example, as part of my research exploring microfinance in the area in 2006, I interviewed Doña Margarita, whose family had been involved in lending credit privately. She was referred to locally as a *residente*—she lived in La Paz and had her main retail business there—but also had family connections in Luribay, where she owned a house and a hostel. She recalls her family's history in the Town and how they would lend to women managing rural production:

> The people here in the Town would lend privately, and then they would be paid back [by the *campesinos* in the hamlets] after the harvest. It was always necessary to borrow money. Sometimes they bought the fertilizer and stuff on credit. It was with interest but not with a contract. My grandma did that and the interest was high: 5 percent a month. (Interview with Doña Margarita, Town, Luribay, July 2006)

The informal loans offered could be notarized by the agrarian union or local notary, and they tended to be at higher rates of interest than those available from formal providers in the city, which for various reasons—including specifications of what could be recognized as collateral, risks associated with rural production, costs of administering small loans at a distance, and explicit discrimination—may not have been available to people, particularly women *de pollera,* from the hamlets of Luribay. Private loans like these, however, generally had a more flexible repayment schedule that could better fit the rhythm of rural production, and they could be managed within the context of community relationships. Doña Margarita, for example, was a sought-after godmother for various fiestas and rites of passage. Loans, although the essential way in which community values and relations become capitalized, could then be at least negotiated as part of broader strategies of reputation management and community politics.

When formal finance did arrive in the Town in the form of the microfinance institution CRECER, private lending such as that described by Doña Margarita declined. As Doña Carol, who ran a hostel and a shop in the Town, recalled, before a formal source of finance arrived in the valley "the people who worked on land would come to us [the people in the Town], they would borrow from us. Now they don't need to come. They've got the bank" (interview, Town, Luribay, March 2006). CRECER specialized in lending to women in rural and peri-urban environments and aimed to build formal, sustainable "financial institutions of development" and capitalize relations within communities by lending on the basis of a "social collateral" group guarantee. Their operations in Luribay increased from one promoter servicing around thirty groups around the valley in 2006, to an established office in the Town by 2018 which offers the financial services that would formerly have necessitated a journey to the city.

The success represented by the establishment of a microfinance institution (MFI) fits the orthodox vision of development—exemplified by economist Hernando de Soto's approach to informality—which is to bring formal financial services to areas where there are none and so marshal informal, cash exchanges that can be lent out by banks to create more capital (see Bromley 1990). Credit is a practical need, given the expansion of capital markets and commerce, but the development of these institutions relies on community support despite the fact that finance can also potentially corrode community relationships and render the labor involved in their maintenance invisible. The inherent mismatch in the schedule imposed by debt and that of rural production places a strain on the very community relations upon which group guarantees depend. This strain was made clear by women in the hamlets I spoke to who had taken out group credit, often at the behest of another community member, in order to support their agricultural production:

> The bank helps us, but it treads on us at the same time. . . . That's the problem with the bank. They don't understand us. The promoter, you can tell him, no, I'm going to get the money as soon as I can sell my peas, but he won't listen. So I have to go and borrow money from somebody else, but that just means that then I have to pay that person too. And I do that as soon as I sell my peas and get some money. (Interview with Doña Sofia, Hamlet, Luribay, August 2006)

The community relations that Doña Sofia falls back on are in effect maintaining the bank, and the financial strategies she adopts involve a delicate, and gendered, balance between community relations and earning a living.

The entrepreneurial activities that best suit the capitalist demands for turnover and profit do not necessarily fit well with community dynamics of interdependence. For example, Doña Veronica in Luribay was a single mother who did not own any land and took out a modest microfinance loan—fifty dollars over six months—and invested in a small shop from which she sold her home-baked empanadas. As she did not have land, she could spend her time on her business and made a regular profit that allowed her to meet repayments. As a single, landless woman she was excluded from community institutions, including fiestas and the agrarian union. The loan allowed her to earn a living from that outsider position, but respecting community relations was her priority, and this precluded entering into competition with other community members:

> Before, when I started with the credit, I didn't make bread, because there was somebody else here who did it, and I'm not one of those people who's going to start a business when there's already

somebody else doing it. That's why I didn't make bread at first. But then, when that person died, I started, because there was no one else around who made bread. So I said to myself, I'm going to make bread. (Interview with Doña Veronica, Hamlet, Luribay, July 2006)

These powerful community relations can be recognized by capital in the form of collateral and joint liability, but the worth of social relationships can be corroded as the demands of capital strain and exploit the relations and resources upon which it builds. Collateral—the guarantee behind the loan—is the way capital extends, both financially and culturally. Once cast as collateral, material goods become valued primarily in terms of their potential exchange value, rather than use value or a sense of identity, history, or belonging. Collateral introduces a requirement of formal ownership, with the implications of individuality and formality that brings. The evidence required to demonstrate ownership—for example, deeds on land—will tend to favor men due to multiple overlaying dynamics of colonialism, inheritance rights, and household headship. However, it is in capital's interest to extend what is recognized as collateral, and the extension of financial services has been enabled by innovating techniques to accept different forms of collateral without incurring disproportionate risk to the institutions, including informal ownership, community property, personal guarantors, and social collateral in the form of joint liability group guarantees (Maclean 2010). However, there is a difference between harnessing this collateral in order to extend capital and valorizing those guarantees on their own terms. If the values of capital are not in turn questioned, capital can corrode the very collateral and trust on which it depends. The comments above from microfinance borrowers in Luribay make clear that their priority is not income generation but rather the maintenance of social relations and belonging. Far from being "free collateral," as it is frequently cast in development literature, loans made on the basis of community ties are hyper-collateralized.

The transition from community to capitalist exchange involves a reconfiguration of the values of care and risk, which creates a gendered distinction. The construction of what counts as risk—an inherently abstract concept—is central to finance and the expansion of capitalist values, as reciprocity is replaced by competition, and the risk taken by the entrepreneur receives higher recompense and praise than those involved in reproductive labor and care. Risk is defined as a technical assessment, as distinguished from the irresponsible boldness of the gambler or the dangers of random hazards. Technical risk assessments involve measurement devices and modeling tools that are placed in contradistinction to traditional indigenous knowledge, which may be seen as handling random danger rather than controllable risk (Maclean 2013). The risk-taking entrepreneur is modeled around colonial, masculinist metaphors of penetrating new ground technologically, or taking on the competition. The recreation of tradition, or the repetitive work of reproductive and recreative labor, is the constitutive other of this risk of the entrepreneur. The value of risk—central to the dynamics of capital—is one of the many values that form a division between "tradition" and "modernity" and between the "feminine" and the "masculine."

Capital creates a gendered dynamic of scale as the reciprocal exchanges that define "local" are coded feminine next to the outward networking that creates the national and global. Credit is the mechanism for this, as greater profits come with leverage and increased levels of production. On a practical level, the income-generating activities that women with family and community responsibilities generally do tend to be qualified as small or micro, whereas manufacturing industries at the national level offer wage labor predominantly to men. Policies to support national modernization projects—the infrastructures required for industrialization and scaling up agricultural production—can overlook this feminine, micro scale of activity. These gendered dynamics explain in part the high proportion of women in the informal economy. Greater rewards accrue to those who already have scale and capital, as the ability for richer people and more developed enterprises to take out larger loans to leverage their projects and benefit from the efficiencies of scale makes it difficult for smaller enterprises and cooperatives to compete. In financial terms, scale constitutes the paradox that it is "expensive to be poor"—an acknowledgment that capital alone cannot "level the playing field" (Bateman and Maclean 2017).

However, despite the gendered, colonial construction of the cultural values of capital, it would be oversimplifying to think that cash and community relations are incommensurate, and while colonial capitalism is central to the construction of race and gender, the political landscape it creates when grounded, reinterpreted, and resisted is complicated and variegated. The rise of the Aymara bourgeoisie in Bolivia, and the historical roots of their wealth, is testament to this complexity. In defiance of the colonial legacy of the phrase, wealthy *chola* market women are frequently referred to as having "*la* plata," and those selling in stalls are assumed to be carrying large amounts of cash, despite their humble attire. This makes them a target for petty thieves, and explains the closed and gruff demeanor, particularly to outsiders, for which they are notorious. The presence of large amounts of cash in popular markets is the explanation offered for the high levels of crime and violence in market areas of La Paz and El Alto, such as La Ceja, Cementerio, and La Rodriguez. The newly emerging consuming Aymara bourgeoisie, who have the most expensive *polleras* and jewels and conspicuous bodyguards, are accustomed to making large payments, even for houses, in cash. Wealth and cash have long been part of Andean traditions, but they circulate and accumulate according to the rules of community belonging and gift exchange. While there has always been wealth in Andean indigenous communities, and it has had a prominent symbolic role, the configuration of cash, indigeneity, and gender is changing in ways that are not represented in either orthodox approaches to the economy or the MAS's heterodox alternatives.

Bolivia's Financial Institutions

The breadth and diversity for which the Bolivian financial sector is famed is attributed to the way the "structure of the finance sector . . . reflects the influence of community organizations" (Thoumi and Anzola 2010, 444). The formal financial system in Bolivia has been shaped by the history of the late twentieth century: the growth of savings and loans funded by the United States in the 1950s and 1960s to promote a property-owning democracy (Garrett et al. 1965); state-backed subsidies to rural production in the 1960s and 1970s; and devaluations and restrictions on public banking in the neoliberal 1980s (Peres-Cajías 2014; Kehoe, Machicado, and Peres-Cajías 2019). Each of these swings between a state-led *dirigisme* to market *laissez-faire* brought with it assumptions about value and what social relations are and should be like (de la Torre, Ize, and Schmukler 2011); there is no culturally neutral finance. Bankarization—the percentage of the population with access to banking services—is greater in Bolivia than in Peru and even Colombia, and a range of different institutions can provide banking services—commercial banks, mutuals, credit unions, *fondos financieros privados* (FFPs; private finance funds), and also unregulated, non-deposit-taking financial entities, typically NGOs offering microcredit (UN-HABITAT 2008). Various forms of collateral are accepted—land, property, goods, usufruct rights, and group guarantees—and institutions differ in their stated development aims, from investment in small enterprises and housing to women's empowerment and sustainable energy. Bolivia's financial sector in the early 2000s hence had the peculiar distinction of incorporating creative approaches to financial technology—experimenting with nontraditional collateral and variable interest rates and repayment schedules—while maintaining the approval of international financial institutions. Nevertheless, commercial banks remain dominant, and the biases in favor of commerce over agriculture and competition over community persist.

Bolivia over the late twentieth century saw the harshest reform of monetary policy and financial regulation after inflation reached rates of over 20,000 percent and the *peso boliviano* had reached a high of 2.2 million pesos to the U.S. dollar (Malloy 1991). In 1985 the *peso boliviano* was floated, which resulted in a 95 percent devaluation; after it had stabilized, a new currency, the *boliviano*, was created in 1986. Following the 1985 adjustment package, savings accounts could be opened in dollars to avoid further capital flight and attract back elite wealth that had fled to bank accounts in the United States during the currency crisis. State banks were privatized and independent financial regulators established—the Central Bank; Superintendency of Banks; and Superintendency of Pensions, Securities Markets, and Insurance (UN-HABITAT 2008). Subsidies to agricultural credit from state-run banks were removed, as the counter-cyclical incentives they created were considered to have contributed to the fiscal and economic instability of the 1980s (Graham and González-Vega 1995). Although these reforms were successful in stabilizing the currency, it was widely held that the potential for growth and production had been damaged; to quote President Suazo, "You have given us stabilisation, but at the price of economic development" (Godoy and De Franco 1992, 618). The removal of state subsidies to agricultural credit was particularly controversial and was seen as a political rather than technical decision that would favor the urban *comerciante* over the rural peasant producer (Godoy and

De Franco 1992). The supposed "technical fix" of structural adjustment overlooked the differential impact of fiscal reforms, and the divides that were created and exaggerated along urban/rural and racialized lines were to frame politics in the 1990s. Debtors' protests were commonplace in La Paz in the 1990s and early 2000s, as interest rates rose and the enforcement of creditors' rights were the priority of international agencies seeking to build sustainable institutions (Rhyne 2001).

A key focus of the structural reforms imposed by the International Monetary Fund (IMF) was to reduce state intervention in the financial system and establish independent regulation. In the late 1980s Bolivia had four state-run banks: two state-owned development banks, one development bank within the Central Bank, and one state-owned commercial bank (Morales 2004). These institutions had high administration costs, were working with poor data, and had high default rates. The leniency toward delinquency distorted the market to the point that loans were considered grants. The IMF strongly advised the closure of state-run banks, and the financial crisis of the 1990s drove more out of business. By 2000, Bolivia's financial sector had no state-run banks. Regulation of creditors' rights had tightened up and debtors' strikes had increased, and by the early 2000s over 90 percent of deposits were held in dollars and 97 percent of loans were given in that currency (Naqvi 2021, 459). The banking sector hence became the symbol of the iniquities of capitalism, as well as Bolivia's lack of sovereignty in the face of the IMF's conditionality and subordination to the might of the U.S. dollar.

Bolivian banks recognized the need to extend trust in order to cover more of the country's economic activity, which led to the eclectic environment that characterizes the Bolivian financial sector. Bolivian financial institutions were praised for their innovation, and developments in inclusive finance in Bolivia were international reference points for the social neoliberalism of the 1990s (Rhyne 2001), but the fundamental precepts of financial orthodoxy that had led to exclusion—the favoring of profit and urban commerce—were not challenged, and Bolivian banks were in effect extending an exclusionary system rather than including "other" economies. The country's reputation for financial innovation comes from its varied microfinance sector, and in particular the flagship MFI Banco Sol, which was one of the first MFIs in the world to achieve financial sustainability (González-Vega et al. 1997). There were also institutions that managed to resist the increasing demands of international funders to achieve sustainability by bringing together the recognized need for Bolivian financial institutions to extend trust with the development imperative to recognize a "social bottom line." For instance, Fundación para Alternativas de Desarrollo (FADES; Foundation for Development Alternatives), one of Bolivia's largest MFIs, developed partnerships to be able to provide nontraditional financial services including loans for infrastructural development such as phone services and rural electrification (Allderdice, Winiecki, and Morris 2007). Microfinance NGOs Pro Mujer and CRECER both argued for their continued use of social collateral despite its requiring subsidy, as it allowed them to achieve greater client loyalty and helped them withstand the financial crisis of 2000 (Velasco and Marconi 2004). These institutions, however, did not challenge the prevailing orthodoxy, which focused on extending sustainable financial institutions, capitalizing social relations, and marshaling the wealth of the informal sector.

Bolivia also has a significant history of mutual and cooperative banking, but these institutions have their roots in the savings and loan paradigm that was supported by the United States in the 1960s, rather than the community dynamics underpinning cooperation in the Andes. The aptly named Mutual La Primera was the first mutual bank in La Paz, set up in 1964. It was a savings and loan bank, supported by the United States Agency for International Development (USAID) and the newly formed Inter-American Development Bank, which gave mortgages for affordable housing (Garrett et al. 1965). The mutual was crucial in the development of a professional middle class in La Paz, to whom it provided mortgages, again supported by USAID, to develop a property-owning democracy. Credit unions were also established in the 1960s by parish groups, which could provide savings and loan facilities. In the 1990s, FFPs were developed as "quasi banks" that could service micro- and small enterprises. At the turn of the century these included Caja los Andes, FIE, Eco Futuro, PRODEM, FASSIL, ACCESO, and COMUNIDAD. However, despite the variety of providers, it was difficult to access credit via formal mechanisms due to the lack of extension of the system as a whole and the dominance of banks, which held over 70 percent of assets, loans, and deposits (UN-HABITAT 2008).

Bolivia's "actually existing" financial ecology represents configurations of community/profit and care/risk that do not conform to the economic orthodoxy that favors profit and commerce. These values can be traced in the cultural flows of capital and identity and in informal community debt, lending, and savings. A range of traditional credit mechanisms in the Andes recognizes different forms of collateral, ideas of interest, and repayment rates. The *pasanaku* is a traditional savings and lending circle in which members of a group each pay in a set amount and take turns borrowing the whole amount to be repaid within a specific time period to the group with interest. Such groups are found worldwide and have become known in development circles as rotating savings and credit associations (ROSCAs), but the *pasanaku* has its roots in *ayni*—the Andean principle of reciprocity and cooperation that underpinned exchange of goods and labor for agricultural production in rural areas. However, *pasanaku* has become generally an urban phenomenon that illustrates how "traditional" mechanisms and rituals are reinvented in a commercial context (Adams and Canavesi 2019). The potential romanticization of the trust and "social capital" that underpins the use of such ROSCAs in development, and evocations of indigenous reciprocity in political discourse, is indicated by the oft-heard axiom *"pasanaku*—es robo" (*pasanku*—it's theft), and there are campaigns for legal backing to these "informal" credit arrangements. Another credit mechanism commonly used in Bolivia is the traditional Andean lending mechanism *anticretico*—derived from Roman law. *Anticretico* is money lent in return for usufruct rights on land or property, and it enables landowners to obtain interest free loans by in effect pawning their land. If the landlord does not repay the loan in full after a determined period of time, the land or property defaults to the lender. Historically this mechanism developed in relation to land ownership, and has become part of the formal lending system, with notaries and banks facilitating these contracts (Delta Financiero 2016).

The financial system in Bolivia exhibits a range of different values in terms of collateral and development aims, but they share the ultimate goal of extending capitalization. The recognition of social collateral is markedly opposed to a decolonial, anticapitalist vision of valorizing community, and the savings and loans, with their roots in the Cold War and U.S. interventions in Latin America, represent a drive to extend the values of capital, property, and ownership. Nevertheless, the variety of these institutions, including traditional lending mechanisms, belies the abstracted "straw man" of neoliberal banking that was prominent in the MAS's narrative. As will be discussed in the following section, MAS financial reforms relied on heterodox theories of the state and capital and aimed to create an institutional framework that forced capital to recognize the social and support cooperative exchange, including at the international level. However, the blindness of these reforms to the preexisting financial landscape, and in particular its gendered dimensions, would have contradictory effects.

MAS Financial Reforms

The aims of the MAS financial reform strategy were to overthrow the dominance of international financial institutions (IFIs), challenge neoliberal banking orthodoxy, and provide appropriate financial support to the National Development Plan of creating a *Bolivia digna, soberana, productiva y democrática*—a dignified, sovereign, productive, and democratic Bolivia. The international economic and political context that developed over its first term in office allowed significant room to maneuver. IFIs had dominated Bolivian economic and fiscal policy since 1985, but after the 2005 election the MAS acquired substantial bargaining power. The strength of Morales's mandate was a key aspect of this, as was the consequent weakening of Santa Cruz–based banking elites (Naqvi 2021). The macroeconomic conditions were also in place: there was a worldwide natural resource boom and a regional trend toward dedollarization, and the 2008 financial crash had underscored the need for bank regulation and state intervention in the banking system. Bolivia had benefited from the debt relief to Highly Indebted Poor Countries in 2005, and the IMF and the World Bank were no longer the only international lenders, as the BRICS (Brazil, Russia, India, China, and South Africa) and regional powers, notably Venezuela, were also able to lend.

The MAS's financial reforms, however, exhibited the tensions between state-led and decolonial visions of reform, as well as demands from members of its political base in El Alto and peri-urban areas who were increasingly reliant on commerce. The reforms made to finance at the regional level and to the Bolivian financial sector scaled cooperative exchange, expanded notions of collateral, and prioritized production over speculation. Despite the unorthodox parameters and the explicit social mission of these reforms, Bolivian banks received high ratings from credit agencies and achieved low delinquency rates. However, as IMF reports from throughout the period in question emphasize, the overvaluation of the boliviano, which was in effect pegged to the dollar, did, contrary to the main aims of the MAS, favor commercial imports over national production (Kehoe, Machicado, and Peres-Cajías 2019). The contradictory directions between political and economic strategy, and the contrast between the effectiveness of cultural and symbolic changes that underpinned policies that for various reasons had limited economic effectiveness, created a space in which many of the gendered and racialized values of competition, ownership, and formality were confronted.

Currency and Sovereignty

Bolivia's participation in ALBA and the SUCRE is an example of scaling up dynamics of community exchange to the level of the nation-state and regional trade, and so changing the logic that made solidarity and cooperation subordinate to competition. The creation of ALBA was vaunted around the world as a potential alternative to the system of global trade that had positioned member countries as providers of natural resources to industrialized nations and had given the U.S. dollar hegemonic power as the international clearing currency. Naomi Klein described it—idealistically—as "essentially a barter system, in which countries decide for themselves what any given commodity or service is worth, rather than letting traders in New York, Chicago or London set the prices for them" (Klein quoted in Cusack 2014, 1). In 2006, Bolivia joined the regionalist project ALBA-PTA—the Bolivarian Alliance for the Peoples of Our Americas–Peoples' Trade Agreement— led by Venezuela and Cuba, which was created explicitly to challenge the dominance of IFIs and the hegemony of the United States in trade agreements. ALBA came to represent the "pink tide" nations of Latin America, all of whom embraced solidarity and community at the level of government and global trade, and these principles were explicit in the treaties underpinning the trading bloc. The aim was to create regional production networks based on solidarity between countries that had been exploited by the world system and were as a result highly indebted. Each country would have specialized national produce— Venezuelan petrochemicals, Cuban medics, Nicaraguan wood, and Bolivian textiles—which could be exchanged in the spirit of solidarity and partnership rather than competition and comparative advantage

(Rosales, Cerezal, and. Molero-Simarro 2011). Surplus from this trade would be paid into a Structural Convergence Fund that would manage aid to less-developed regions.

In order to reduce dependency on the dollar, members of ALBA, chiefly Presidents Rafael Correa of Ecuador and Hugo Chávez of Venezuela, proposed a "new financial architecture" along the lines advocated by Keynes during the Bretton Woods summit. This would include the creation of a Banco del ALBA and Banco del Sur, which would be able to invest in development and infrastructure projects, and a regional clearing currency, the SUCRE (Sistema Unificado de Compensación Regional de Pagos; Unified System for Regional Compensation), which enabled trade within the ALBA group without reliance on the U.S. dollar. The creation of the SUCRE was inspired by the Keynesian idea of the "bancor," which would be based on the price of gold and enable international trade without the domination of the richer countries. The SUCRE, mirroring Keynes's scheme, was to be based on donations from member countries, proportionate to GDP, and has been referred to as a "monetary tool toward economic complementarity" (Rosales, Cerezal, and Molero-Simarro 2011, 4). Chávez also declared it "an important step towards the sovereignty of our peoples and freedom from the dictatorship of the dollar, the neoliberal dictatorship and the dictatorship of transnational corporations" (Vaca 2009). The vision of the SUCRE went beyond other regional trading currencies—for example, the euro and its predecessor the ECU—and its founders sought to develop a new form of value, based on solidarity and reciprocity. To this end, in addition to the Regional Monetary Council and ALBA Executive, which set rates, a Social Movements Council was established, consistent with the long-term vision of decolonizing the state and the global order in favor of community dynamics of social and civil society organizations (Artaraz 2011). This coincided with the theory driving the MAS of using community ideals of reciprocity and solidarity, rather than competition, to structure the economy at national, regional, and global levels.

By replacing the dollar, the SUCRE would favor intraregional trade and regional development, as fewer foreign reserves would need to be spent on facilitating trade. It would allow small and medium-sized enterprises (SMEs) with limited facilities to deal in dollars to participate in intraregional trade, which could potentially be of benefit to those working in informal markets. However, there were several downfalls in implementation. The Social Movements Council lacked legitimacy and was trumped by the imperatives of other regional trade agreements with which ALBA needed to negotiate (Rosales, Cerezal, and Molero-Simarro 2011). Similarly, the Structural Convergence Fund, despite being described frequently as a "cornerstone" of ALBA, did not really exist. Only the four largest economies in ALBA—Venezuela, Ecuador, Cuba, and Bolivia—joined the SUCRE, but the vast majority of use of the SUCRE was between Ecuador and Venezuela—consistently over 80 percent (*IP Nicaragua* 2020), with Ecuador mainly exporting and Venezuela mainly importing. The height of the number of transactions conducted using the SUCRE occurred in 2012 and included multinationals as well as state enterprises. This was, however, in the midst of a commodity boom that had greatly buoyed the Venezuelan economy. The number of transactions using the SUCRE has since fallen with the fortunes of the Venezuelan economy (Cusack 2018).

Bolivia's participation in the currency was minimal, reflecting the relative size of its economy and lack of existing trading relationships. There have been sporadic incidences where Bolivia has benefited from trade—for example, in 2010 when Venezuela bought up textiles after trade deals between Bolivia and the United States collapsed (Cusack 2014). However, this was not indicative of a longer-term commitment to integrate Bolivia into intraregional supply chains, despite that being the specific purpose of ALBA and intended function of the trading currency. The SUCRE—despite its commitments—could not break away from the international trading system and economic basis, shaped by the international order.

However, symbolically the SUCRE has been important in Bolivian and Latin American politics in terms of autonomy and legitimacy. The currency was dismissed by the United States initially as "economically meaningless" (Cusack 2014, 128) but was part of a trend toward regional currencies throughout the world. The challenge to the hegemony of the dollar—a central aim of Rafael Correa, whose country had been forced to adopt the currency as its own—also spurred Bolivia's attempts to dedollarize its economy. It is hard to argue that the innovations around the SUCRE can be seen as more than economic nationalism and protectionism rather than a reinvention of the way that money functions. However, the SUCRE and Bolivia's participation in ALBA were also symbolic, cultural factors that had economic effects in terms of the country's monetary sovereignty against the dollar.

Bolivianización

Establishing a sovereign currency was a pillar of MAS financial policy. Following the structural reforms of 1985, the boliviano had lost 95 percent of its value, and accounts were allowed to be opened in dollars to prevent capital flight. Various periods of dollarization and redollarization ensued, and by the 1990s the boliviano was in effect pegged to the dollar. The dollar soon became the main currency for bank credits and deposits, and by 2001 more than 90 percent of deposits (93.2 percent) and credits (94.4 percent) were in dollars (Morales 2004). The dollar was the currency of the wealthy, who could benefit from its stability and transferability, and the existence of dual currencies increased inequality and financial exclusion, heightened the risk of capital flight, and politically restricted fiscal policy and central banks' ability to moderate their currency in the face of shocks (Peres Cajías 2014; Kehoe, Machicado, and Peres-Cajías 2019). The U.S. currency was also favored culturally as a symbol of wealth across the economy, whether by investors or in rural communities, where the expectation was that good godparents would gift in dollars. Popular economies, which by definition functioned predominantly with cash rather than bank transactions, dealt in both currencies, with dollar bills preferred for large purchases. Forgery of boliviano notes was a widespread problem, and the symbols of wealth used in ritual offerings were sugar tablets in the shape of the U.S. dollar. By the early 2000s the boliviano had lost legitimacy as a store of both monetary and cultural value.

For both symbolic and financial reasons, returning to the boliviano and reducing dollarization was a central plank of the MAS's fiscal agenda and approach to finance. Regaining control of a national currency would allow domestic institutions—the state and the Central Bank—to have more control over fiscal and monetary policy. Lack of control over a dollar-denominated sovereign debt had caused the crisis of the 1980s, and regaining the seigniorage that was lost at the behest of the IMF would be a triumphant overthrow of neocolonial global finance. It would also bolster the internal market and be particularly important to giving those micro- and small enterprises and low-paid workers in the informal economy more trust in a banking system that facilitates loans and deposits in the same currency in which they earn. However, greater fiscal control would also give the state more power, which was in itself controversial within the MAS movement and other organizations arguing for the decolonization of Bolivia's politics and economy.

Dedollarization had been a trend across Latin America since the turn of the century (García-Escribano and Sosa 2011), but Bolivia's process was particularly dramatic. According to the president of the Bolivian Central Bank at the time, Juan Morales (Morales 2004, 106), dollarization in Bolivia was "close to complete" before the MAS came to power. By 2010, rates of dollarization of deposits and credits had been reduced to 51.4 percent and 53.8 percent, respectively, representing a significant shift toward the boliviano of over 40 percent from 2001 (Luján Chávez 2012). This trend was reflected across the region and was due in part to macroeconomic changes that had stabilized inflation, GDP growth, and exchange rate appreciation. In Bolivia dollarization was down even further by 2016, to 16 percent of deposits and just 3 percent of loans. This reduction was achieved with assertive policies to encourage dedollarization by the government and regulators, including higher taxes on foreign currency transactions, higher requirements for foreign currency loans and deposits, higher capital requirements for trading, and a currency ceiling on foreign deposits in banks (Laframboise 2017).

This process of *bolivianización* was praised by international institutions for being a "successful market friendly" process (García-Escribano and Sosa 2011, 3) and was compared to the dedollarization processes in Peru and Paraguay, where the governments of the time did not share Bolivia's socialist aims. The Bolivian process saw the most dramatic decline, particularly in credits, which was a point of interest for international commentators. However, commentators within Bolivia saw dedollarization as a political and cultural as much as a financial issue and attributed diminished reliance on the U.S. currency to increased national confidence. The rapid dedollarization in Bolivia was seen as an "expression of the recuperation of monetary sovereignty" (Mendoza Hernández 2020, 102), and the increase in the proportion of bolivianos in circulation was taken as a sign that there was greater trust and confidence in the boliviano as a store of value.

However, there was also a concern that the main driver of the rapid dedollarization process has been the dramatic appreciation of the boliviano, the value of which rose sharply over 2005 and 2006. In 2011 the Central Bank adopted a de facto fixed exchange rate with the dollar of 6.96 bolivianos (Kehoe, Machicado, and Peres-Cajías 2019). This was made possible by the influx of foreign reserves following the boom in the price of hydrocarbons, which provided the Central Bank with the dollars to maintain this rate. A sovereign wealth fund, Fondo para la Revolución Industrial Productiva (Fund for the Productive Industrial Revolution), was instituted in 2012 on the basis of reserves generated from the nationalization of hydrocarbons. The development of a sovereign wealth fund was the crucial precondition for the industrial reforms that the MAS was to put in place and was a key element of the MAS's strategy to avoid the resource curse, following the Norwegian example (Quiroga 2012). Nevertheless, the boliviano was largely considered to be overvalued (IMF 2016), and it has been estimated that a real appreciation of the boliviano commenced in 2005 and continued for at least a decade (Kehoe, Machicado, and Peres-Cajías 2019). The overvalued but stable boliviano provided an incentive to take out loans in that currency, which was also encouraged by rumors of an imminent devaluation, and favored commercial imports over manufactured exports, contrary to the aims of MAS economic strategy.

Many aspects of the "new financial architecture" question orthodox ideas of value, risk, and exchange. The SUCRE challenged notions of value and scale and attempted to facilitate and valorize cooperative solidarity at the international level. Both the development of the SUCRE and *bolivianización* represent significant political, cultural, and symbolic steps toward reestablishing the legitimacy of national sovereignty against the hegemony of IFIs. The economic aim of these monetary developments was to potentiate the internal market, which would in turn benefit national production and small-scale producers in Bolivia's popular economies. However, the sovereignty in question remained in the hands of a state that was increasingly buoyed and centralized due to the influx of capital from natural resources, which exacerbated the tensions among Marxist, Indianist, and communitarian agendas. The overvaluation of the boliviano favored commerce and importation rather than production, which in turn created competition for Bolivia's producers and concerns for food sovereignty as national production dropped. As we will see in subsequent chapters, those who stood to gain most from these contradictions between symbolic sovereignty and an overvalued currency were the popular markets that had been so important to the MAS electorally.

Banking Reform

The MAS achieved significant banking reforms, particularly in its second term. It reestablished a role for state-owned banks and in 2013 passed the Financial Services Law, which allowed the ministry to direct finance, control interest rates, and compel lenders to recognize non-traditional collateral. These moves had been vehemently opposed by the banking sector but were not as extensive as had been feared, as some within the government were advocating full nationalization. Nevertheless, the reforms were controversial. The banking sector objected to the power accorded to the ministry to direct banks to lend to "productive" sectors and requirement to recognize nontraditional forms of collateral, both of which could increase delinquency and be potentially inflationary but were also crucial to supporting inclusion and reducing the urban bias in finance. The considerable power the state gained in this process and its reliance on income from hydrocarbons also exacerbated fears that the promise of plurality was being subsumed beneath what was in effect a modern extractivist economy.

The Banco de Desarrollo Productivo (Productive Development Bank) came into being in May 2007 as a second-tier state-owned bank, incorporating the activities of two state-owned second-tier banks formed in the 1990s—Nacional Financiera Boliviana and Fondo de Desarrollo del Sistema Financiero—with $60 million U.S., to support productive SMEs. Its remit was to support the National Development Plan by channeling credit to financial institutions that would boost national production with funding from the national treasury (Villarroel and Hernani-Limarino 2015). The BDP was explicit in its social mission to support micro- and small enterprises that had been underserved or exploited by mainstream and microfinance banking institutions by offering low interest rates and recognizing a range of forms of collateral.

This "social mission" was directly against the prevailing orthodoxy that the main duty of banks was profitability and therefore the extension of sustainable financial services. Although Moody's, in a 2015 report, praised the bank's low delinquency ratios, due largely to the fact that its role was on-lending to other banks and cooperatives, it expressed concern that "modest profitability" was "a direct consequence of the bank's social mission to promote the development of SMEs by providing them with access to financing at below-market rates" (Moody's 2015). Economist Luis Arce, who was appointed minister of economy and public finance in 2006, saw banks "purely as a tool for productive sector development," such that profitability was a secondary concern that should even be treated with "suspicion" (Naqvi 2018, 17). Arce's heterodox approach dovetailed with the idea that capital inherently favored urban, commercial enterprises rather than rural production, and it had the support of both large-scale industries and small businesses in the productive sector. The BDP's aim was to address this by offering larger loans, at lower interest rates to specifically productive enterprises. In 2014 the provision of various credits, subsidized by government reserves, were announced to promote inclusion and economic production. These included credits available only to those who had productive enterprises and offered at an annual rate of 6 percent (Chipana 2013). This allowed "producers," including manufacturing cooperatives and farmers, to benefit from larger loans with longer repayment terms, hence offering a promise of growth and formalization. However, in focusing on national production, the BDP approach risked replicating gender biases of scale and repeating the errors of the MNR modernization era in attempting to create a national rather than a "motley" or plural productive economy.

The FSL further reinforced the state's powers to direct banks and ensure that their activities supported the economic *and social* development of the country. This was a radical change from the previous law, passed in 1993, which had guaranteed the power of banks to set interest rates that "will be freely agreed between financial intermediaries and users" (A. Méndez 2014). Using provisions in the FSL (Article 66), in 2015 the government stipulated that banks have a maximum term of five years to bring at least 60 percent of their loan portfolio to the productive sector and social housing, and that mutual financial institutions should allocate 50 percent of their loans to social housing (Supreme Decree 1842, Article 4). The law also required banks to provide credit for social housing and productive enterprises at interest rates of around 6 percent. The aim of this law, which again resonated with both heterodox and colonial critiques of the role of capital in the economy, was to overturn the tendency of banks to lend to urban commercial enterprises, which were relatively low risk, high turnover, and less costly to administer.

The FSL capped interest rates on credit to productive sectors, ranging from 6 percent for large loans to 11.5 percent for microfinance loans (Knaack 2020, 247). These caps were a particular concern to MFIs, whose vision was to charge market-based—although in many cases partly subsidized initially—interest rates in order to create sustainable financial institutions and an active formal credit market that would itself eventually lower rates. However, they had been criticized for charging high levels of interest and for in effect exploiting their beneficiaries for the sake of developing institutions. Organizers of debt protests had argued that the interest was unaffordable despite the apparent high payment rates, which disguised the actions that borrowers took to repay (Rhyne 2001). The oft repeated phrase "We're just working for the bank" gave a sense of the futility felt by people whose arduous labor was beneath the small profits which then had to be used to repay (Maclean 2013).

The FSL recognized nontraditional forms of collateral specifying that banks were duty-bound to "grant credits and make short-, medium-, and long-term loans, against personal guarantees, mortgages, pledges or other unconventional forms of collateral" (Article 119, paragraph I.a, my translation). This caused concern within the banking sector, where it was feared that this would increase delinquency and risk, and ultimately reduce the expansion of financial services and therefore financial inclusion. Orthodox definitions of collateral, however, favor those who have benefited from colonial patterns of property and can demonstrate formal ownership. This presents a barrier to women's access to credit, as under colonial administration property would be registered in the man's name, and the extensive history of bilateral inheritance rights in the Andes, including women's right to property, would be overlooked. The recognition of nontraditional collateral would hence correct biases in the documentation of ownership and what could be valued in the capitalization process. The list of acceptable guarantees that could be used to obtain credit to finance productive activities was extensive:

> Among others, the types of unconventional acceptable guarantees are: guarantee funds, agricultural insurance, documents in

custody of real estate and rural properties, machinery subject or not to registration with or without physical delivery, contracts or commitment documents for future sale in the domestic market or for export, endorsements or certifications from community agencies or territorial organizations, products stored in their own or rented premises, livestock guarantees, registered intellectual property and other unconventional alternatives that have the character of guarantee. (Article 99, paragraph I)

The inclusion of endorsements and certification from community authorities changed the institutions that had the power to confirm value and therefore could recognize different patterns of ownership. The collateral specified, however, prioritizes manufacturing and agricultural production, and it could be argued that some of the techniques used by MFIs—chiefly social collateral—were more innovative in terms of recognizing social value beyond economic production.

The stipulation that banks and financial institutions had to give 60 percent of their lending portfolio to "productive industries" was intended to support the government's National Development Plan, which focused on support to agricultural production and manufacturing industries. The banks objected on the grounds that this *dirigiste* approach would create financial and economic imbalances that could lead to inflation. While small cooperatives and productive units would be included in this lending, informal commerce—an important livelihood strategy in the popular areas of Bolivia's cities—was here constructed as a problem to be solved, namely, that the "informal sector" had expanded precisely because the urban, commercial biases of neoliberal capitalism had undermined productive industries. However, the fact that the division between productive and nonproductive is gendered, both culturally and in terms of the numbers of men and women working in each sector, was not taken into account.

The productive and nonproductive industries originally identified are listed in Figure 4. There is—of necessity—significant discretion and flexibility in the application of these categories. For example, a loan to a restaurant is legitimate if it is being invested in construction. Despite the financial targeting of the productive sector, the informal sector and petty commerce increased in size and wealth over the course of the MAS administration (Medina and Schneider 2018).

PRODUCTIVE SECTOR	NONPRODUCTIVE SECTOR
Agriculture and livestock	Hotel and restaurant
Hunting, forestry, and fishing	Transport, storage, and communications
Extraction of crude oil and natural gas	Real estate and business services
Metallic and nonmetallic minerals	Public administration services
Industrial manufacturing	Social, community, and personal services; other services
Production and distribution of electricity, gas, and water	Wholesale and retail (commerce)
Construction	
Tourism and intellectual production	

FIGURE 4. *Productive sector versus nonproductive sector.*

Overall, the aim of these reforms to the banking sector was to create a productive and inclusive economy in which finance was at the service of society and not the other way around. The FSL has been seen as a remarkable achievement both politically and in terms of the changes that were made (Naqvi 2021; Knaack 2020). The banking sector expanded significantly over Morales's first two terms, due in part to greater liquidity in financial markets in general and Bolivia's rapid economic growth. The number of financial service points in the country tripled from 2007 to 2015, with significant increases in rural areas, and the number of microcredit borrowers grew by 70 percent from 2008 to 2015 (Knaack 2020). However, since 2015, when economic growth began to slow, the number of microcredit borrowers consistently decreased, and lending to SMEs stagnated (Knaack 2020, 254). The number of women with loans was also stagnant from 2007 to 2015, despite significant increases among men, and women were also overrepresented among those who only had informal loans (Calle Sarmiento 2016). Representatives from small enterprises, and particularly from those operating informally, complained that it was more difficult to access credit following MAS reforms. For example, to qualify for a productive loan from the BDP, potential borrowers had to demonstrate that they had a clean credit record and had to have a guarantor who was prepared to secure the loan against property (Chipana 2013).

These findings are consistent with concerns, first, that the focus on "productive" enterprises would limit the scope of operations that mostly serve women, and second, that the focus on larger loans to certain sectors had a gendered effect. Nevertheless, the banking sector did not implode, as orthodox commentators had predicted, and Bolivia is held up as an example internationally of a country that was able to provide an alternative to orthodox economic rules of finance that did not succumb to the inflationary predictions of neoliberal monetarists cautioning against the "resource curse." It does seem, however, that a gendered analysis falls between an approach that prioritizes the extension of financial services, and so constructs the social as collateral, and a heterodox vision based on large-scale production and an extractivist state. The disruptions to this orthodox/heterodox divide came from the popular economies where those informal loans that women were more likely to have would be found.

Cash and Popular Markets

Despite the structuralist, production-focused approach and the explicit designation of informal economies as a symptom of the destruction of rampant neoliberalism, popular markets expanded significantly over the period of MAS rule. Import commerce gained strength, artisanal cooperatives closed in their thousands (*VOA News* 2019), and in 2018 the IMF concluded that Bolivia had the largest informal economy in the world (Medina and Scheidner 2018), with informal employment in the nonagricultural sector in 2019 estimated to be 79.1 percent, 81.2 percent for women (Gómez-Ramírez and Handland 2021, 3). There are both monetary and political explanations for this. First, the overvalued boliviano encouraged imports over production for export. Despite measures to strengthen agricultural production and manufacturing, the Bolivian market was flooded by imported clothes, white goods, electronics, car parts, and even fruit. This favored *comerciantes* and was a boon to the networks of Aymara traders who are famed for their effectiveness in commerce. The second explanation for this is a political unevenness in the collection of import duty and other taxes. The apparent impunity with which global corporations avoided or paid minimal tax in Bolivia was one of the main injustices that galvanized social movements in the early 2000s, and the MAS increased enforcement of tax regulations on large formal and international businesses, with conspicuous closures for nonpayment of tax (Paredes 2012). In order to facilitate formalization and payment of sales tax from small businesses, taxation categories were divided between a "general" and "simplified" regime, the latter of which was a flat-rate fee for small businesses with a turnover of under 13,600 bolivianos annually—approximately $1,973 U.S. (Bolivia Impuestos 2021). There were frequent accusations, however, that the enforcement of tax collection was uneven and favored Morales's power base in peri-urban informal economies, where it is an open secret that businesses, including wealthy importers, do not pay tax on their significant profits (Ugarte Quispaya 2015). Complying with taxation is definitive of formality and legitimacy, but in a context where "formalized" activity is a minority of the economy and the state lacks legitimacy and extension, these boundaries do not hold.

This accumulation of wealth that MAS policy, albeit unintentionally, enabled has led to the rise of the Aymara bourgeoisie, and in particular the powerful, wealthy, modern *chola*. The character of the wealthy *chola* has come to exemplify the changes over the MAS administration, but this figure represents a form of economic and financial subjectivity that is not predicated on either the neoliberal romanticization of women's labor in the informal sector or the heterodox, national production–focused alternatives that framed MAS policy. However, the symbolic changes and cultural confidence that accompanied ALBA, SUCRE, and *bolivianización* are factors in the rise of wealth in popular markets and the dramatic increase in consumption. The wealthy *chola* is a woman who is in charge of key investment decisions as part of a family and community unit, leads negotiations, often transacts in cash, and whose conspicuous consumption is accompanied by reinvestments in community networks, where her main ambitions lie. The emergence of the trope of the wealthy *chola* is due to the confidence associated with *bolivianización* as much as to the strength of the currency itself. It is no secret that *chola* market women have always had wealth, but the depth and breadth of the phenomena of Aymara wealth, coupled with the political and cultural transformations that allowed this wealth to become conspicuous, led to the wealthy *chola* being viewed as a transgressive character on the basis of gendered and colonial assumptions about financial propriety.

The main sources of suspicion were the rumors that the wealth is associated with narcotraffic and that the boom in conspicuous consumption, particularly of real estate, is due to laundering rather than any newfound confidence. There is some evidence to support there being greater liquidity in the Bolivian economy due to escalated involvement in the cocaine trade, and the number of incidents of narco-related violence along the border with Brazil and in Santa Cruz have risen (UNODC 2018). The possibility of involvement in narcotraffic is broadly recognized, but the assumption that Aymara wealth is necessarily due to illicit trade is problematic. To illustrate, as part of a seminar at the Universidad Pública de El Alto (UPEA) I presented the official statistics on cocaine production in Bolivia and asked the students what they thought of them. Students at UPEA generally live in El Alto, come from bilingual families, and are of indigenous descent. The university is one of the country's more radical and critical institutions, and it was a base for the social movements that led to the water and gas wars of the early 2000s. Students at UPEA are well versed in the decolonial critique of U.S. hegemony and the problematic assumption that coca is necessarily linked to cocaine. However, in response to the statistics I presented showing quite minimal levels of narco-activity in Bolivia, there was open laughter and gestures indicating that the estimates were far too low. Nevertheless, the blanket generalization that the *only* way to become wealthy is via narcotraffic or corruption, which is frequently and vociferously stated in traditional elite circles, is met with astonishment and offense among those in the north of La Paz and El Alto who work and frequent popular markets. While the possibility that illicit trade is an element of the boom in wealth is acknowledged, the assumption that it is necessarily involved is emphatically rejected. A student living in the neighborhood of Kollasuyo put this succinctly when I described the frequency with which narcotraffic came up as an explanation for wealth in El Alto: "Of course you can get rich through commerce. It's what they all do" (interview, Kollasuyo, 2017).

The implications of laundering are also not without foundation, but the notion of laundering itself assumes a division between formal and informal that does not apply in a country where the majority of economic activity is in popular markets and where "formal" mainstream institutions lack legitimacy. Technically, money can be laundered into the formal system in various ways, most of which involve numerous purchases of goods and multiple "layers" of interaction that can disguise provenance. Transactions in "informal" markets are frequently in cash. Cash, with its relative untraceability, is a key tool in money laundering, to the point that various governments have made moves to demonetize the economy in order to deal with corruption, despite devastating effects on informal income-generation activities (Dash 2017). In a Bolivian context, the use of cash is associated with the wealth of indigenous informal markets, and that it provokes immediate suspicion represents the erroneous assumption that informal activity necessarily involves trading in illicit goods.

Among those who earn a living in informal markets, there is particular astonishment that the use of cash should provoke suspicion. "No one trusts the banks!" exclaimed Doña Beatrice, who lives in the north of La Paz, as she explained to me why people prefer to keep their money in cash—specifically, dollars—and invest it in land rather than going through formal institutions. She took out a collection of now worthless large-denomination boliviano notes from the 1980s, at a time of the most extreme inflation and devaluations. "If you keep money in the bank you'll lose it if there's a devaluation." She gave the example of her sister, who had savings in the bank but lost it all in the devaluation of 1985. "As soon as you get cash you want to put it in land. That way you know it's safe" (interview, May 2017).

The *chola* has accumulated her wealth as part of a community economy built on gift exchanges, expansive trading networks between communities rooted in Andean traditions of reciprocity, and competitive bargaining in urban markets. The economic subject that the *chola* represents embodies the importance of community reciprocity to the possibility of functioning in a competitive market that is erased in the fantasy of the liberal individual relating to others solely by contract. As the wealth and conspicuous consumption of the Aymara bourgeoisie increased over the period of MAS rule, they hence rewrote the unwritten rules of liberal propriety and the invisible boundaries of belonging that demarcated power and space. The fear and suspicion that the image of a wealthy *chola* making large purchases with a suitcase of cash generated were in part because she overturned the liberal, contractual order of things and was accumulating on behalf of a community that was, in the words of one newspaper headline which was later corrected, "colonizing" traditional elite spaces (Juárez 2014). However, while some critics argued that accusations of clientelism and patronage were simply a denial of the cultural biases of liberal good governance, others, including informal workers who had not seen their wealth rise to the spectacular levels of the Aymara bourgeoisie, pointed out that the mechanisms to distinguish community reciprocity and the redistributory mechanisms of *compadrazgo* from networks of clientelism and corruption were not always apparent. Nevertheless, the economic subject which the *chola* represents cuts through the multiple gendered contradictory binds created by liberal binaries—community/individual, reproduction/production, tradition/modernity—and her riches represent an economic imaginary in which gender, wealth, power, and indigeneity coincide.

Conclusion

There were multiple contradictions in MAS policy to establish the financial architecture that could support communal solidarity and a production-focused economy. Some of these contradictions reflect the "creative tensions" that had been observed between reinforcing the powers of the state to ensure sovereignty and defending against the iniquities of the neoliberal decades when the demands of finance had taken such a corrosive toll. However, other contradictions stemmed from the application of heterodox theories that, just like their orthodox opposites, were developed with reference to industrialized economies and were blind to gender and the complexities of community. Nevertheless, the plans to institutionalize the values of community exchange at the national and international level, to reinstate the sovereignty of the boliviano, and to make finance subordinate to social values broke the molds of liberal economic orthodoxy. The symbolic effects of these initiatives were highlighted by proponents of the MAS project and were not "merely cultural"; the confidence engendered changed livelihoods and patterns of consumption and mobility, as we will see in later chapters. However, the economic effects of these policies were not as intended, and the gender blindness of the focus on production and the implicit assumptions about scale and collateral coincided with a decrease in women's access to formal capital.

However, the contradictions of the policies themselves—particularly between national production and the overvalued boliviano—when grafted onto a varied financial sector and popular markets in which women were traditionally powerful, created a landscape in which the wealthy *chola* came to the fore. The woman who handles large purchases in cash, operates as an integral part of an extended family unit, and prioritizes reinvestment in community over tributary payments is far from the *Homo economicus*, and also unimagined in heterodox financial policy. Her behavior and the suspicion it aroused demonstrated the alienation that those working in popular economies experience as associations with illicit trades, laundering, and feminine power provoke fear of an Other.

Many elements of MAS management of finance were inequitable—the uneven application of tax laws, the detrimental effects on a varied financial sector, and the difficulties involved in distinguishing communitarianism from patronage and clientelist networks. However, the symbolic changes in finance, and the communities who gained power through these changes, generated notions of confidence, trust, and value that enabled a transgressive form of gendered financial subjectivity and, as we will see in the following chapters, provided a space in which the fundamental precepts of modernity can be reimagined.

5

Clothes

Nation, Production, and Contemporaneity

Clothes might not always be deemed central to questions of governance and economy, but these most everyday items are inherently political. Clothes are intimately connected with identity, and this is transparently the case in Bolivia, where the nomenclature of cultural and ethnic identity comes from clothes—*de pollera, de vestido,* or *de corbata.* The distinction evoked, however, between clothes as demarcating an ethnic identity as opposed to expressing an individual sense of style is a sustaining myth of fashion, and definitive of the difference between tradition and modernity, use value and exchange value, and, therefore, the modern world and the colonized rest. These divides are reflected in the narratives of globalization that contrast the sweatshops of the global South with the throwaway consumption culture of the postindustrial North, which is emblematic of the destructive inequality of unbridled global capital. Textiles, clothing, and fashion hence forge a divide, both materially and culturally, between the individualist, self-expressive consumer of the modern world and the traditional, exploited "third world" producer, who is figured as so submersed in everyday survival that the possibility of choice or taste is erased.

This narrative of globalization and modernity is apparent in both orthodox economic approaches and heterodox alternatives, which both focus on the development of exchange value, consumption, and capitalist social relations. This shared narrative relies on a vision of production and progress that implies a particular construct of time and the contemporary. The disciplining mechanisms of capital create an arrow of time that makes order out of chaos by producing coherent objects from the morass of nature, thereby evoking a sense of progress while implicitly denying the destruction of resources and labor that such production implies. Fashion is predicated on a sense of "now" and creates a fantasy of contemporaneity that is reliant on dismissing "other" aesthetics as belonging to an out-of-date, traditional past. Both capitalism and fashion depend on myths of progress and time, which imply an increasing order and mastery over nature and the possibility of constant production and creation, which is in effect an ideological denial of the destruction upon which the values of capital and modernity rely.

The development of the national production of textiles and apparel had a prominent place in the MAS's industrialization strategy. The plan was that state-owned companies and worker-led cooperatives would produce textiles to be exchanged with other countries in ALBA, and the emphasis would be on national production. The focus on textiles was inspired by the long history of woven fabric in Bolivia and its importance to Andean culture (Howard 2010), as well as the need to revive what were once promising textiles and leather industries that had been decimated by the trade liberalization of the 1980s with the loss of over thirty-five thousand manufacturing jobs (Kohl 2006, 311). State support of textiles manufacturing and an emphasis on national production and consuming *lo nuestro* was an attempt to protect against the global flows of cheap textiles that were flooding the world market. The ultimate failure of these attempts was due to various economic factors, including the government's underestimation of the importance of taste, creativity, and fashion among its supporters.

This same period of time saw a boom in two areas that disrupted the standard scripts of globalization, progress, and production. First, there was significant growth in the informal market in used clothes, mostly from the United States. This constituted a fertile source of income for women working in the markets of El Alto or selling in the street. The arrival of cheap, secondhand Western brands attracted wealthy women from Bolivia's traditional middle and upper classes to the Sixteenth July market held biweekly in El Alto. This market in effect "shorted" the flows of consumption and production that placed indigenous women as low-paid producers and traditional artisans, on the one hand, and middle-class white women as modern consumers, on the other. And second, over this same time period, *la moda de la chola paceña* (luxury fashion brands of the distinctive *chola* outfit) gained a place on the global stage, and the *pollera*—a quintessential marker of tradition and identity—was recognized as fashion. Both the used-clothes trade and *la moda de la chola paceña* created controversies, as we will see, but the flourishing of these trades demonstrates different possible scripts of time, production, modernity, and value. The cyclical material and cultural flows of

CLOTHES   151

clothes, marshaled by *chola* women selling in La Paz, challenge these concepts and open the possibility of a decolonized idea of progress and capitalist time without resorting to problematic scripts of tradition, identity, and production.

In this chapter I will explore developments in Bolivia's textiles and clothing sectors from 2006 to 2019 to illustrate the ways in which precepts of modernity that erase the value of the feminine and the colonized have been challenged. Some of the most dramatic examples of the MAS's post-neoliberal agenda were seen in this sector, including the state closure of high-profile Bolivian firms and the workers' takeover of luxury textiles manufacturer Ametex. The way these changes were administered demonstrates the continued reliance on a script of modernity—production and nation—that reproduced gendered and racialized values and exclusions. The expansion of the used-clothes trade and *la moda de la chola paceña* are the results in part of the favoring and minimal regulation of popular markets due to their political power and their importance to the MAS. These markets are based on the popular, community dynamics that constitute modernity's other, and the fact that they were empowered and enriched led to notions of progress, contemporaneity, nation, and production being dismantled and recast.

Textiles, Clothes, and Identity in Bolivia: Evo's *Chompa*

The MAS targeted the textiles and apparel sectors to reverse the damage that had been done to national industries since the liberalization of the economy in the 1980s. These sectors also had the potential, given the importance of textiles to Andean culture, to reassert national sovereignty and indigenous identity. The steps the MAS took to bolster and protect national textiles and clothing production included state subsidy, trade agreements within ALBA, constitutionally sanctioned worker takeovers, social enterprises, and cooperatives. These measures were emblematic of the way pluri-economy was being institutionalized. However, despite the potential of the textiles and clothing sector to unite the MAS's economic and cultural agendas, by the end of 2019 the worker-owned—and subsequently state-owned—firm Enatex had collapsed, the owner of Bolivian clothing retailer Punto Blanco was in jail, and the used-clothes trade was flourishing, despite being banned multiple times. Yet these direct attempts to "reverse" neoliberalism still relied on the same script—nation, scale, production—as the orthodox economic recommendations they were resisting.

The history of the clothing and textiles industry in Bolivia shows how firmly textiles are rooted in Bolivian national and indigenous identity. Healthy potential industries in llama leather and woven materials were devastated by the economic recession and neoliberal globalization of the 1980s (Kohl 2006). During that time, production had been outsourced to small family units and home workers, who were less able to negotiate than a unionized industrial workforce, and the knitting cooperatives set up by international NGOs seemed a painfully inadequate response to the loss of national industries. When the MAS came to power it was estimated that the garment sector formally employed 7,800 people, but nearly 60,000 if the informal sector was taken into account, the majority in small family units (Frazier, Bruss, and Johnson 2004). The clothing industry was emblematic of the neoliberal destruction of Bolivian national production and identity. It would seem, on looking at the landscape of both textile manufacturing and clothing retail in 2006, that the potential for Bolivia to have a thriving leather- and textiles-manufacturing industry had been destroyed. In its place, informal markets had developed as a survival strategy where cheap imports from China were sold by people with no prospect of formal employment, and used clothing was turning Bolivia into the *vertedero de los EEUU*—the garbage dump of the United States.

The state of Bolivian textiles manufacturing at the start of the MAS administration is illustrative of the dispossession, inequality, and exclusion that poor, rural, and indigenous people had experienced in Bolivia since the 1980s. However, there is plenty to disrupt this structural analysis that, while highlighting exploitation, also reaffirms the terms of the debate that in part create it. An illustration of the potential for disruption is the outfit of Evo Morales himself. When Morales first came to power, his tour of world leaders made headlines even in the United States and the UK, where Bolivia does not as a general rule feature. He made the papers not because of his meetings with various heads of state but because at each meeting—with Thabo Mbeki of South Africa, Hu Jintao of China, and José Luis Rodríguez Zapatero of Spain, all of whom were in tailored suits—he was wearing a *chompa* (sweater) and a leather jacket (BBC 2006). The tone of the international press coverage, as well as his reception by the other heads of state, was lighthearted but mocking. The debate around Morales's *chompa* in Bolivia indicated the identity dynamics at play and the consequences for economic policy. The view of many was that he had been disrespectful: "It's not about the suit and tie, he could have worn something indigenous—they have such lovely clothes" (interview, NGO executive, Zona Sur, February 2006). This throwaway remark evokes Silvia Rivera Cusicanqui's criticism of the "permitted Indian" and illustrates the importance of changing the framing of debates on identity to avoid reinforcing colonial dichotomies of tradition and modernity. One Aymara woman working in retailing crafts put this succinctly: "Evo's representing his people, and that's what they wear. . . . Although I would have liked it if he had at least put on different *chompas*" (interview, crafts trader, El Alto, February 2006).

The *chompa* controversy illustrates how Morales's personal charisma and the political processes that led him to the presidency did not necessarily conform to the conceptual schemes underpinning debates in Marxist and Indianist thought, despite the prominence of this theorizing in electoral strategy. However, commentators also observed that his choice of *chompa* was continuing the Andean tradition of using clothing as political language (Howard 2010). Morales's persona represents a live culture that has engaged with modernity, not ossified traditions of the essentialized permitted Indian. The *chompa* scandal brought a number of divisive reactions, but it also enabled a reassessment of dynamics of identity, modernity, and nationhood, exemplified by Bolivian clothing retailer and manufacturer Punto Blanco responding to the controversy by producing its own version of the *chompa*, made of alpaca, as a "symbol of the new Bolivia" (Forero 2006).

MAS Interventions in Textiles and Apparel: Punto Blanco, Ametex, and Enatex

The textiles industry, clothing manufacturing, and retail constituted complicated ground for the MAS. On the one hand, the state of the textiles and clothing sectors that it inherited in 2006 provided compelling support for its position that the Bolivian economy had been ravaged by global neoliberalism and that Bolivian cultural identity had been undermined. However, the ability of Bolivian institutions to enact measures that could offer protection from the pressures of global competition remained limited, particularly given the strength of the U.S. market, which dwarfed Bolivia's internal market and even that of the regional trade organization ALBA. The practical, political challenges of the textiles industry were substantial, and the scandals and failures that ensued brought out the conceptual fault lines that had been glossed over in electoral campaigning.

By Morales's second term, the textiles industry and the clothing retail industry were under pressure from increased textiles and clothing production in China and the continued influx of used clothes (Farthing and Kohl 2014). It was clear that the textiles industry was a race to the bottom and that the protectionist measures enacted by the MAS—particularly of regional trade, vertically integrated industries, and boosting internal consumption—were a popular response to this. Its aim was to establish national businesses and social enterprises in textiles and clothing production, but the competition would remain fierce, and global flows of material and clothing had become such an established element of people's livelihoods that any notion of "national production" was difficult to define.

The fortunes of the Bolivian textiles and retail industry can be illustrated by the decline of Punto Blanco and the arrest and imprisonment, in 2014, of its CEO, Raúl Varda, who had, ironically in hindsight, been featured in the advertisements for Punto Blanco's version of Morales's *chompa* as a symbol of the new Bolivia. Punto Blanco started business in the 1970s, employing two hundred people and aiming to provide for the internal market (Filomeno 2017). In 2014 it fell into dispute with around thirty employees who claimed that they had not been paid for months and that the company was not making the required pensions contributions (Rojas 2014). The workers and management agreed that competition from China, Brazil, Peru, and the used-clothes trade—which one union leader described as "disloyal" (*Página Siete* 2019a)—was the basis of the company's problems. Workers accused management of having been negligent in their duty of care and of having allowed conditions to deteriorate to the point that some employees had been left homeless (*Página Siete* 2014a). Management responded that the minimum wage and triple bonus mandated by the state did not give them the flexibility to react to market pressures and that the protests against them were being provoked by outsiders who wanted the company to be taken over by the workers (Rojas 2014).

The company passed into the management of its workers in May 2014, and Varda was found guilty of reneging on his responsibilities to his workers that September (*Página Siete* 2014a). Punto Blanco was later one of the first of four companies to be reconstituted under the Ley de Empresas Sociales (Law of Social Enterprises) (Filomeno 2017). Social enterprises were recognized in the 2009 Constitution in order to facilitate worker takeover of businesses that are in bankruptcy or closed without justification. This was intended to result in greater redistribution of wealth and a more inclusive economy, and to force companies to take responsibility for workers' welfare during difficult economic times (*El Deber* 2018; Kempf 2019). Under the law, governance of social enterprises was to mirror those of rural communities, and have rotating leadership and a horizontal structure: "We have a General Assembly which is the highest authority in the company, which supervises the work of the board, which rotates, and in turn is supervised by the workers," explained worker and technical director of the newly reconstituted Punto Blanco, Rubén Vargas (Filomeno 2017). When the law was introduced on Labor Day 2018, May 1, Morales declared that it was a "revindication of the working class" that was intended to reinvigorate the internal market (TeleSur 2018).

However, it was not clear that these processes were in workers' best interests, and this would go on to strain relations between the Central Obrera Boliviana (COB) and the MAS. Like Punto Blanco, the La Paz–based textiles manufacturer América Textil SA (Ametex) had found itself in extreme difficulties during Morales's second term due to competition from imports and contraband and from the loss of trade deals with the United States (Gonzalo Chávez 2016). To manage this situation, new trade deals were developed within ALBA—for example, T-shirts for tourists in Cuba—and a deal worth $20 million U.S. was also struck with Brazil. However, these were weak and volatile markets that, in consumption capacity terms, would not begin to approach the size of the U.S. market that had been lost (Achtenberg 2016b). Teresa Morales, minister for productive development and plural economy at the time, also discussed the possibility of raising import tariffs to 35 percent on textiles (Farthing and Kohl 2014, 88), but nevertheless, as for textile manufacturing worldwide, this was a time of crisis. Enatex had come into being in 2012 when Ametex, owned by the entrepreneur Marcos Iberkleid, was failing, threatening thousands of jobs. The workers took the company

over and created the Empresa Pública Nacional Textil—Enatex. This was
under the stewardship of Teresa Morales's brother, Manuel Morales. His
vision was to protect jobs by integrating the production chain vertically;
the factory would be responsible for every stage of production, from raw
materials to thread to shirt making, and would sell to the internal and
regional market (*Los Tiempos* 2016). Despite these steps, the company
continued to decline, and consequent cuts to production were met with
industrial action by workers, which in turn led to an erosion of the relationship between the MAS and the COB. In July 2016, after numerous
strikes from workers who had not been paid, Enatex was closed and all
jobs were lost (Achtenberg 2016b).

Ametex represented the neoliberal colonialism that the MAS defined itself against. It was set up in 1965 by a European family that had
migrated to Bolivia after World War II. By the turn of the twenty-first
century the family had accumulated considerable wealth and, like many
European migrants, had property investments in desirable areas of La
Paz (*Los Tiempos* 2016). Ametex had benefited substantially from favorable trade with the United States under the 1991 Andean Trade Prefer-
ences Act and the subsequent 2002 Andean Trade Promotion and Drug
Eradication Act (ATPDEA). These treaties eliminated import tariffs for
Andean countries—Bolivia, Peru, Ecuador, Colombia—on condition
that they cooperate with counter-narcotics measures. As a result, Ametex was able to provide textiles to U.S. clothing manufacturers at favorable prices. Once Bolivia left ATPDEA, export costs to the United States
increased by 20 percent (Gonzalo Chávez 2016).

Ametex hence exemplified the narrative of Western powers coordinating to exploit Bolivian resources—cotton and labor—to feed Western consumption at the expense of its own traditional crop—coca. In
the United States, the example of Ametex featured prominently in the
2009 House Committee on Foreign Affairs' hearing on U.S.–Bolivia
relations (Committee on Foreign Affairs 2009). Iberkleid himself testified, and the chair of the committee, Eliot Engel, introduced him as
his friend. Engel detailed how Iberkleid had come to Bolivia after World
War II as a Polish Jewish immigrant who had started working in the
mill at age sixteen and worked his way up to being the CEO. Throughout
the hearing, Ametex, whose factories Engel had visited, was held up as
an example of how ATPDEA was helping reduce poverty in the region.
Engel referred to the company as a clear example of how ATPDEA can

provide "quality jobs to the country's poor, including indigenous women who are among historically the most marginalized members of society in Bolivia" (Committee on Foreign Affairs 2009, 53).

There are different meanings of Bolivian national identity at play in the differing accounts of Ametex's decline. Ametex fits a particular view of the possibilities of the Americas for refugees after World War II who were able to work their way to the top. The view articulated from the United States of the value of bringing jobs to "indigenous women" elides indigeneity and poverty and recreates a trope of indigenous women needing to be rescued. Ametex, even after its collapse, continued to be invoked as an example of the high-quality production of which Bolivia was capable. It was a low-quantity, luxury manufacturer that produced textiles for top U.S. designers, including Tommy Hilfiger and Ralph Lauren Polo. Bolivian elites, often made to feel ashamed of their country by the greater economic strength and technical expertise of Peru and Chile, pointed to its success as evidence that Bolivia could be as good as them—it was a "national pride" (*Los Tiempos* 2016). This represents a particular imaginary of development that is predicated on Western, modernizing norms and cultural values of what quality, expertise, technology, and infrastructure should look like. The notion of Bolivian indigenous sovereignty espoused by Morales and the movements involved in the MAS was defined against this vision. Nevertheless, Ametex did employ people, and its decline was a blow to the people who lost their livelihood as well as the Bolivian economy, all of which created tensions between the ruling party and the COB (Achtenberg 2016b).

Once Enatex was brought under worker control in 2012, its vision was to develop its own vertically integrated company. Bolivia had the expertise, resources, and equipment to do this. However, this was at a time when the global competition in textiles, thread, and clothing markets was unprecedented; China and India were dominating global production, and industries around the world taking advantage of cheaply manufactured materials from Asia. Bolivia was trying to reverse what seemed like an unstoppable trend (*Los Tiempos* 2016). In addition, the MAS had mandated a minimum wage and a triple Christmas bonus. This protected workers against the possibility of "sweatshop" textiles and clothing manufacturing conditions, for which the industry is notorious. However, given that production, particularly in Asia, was based on low-wage labor, Bolivian goods would not be able to compete.

Enatex produced for the internal Bolivian market, and it had branded retail outlets dedicated to those clothes. However, the competition from imports and contraband was overwhelming, and the nondescript, mass-produced designs did not attract consumers. The response was to encourage a market based on patriotism and to persuade people to shop at Enatex to buy Bolivian—*consumir lo nuestro* (Achtenberg 2016b). The internal market was growing during this time, GDP was booming, and there was an increase in the number of middle-income households, but this also meant that consumer tastes were developing, and those most likely to hear the call to shop for the nation were those least likely to have disposable income. Enatex was soon retailing its clothes at far less than the cost of production.

What finally led to Enatex's closure was its worsening relationship with striking workers, and its eventual closure led to a rift between the MAS and the COB. In July 2013, workers went on strike because of delays in the 20 percent pay raise they had been promised. Teresa Morales met with them and immediately paid their claims, and they then got a further 100 percent pay raise in October 2013. Nevertheless, after various strikes and increasing conflicts with the COB, in May 2016 the decision was made to close Enatex because, according to the then minister for productive development, Veronica Ramos, the government had sustained jobs for eight years and made the company healthy, but now the costs of production were too high. They therefore reformed the company—which was later to be known as Senatex—to just provide services (*Página Siete* 2016b).

It is easily argued that nationalism and political symbolism, rather than economic strategy, had driven decision making at Enatex. Manuel Morales had also been in charge of negotiations with hydrocarbons companies after nationalization in 2006, and he had explicitly adopted a policy of having key documents written in Aymara and serving coca tea at meetings. "They had to speak our language," he explained to me in an interview in 2011, just before taking on the role at Enatex. However, the Enatex example also indicates the cultural tension among the Marxist nationalist vision of the economy, the indigenous vision of the economy, and the power of the informal market. Assumptions made about the growing internal market and consumer culture seemed to be in conflict, as the rise in wealth also meant a change in tastes, as we will see in the following section.

Informality, Identity, and the Global Trade in Used Clothes

The "informal" market in used clothes was banned multiple times by the MAS and prior administrations on the grounds that it undermined national production and represented the economic indignities that had been foisted on Bolivia by decades of economic restructuring. On the surface, the contraband trade in used clothes is a clear example of the iniquities of a neocolonial globalization upon which support for the MAS was built. This trade is also referred to as *ropa americana*—American clothes—and is a clear example of global neoliberalism debasing Bolivia's sovereignty, economy, and cultural identity as Western castoffs flood Bolivian markets. The formal ban on used clothing is based on a Chamber of Commerce report from 2005 which argues that the used-clothes trade incurs a cost to the Bolivian economy of some $513 million U.S. in terms of jobs, tax, and sales tax, as deduced from the assumption that Bolivian production of clothing would have more of the market if the contraband was stopped (IBCE 2005).

The MAS alternative to the rapidly growing market in used clothes was to encourage cooperative units that could engage in production, but it was an open secret that the size and strength of the informal economy rendered the government comparatively powerless to regulate it. "The government itself depends on the folks in the Sixteenth July" (interview, La Paz, May 2017), a municipal worker chuckled, referring to the vast market dominated by contraband goods from outside Bolivia's borders, including over a dozen city blocks dedicated to used clothes. He then outlined a number of examples—from electricity generators to software—where state and municipal departments had resorted to the distribution networks of those working in the very markets the government aspired to regulate to access the basic material they needed to run the administration. "Even the minister of the presidency is a contrabandista" (interview, El Alto, August 2011), said one informal trader, referring to Juan Ramón Quintana, who had been caught in various corruption scandals including the coordination of vehicles transporting contraband from Iquique in Chile to Bolivia and beyond to Brazil (*El Mundo* 2008).

Despite the official rhetoric on the need to formalize popular markets and bring them within the state bureaucracy, the situation in Bolivia is a stark illustration of how merely seeing those markets as "informal" is to completely misconstrue the power dynamics and exchanges that structure them. Neither the neoliberal romanticization of the creativity and ingenuity that can be found in such an apparently unregulated space nor the structuralist assumption that informality is inherently exploitative is adequate to understand its power and role in the "national" economy, community, and livelihoods. Nowhere is the need to "change the script" more evident, as ministers who had had to deal specifically with the used-clothes trade openly acknowledged. "Informality—it's the mother of all problems" (interview, La Paz, August 2011), said a minister from the first MAS administration who had seen the used-clothes trade flourish despite being banned. "Oh yes, please tell me what I'm supposed to do about that" (interview, La Paz August 2011), said a minister from Morales's second administration, who could see the value of used clothes as a source of cheap clothing and as a livelihood but also recognized that the en masse contraband in secondhand garments significantly undermined attempts to develop formal national industries.

The used-clothes trade is hence a fertile site from which to reimagine the discourses and the inherently gendered values that render informal markets female-dominated spaces worldwide and frame them as "the mother of all problems." The markets where women—many of them *de pollera*—are selling fashion labels from the United States to a clientele that includes rural mothers impressed with the durability of the children's clothes, *alteños* who need smart clothes to work in wealthier areas of La Paz, and women from the middle classes and elites who value a designer bargain overturn configurations of tradition, identity, quality, work, and nation. The flows of clothes "returning" from centers of consumption in the global North disrupt the global script that places the "first world consumer" in opposition to the "third world producer" (Larner and Molloy 2009) and breaks the association of indigeneity with "authenticity" and "tradition." It problematizes capitalist notions of "progress" as the linearity of production and commodification mastering natural resources is disrupted by these cyclical flows of goods; and the arrow of time, which is imposed by both economic orthodoxy and Marxist critiques of capitalism, is shown to be far more chaotic and recreative than the official discourses of technology and governance would suggest.

However, some of those worst hit by the informal market in used clothes are the small and medium-size producers whose business model is to develop production of Bolivian materials. Some of these formal businesses have been built up from the NGO initiatives of the 1990s, in which entrepreneurialism was a central pillar, and work with producers in El Alto and the north of La Paz. Formal SMEs have campaigned and protested against unfair measures by the MAS government, specifying an undue burden and uneven implementation of tax and wage regulations (C. Méndez 2019). One campaign to illustrate the pressures they were under featured a white businessman in a suit being crucified, surrounded by the burdens of tax, regulation, and unfair competition from new and used imports, and enumerated the sacrifices this implied in terms of national production (Figure 5). While many aspects of the campaign were clearly substantiated, this image aptly illustrates the colonial divisions that persist in what counts as formal and informal business.

It is difficult to define strictly what counts as "national" production in clothing, in either economic, political, or cultural terms. Several luxury Bolivian knitwear companies, such as Intiwara and Walisuma, focus on the external market and have expensive outlets in tourist and rich

FIGURE 5. *Protest leaflet from the Cámara Departamental de la Pequeña Industria y Artesanía, 2015.*

areas of La Paz. Although they are using Bolivian raw materials, they are catering to the tastes of the external market and arguably an exoticized view of "authentic" Bolivian designs. Luxury products for export are made by a multitude of NGO-sponsored knitting cooperatives. Cooperatives are a central part of the MAS's vision for a pluri-economy, and the minister for productive development and plural economy at the time of my research on the used-clothes trade—Antonia Rodríguez Medrano—made her political career in the cooperative movement. These groups trade on the authenticity of their hand-knitted designs, but it is notable that there is a very limited market for this "traditional" Bolivian identity within Bolivia itself. Some of the most vociferous opponents of those selling used clothes are the *mañaneras*. The *mañaneras*—early morning ladies—are so called because they start selling at 4 a.m. on the Calle Illampu in the textiles market area of La Paz. They offer a variety of clothes, jackets, T-shirts, and sweatshirts that are assembled in small, often family-based cooperative units and sell mostly wholesale to retail outlets throughout the country. The *mañaneras* have a legitimacy in political discourse that those retailing used clothes lack, as they are seen to produce rather than just sell. However, a critical eye could be cast on the construction of their work as "Bolivian": the material is imported from Korea and China, the designs are Western, and the labels copy European and American brands—Versace, Wrangler, and Chanel.

Selling used clothes at retail is seen as "earning money almost without working" (Foronda 2009), as it does not involve production. Those involved in the used-clothes trade are frequently villainized for undermining national production and for their overall lack of contribution to the economy by engaging in tax-free retail rather than manufacturing and by not creating "dignified employment." The majority of those selling are women *de pollera* who face gendered and racialized epithets implying that they have let down their culture; the insulting term *chota*—an indigenous woman who has sold out to Western culture—is an example. However, this mischaracterizes the complex reasons why people took up the trade. For example, Alejandra started selling used clothes and toys after she injured herself and had to leave her job cooking in a little streetside restaurant. She does not have a stall, but she sells tops on the side of the street and has been chased away by the municipal police several times. She explains that she sells used clothes precisely because it is the kind of light work that she can do given her physical ailments and her age—sixty-seven. Nevertheless, she takes pride in making the clothes presentable. This involves repairing, washing, ironing, and cleaning off the wool bobbles that hang on older sweaters, as well as getting to the market by 4 a.m. on days she goes to sell. The characterization of this work as "easy money" in the press fails to recognize the labor involved, the feminine nature of this labor, and the various motivations for being involved in this trade.

In contrast to the dismissive characterization of the labor involved in retailing used clothes in popular discourse, retailers accord great value to their work. Alejandra's daughter Sandra, who also sells used clothes, put this very clearly, comparing her current livelihood—selling clothes on the streets of La Paz—to an imagined future working in an industrialized garment industry: "This way I work for myself, I don't need to subordinate myself to a boss" (interview, La Paz, August 2010). Interestingly, Charo drew on the discourse of national identity to explain the dominance of women in informal markets in Bolivia: "The Bolivian woman has to work—we're not like you Europeans, we don't want to stay at home. This is what we're good at" (interview, La Paz, August 2010). Similarly, her colleague Sylvia, who is in her twenties and sells children's clothes, confirms that "I can have my baby beside me and work and care for him at the same time. I don't want to stay at home— I'd go crazy there" (interview, La Paz, August 2010).

One of the most frequent arguments in favor of incorporating the used-clothes trade into the Bolivian economy rather than banning it, is that it provides a source of cheap clothing for those who cannot afford it. There are elements of truth to this: there is a section of the Sixteenth July known as The Rail where the lowest-quality bales of clothes are opened up and sold at one or two bolivianos apiece. Representatives of Bolivian clothing retailers Gav Sport and Batt claimed to me in an interview that despite the polemic in the press, they did not see that the sale of used clothes affected their business, on the assumption that it was covering a part of the market that did not have disposable income to shop with them. However, as the Instituto Boliviano de Comercio Exterior (IBCE; Bolivian Institute of Foreign Trade) report states, "contrary to popular belief," the used-clothes trade is valued not only as a source of cheap clothing but also for "the possibility of finding a 'label' at possibly one thousandth of its original cost" (2005, 41). At a discursive level, however, the prominence of the argument that the trade in used clothes should be legal if it is providing a source of clothing for the poor perpetuates an association of indigeneity with poverty and need and villainizes women who are associated with profit and consumption. The tight association of indigenous femininity, tradition, and community, defined in terms of gift rather than capital exchange, means that the idea of the indigenous woman consumer is tantamount to a contradiction in terms.

However, the women—many *de pollera*—who work in the retail of used clothing have a thorough knowledge of which Western brands are the most sought after in the market by people who have to wear Western dress to work in the city or people who come up to El Alto from the Zona Sur in search of a bargain. The desire for known brands has led to the creation of another market in La Paz, where labels of high street and couture designers can be bought on rolls to be sewn into otherwise less valuable clothing. These exchanges run counter to the way luxury goods generally flow and constitute an unusual instance of goods sold by the indigenous working class coinciding with middle- and upper-class tastes. Unlike the knitting cooperatives producing "authentic" Andean goods or the *mañaneras* producing cheap clothing for wholesale, people selling used clothes can access the internal market.

Nevertheless, the influx of used clothing and the popularity of the brands play on postcolonial legacies of "good taste" and "quality." Many stall owners pointed out that, in addition to seeking Western labels, customers would actively denigrate the quality of Bolivian production. Charo found that this was reflected in comments from her clientele: "Bolivian people almost don't want Bolivian shoes. It's foreigners who buy all the Bolivian stuff. I don't understand it—people have got used to saying, 'Oh, these boots are American, or Brazilian maybe'—but Bolivian material is good!" Charo's shoe stall has Bolivian and used wares— and she took pains to point out to me how durable the Bolivian produce was. But, as she says, "people always want foreign stuff. . . . The first question is always 'Where's this from?' A woman just came past and asked me that, and said, 'Oh, I thought it was American,' and walked off" (interview, La Paz, August 2010).

In terms of the discursive framing of this debate, however, the relationship between traditional femininity and the consumption of used clothes is telling in terms of which identities are "permitted." To wear Western clothes as a matter of need fits with the narrative of indigenous people being excluded from and oppressed by the global market. The iconic *pollera* is, predictably, not available in the used-clothes market. Stall owners commented that although the women *de pollera* who bought used clothes were generally buying for their children, they would also buy used clothes for the quality of the material and make them into underskirts or blouses. In this market there are also examples of the agency and strategy involved in people making a living in a global marketplace, where the cultural and material flows of globalization can be reshaped to reinforce rather than destroy local customs. Numerous stalls in the used-clothes area of the Sixteenth July market sell ponchos made from American sweaters that have had the sleeves removed and been restitched into the triangular shape of this typical Andean item. As one stall employee told me slightly mischievously, "It's just that Americans are so big. These huge sweaters arrive, and how are we going to sell them here? So we turn them into ponchos. It's perfect" (interview, El Alto, August 2010).

La Moda de la Chola Paceña

The accumulation of wealth in the informal, popular markets of La Paz and El Alto has led to a flourishing *moda de la chola paceña*. Dressmakers, themselves *de pollera,* who started in small shops renting out costumes for fiestas, are now high-profile designers and fashionistas. They include Eliana Paco Paredes, whose collection was shown in New York; the embroiderer Jaqueline Tarque; modeling agency director Rosario Aguilar; and numerous small-boutique owners who have been able to build businesses on the strength of this growing trend. The area of Kollasuyo in the north of La Paz, where Paco Paredes had her first workshop, boasts new *galerías* in the distinctive Andean *cholet* architectural style dedicated to the fashion. A style magazine—*Warmi*—was launched in 2014 to "discover the wonderful human world of the makers of magic that embodies the clothing of the *Chola Paceña*" (*Revista Warmi* 2014), and the secondary industries of modeling, makeup, and photography are thriving.

There is at first glance a simple economic explanation for this phenomenon—the increase in disposable income that came with economic growth led to a rise in conspicuous consumption which is exemplified by the idea of "fashion." This would, however, be an oversimplification of the community structures and social relations behind the rise of the Aymara bourgeoisie and of the overhaul of fundamental precepts of modernity that the juxtaposition of the words "indigenous fashion" represents. As clothing associated with ethnic identity, the *pollera* is quite specifically "anti-fashion"—the clothes associated with tradition and utility against which the fashion of Western modernity has defined itself (Jansen 2020). Traditional clothes are assumed to belong in the "past" whenever and wherever they are worn, and are the constitutive other of a Western-centric modernity that appoints itself to define contemporaneity and futurity. The *moda de la chola paceña* challenges modernity's "'now' as a property of the self . . . defined through seeing the other as traditional, as passé, as backward, as a belated copy" (Rolando Vázquez quoted in Jansen 2020, 826). *Chola paceña* designers have thus succeeded in decolonizing the cultural meanings and aesthetics of modernity by using the global trade of textiles from East Asia and the flourishing "informal" popular markets that Bolivia's decolonial state has attempted, and failed, to limit and control.

These changes in cultural dynamics were on display at a fashion show held in the gardens of the residence of the Brazilian ambassador to Bolivia in August 2016 (*Página Siete* 2016a). The ambassador's wife had developed quite a penchant for *chola paceña* jewelry, and she had taken to organizing a minibus to take the Damas Diplomáticas (the Ambassadors' Wives' Club) from their exclusive residences in the Zona Sur to the *chola paceña* jewelry boutiques in Villa Adela, on the other side of El Alto, which in itself constituted quite a change in the city's cultural geography. The fashion show that she organized placed the *moda de la chola paceña* at the center of La Paz high society. Aymara designers showed their collections to *paceña* society, which included the mayor and his wife, a beauty queen from Santa Cruz, who chose to wear a bright pink *pollera;* society ladies from the Zona Sur, many of whom had also worn luxurious *polleras* for the evening; and the feminist activist María Galindo, who was there with *de pollera* members of Mujeres Creando. The designers on show were Aymara, as were the models, and the presenters, both also urban Aymara, made a point of describing the colors in Aymara terms—*chuño* black and *tunta* white. Far from being co-opted for mainstream consumption, the target market for these designers was wealthy Aymara people who had benefited economically from government policy and the favorable conditions for commerce. But this fash-

FIGURE 6. *One of the* escaladoras *modeling at the* chola paceña *fashion show in La Paz, 2016. Author's photograph.*

ion show was not just the revaluation of the *pollera* as a consumer item; it represented a shift in the traditions and identities that frame what counts as fashion, beauty, contemporaneity, and economic femininity.

The fashion show is the quintessential space of the wealthy woman as consumer—an economic trope that does not fit the economic femininities of the Andes, as we have seen in chapter 3. As if to reinforce this point, the first five models to appear at the show at the Brazilian ambassador's residence were a group of Aymara women of various ages who are known locally as *las cholitas escaladoras* (the women mountain climbers) (Figure 6). Earlier that year these women set themselves the challenge of climbing some of the highest peaks of the Andes while dressed in the *pollera,* motivated by the discrimination and violence that indigenous women face (*Guardian* 2016). They opened the fashion show dressed in the luxurious designs but were also wearing their climbing gear. One came out in a *pollera* with a hard hat and a light, another with an ice pick, another with ropes, and all wearing climbing boots. This is not the image of femininity that is expected with the development of a consuming middle class. The *escaladoras'* use of the *pollera* positions them as indigenous women activists, but they emphasize that this is simply what they wear—"We are indigenous women and *de pollera*. . . . We've never taken them off, so that's how we climbed the mountain" (Lat Fem 2020). The inclusion of the *escaladoras* in the fashion show brought the importance of identity and empowerment to the notion of the *pollera* as fashion.

The big names in the Aymara fashion industry are made by the exclusivity, status, and wealth of their clientele. Paco Paredes cites Aymara women politicians as some of her most important clients. These women are *de pollera* in their everyday lives, and in the public office they take pride in wearing the indigenous outfit that was for so long banned from public spaces (Stephenson 1999). They seek *polleras* that communicate power and status. As Paco Paredes puts it, "the *pollera* has become a symbol of empowerment, strength, and the fight against discrimination" (interview, La Paz, January 2018). The *moda de la chola paceña* indicates a shift in the aesthetic frame of reference and a displacement of the mainstream that has not been the case in instances of traditional identities being adopted, and arguably co-opted, by commercial designers, for example, "favela chic" or the Mexican-inspired *"chola* style"—indicating urban Hispanic chic—in the United States. The popular markets in Bolivia where wealth has accumulated and luxury *pollera* designs have taken off are constituted by networks that are reliant on the cultural exchanges of which the *pollera* is definitive—the fiestas, with accompanying exchanges of gifts, favors, loans, and opportunities to extend *compadrazgo* networks. Although the boom in wealth there has brought the *pollera* to the attention of New York fashion week, the categorization of the *pollera* as "merely" traditional, or as costume, had never been fully inculcated into the aesthetic sense of Andean communities and markets.

The sense of confidence that the shift in aesthetic sensibilities generated thus changed the value of the networks and cultural capital that function in the popular markets of La Paz. While the big-name *pollera* designers rely on the wealth of a new political and professional class of Aymara women, the popular markets of La Paz where they started—notably, the areas around Kollasuyo, Cementerio, and Gran Poder—now boast *cholet*-style *galerías,* which—quite literally given their glossy surface—reflect the style, identity, and culture of those around them. These reflections can have a number of meanings: the sense of one's appearance that is a precondition for the fashion consumer and the modern subject, but also the recognition of the legitimacy of the *pollera* in urban space, a battle that has been and continues to be hard fought as the outfit, although no longer banned, remains a transgression in many spaces. This boom in *pollera* fashions has transformed the sense of possibility for those of more modest means earning a living in the informal markets of La Paz and El Alto. The shopping galleries of Kollasuyo, where Paco Paredes still has her boutique, are mostly populated by midrange designers, many operating informally, who make custom outfits for dancing groups for festivals, drawing on their own contacts to do so. These designers are young and *de vestido,* and appeal specifically to the trend for wearing the *pollera* in dances, rather than the identity of being *de pollera* itself. Naomi has a shop in one of the galleries on Kollasuyo Avenue that she runs with her mother. She has bought the various brightly colored materials from suppliers in the center of town, imported from East Asia, and her clientele are mostly girls whom she knows from her college and dancing. She is of indigenous descent but does not speak Aymara, and both she and her mother are *de vestido.* "I mostly work with the *señoritas,*" she says, using the term to indicate young urban women. "They want bright colors and more modern designs" (interview, La Paz, August 2017). She rents out *polleras* specifically for fiestas, and tailors bespoke outfits. She also designs her own jewelry. Naomi's own narrative of how she became involved in fashion presents her specialization as a shift from a livelihood strategy to a career in which her particular experience, cultural expertise, and tastes are an advantage. "I'd tried loads of things—selling used clothes, making and selling fried chicken and chips, but this really took off. . . . I used to dance myself, so I know what young girls want, and I already have the networks."

Despite the association with tradition, there has always been a sense of contemporaneity to Andean fiestas and the dances that are essential to the communities, neighborhoods, and markets of La Paz and El Alto. One of the *prestes*—lead organizers and sponsors—for the fiesta of Gran Poder in 2017 took me through a photo album of the various festivals he had taken part in over the years, emphasizing the changing trends and little innovations in each outfit. "This year it's all about boots—the old-style *pollera* and lacey shawl, that's what's most wanted now" (interview, La Paz, August 2017). "You absolutely have to have the latest designs, the latest music," said one photographer who specialized in festivals,

"or else people will know immediately and will speak badly of you—
and that's really not the point!" (interview, La Paz, August 2017). His
tone expressed the contemporaneity of these "traditional costumes" as
a given rather than a triumphant reassertion against an exclusionary
modernity.

However, the rise of the wealth and fashions of the Aymara bourgeoisie has been accompanied by a number of rumors and accusations that
reinforce exclusionary logics of colonial modernity. A frequent charge
levied is that those participating in the trend, both as producers and
consumers, are associated with narcotraffic. There is some suggestion
that the increased liquidity in Bolivia is due to money laundering from
illicit trades (UNODC 2020). However, to those familiar with the markets of La Paz and El Alto it is clear that while there may be particular examples, there is not a necessary association between wealth and
narcotraffic or laundering and that it is also possible to make money in
other ways—most notably by commerce. By contrast, discussions outside of those areas tend to assume that narcotraffic is the *only* explanation for the rise in wealth, and discourses employed tend to draw on
colonial tropes that erase the value of indigenous labor. Insinuations
of money laundering are drawn on to explain the apparently inflated
prices, and there is a general aura of suspicion around the success of
the trend. One professional woman from the affluent Zona Sur who attended a presentation I was giving about the fashion in May 2017 expressed incredulity that a vicuña shawl could possibly cost the rumored
price of $20,000 U.S. on the grounds that the raw material could not pos-
sibly cost that much. The shawl was made of expensive fabric—vicuña
is one of the world's most valuable woven textiles—but, she claimed, it
would not be possible for the weight of the shawl to justify that cost. A
discussion ensued about how price is determined—supply and demand,
the market being flooded with narco-money, and the value added of the
labor involved—and eventually, following this discussion with her colleagues, she conceded, "Oh, okay, so it's like when I buy something by
Calvin Klein, it's worth more than just the fabric."

This exchange illustrates a number of racialized aspects of the construction of value in the fashion industry. The price of the shawl was
seen to be entirely a function of the raw material, which would not be
the definitive consideration when assessing the value of work from a
Western designer. This recalls the equation of indigenous labor with

natural resources, and the Western construction of "civilization" set against the construction of the colonial other as "natural." The labor of the colonized is part of the process of extracting natural resources, but in itself it cannot add value. The value added by the skill and creativity of the designer was also erased. *Chola paceña* designers are often accused of being *confeccionistas*—just bringing together materials rather than creating something new—recalling the way women's labor is generally naturalized in the sphere of social reproduction rather than valued as a cultured skill (Socolow 2015). Part of the logic of the values of modernity is that tradition is seen to be repetitive rather than innovative, in opposition to the creativity of art. The power of this logic is it erases the possibility of indigeneity penetrating new ground, and therefore joining the modern world of fashion (Craik and Jansen 2015).

The fascination with the *moda de la chola paceña* on the international stage, however, does not fully embrace the trend into the fashion arena. The fashion show in New York did receive coverage, but in *National Geographic* (Little 2016) rather than *Vogue* or *Cosmopolitan*. There is hence an element of self-exoticization of indigenous culture entangled in the aesthetics of the *moda de la chola paceña*. The *pollera* can function as costume even within the cultural landscape of La Paz. The long-standing *chola paceña* beauty contests, the fiestas, and the fashion show in New York are all sites where the outfit is donned as a sign of identity rather than style, in an extraordinary, rather than everyday, context, and by women who are not necessarily *de pollera*. The *pollera* is also, however, an everyday dress that is worn by women who are working in the fields in rural areas and selling in markets. *Polleras* can be for functional, everyday wear or for fiestas and events. However, the *pollera*, even in its designer form, is not just an outfit—it *is* an identity. One does not just wear a *pollera*, one is *de pollera* (Gill 1993; Baudoin 2016), and, unless as costume, one cannot be *de pollera* one day and *de vestido* the next—*esto no se hace*—it is just not done. The *pollera* is hence a reflection of postcoloniality as it crosses the borders between colonial imposition and indigenous resistance, and between costume and fashion. It is a symbol of women's everyday work, and a consumer item. It can be worn as costume in fiestas, but at the same time is a marker of identity that cannot be mixed and matched.

The rise of the *moda de la chola paceña* is, however, shifting this aesthetic frame of reference that constructs the *pollera* as "in between." As the *pollera* is increasingly recognized as fashion, the dynamics among pastiche, costume, exoticization, fashion, and political symbolism are changing. For example, the *de pollera* designer Rosario Aguilar, who is known for her modeling school in La Paz, famously dressed the Santa Cruz–based beauty queens Las Magníficas in *pollera* designs for a show in 2017. Santa Cruz is Bolivia's second city—the economic powerhouse based in the east of the country, with a predominantly white population. It is said that Bolivia's most beautiful women come from this city, and it is renowned for consistently being the home of Miss Bolivia. The racial aspects of what counts as beauty have been conspicuous in this contest, and were highlighted in 2004 when one *cruceña* Miss Bolivia chose to emphasize in an interview at the Miss World contest that, contrary to popular belief, Bolivia was not just inhabited by indigenous people (*El Universo* 2004). In this context, for Las Magníficas to be dressed in *polleras* by a recognized Aymara designer, rather than as a pastiche of indigenous tradition, is an illustration of the revolution in cultural constructions of beauty that the rise of the Aymara bourgeoisie has advanced.

Conclusion

The mixed fortunes of the textiles and apparel industries in Bolivia indicate the inadequacies of economic narratives that rely on ideas of production, nation, and formality. The vision for Bolivia as the textiles producer within ALBA brought together the two primary concerns of pluri-economy: the reversal of the damage done by neoliberalism, and the valorization of Andean culture and traditions. However, it also brought out the tensions between state-led political economy, decolonization, and the livelihoods of those who constituted the MAS's political base. Worker-led social enterprises and state control of failing companies were measures intended to enact the ideas of pluri-economy and create institutions that would valorize cooperation and compensate for the implicit cultural biases of a solely financial bottom line. The failure of these approaches in the cases of Punto Blanco and Enatex can be attributed, among other things, to misconceptions of nation and solidarity in the formulation of these policies. The political significance of the decline of these companies is underscored by the relative success of the markets in used clothes and the *moda de la chola paceña*. These contrasting tales show the economic plurality of popular markets of La Paz and

El Alto, where the contradictory pressures of community, globalization, identity, and modernity were not merely being resisted but being interpreted and engaged with in a way that escaped the theoretical precepts of economy and modernity.

Controversies around the construction and role of the state were prominent in the theorizations of the Grupo Comuna and negotiations in the Constituent Assembly. The state takeover of Enatex and protectionist measures taken against the import of used clothes were the actions of a modernizing state that supports industries the market cannot sustain. This role betrayed the complexities of the plurination defined in the Constitution and fulfilled fears from social movements that the state would become too powerful and centralized, but it was true to the calls for the active defense of Bolivian sovereignty against global economic forces that had been so prominent in electoral campaigns. However, these interventions demonstrated both economic and cultural inadequacies inherent in the idea of the modernizing nation-state. The influx of clothing and textiles, both by contraband and legitimate import, was insurmountable, and the state had neither the infrastructure nor the extension within Bolivia adequately to police the bans and restrictions imposed. The importance that was accorded to the internal market or the regional trading bloc could not counterweigh the power of global trade, particularly when Chinese and Korean production of textiles was becoming dominant worldwide. Culturally, the markers of Bolivian identity and solidarity that were marshaled in criticism of those involved in the used-clothes trade did not reflect how those working in the "informal" sector, which had indeed expanded as a result of economic restructuring, had engaged with the pressures and contradictions of global markets, which was in their view entirely compatible with the maintenance of Bolivian tradition and identity.

A decentralized view of the used-clothes trade shows a reworking—quite literally in the case of the poncho—of discourses of nation versus globalization and illustrates how the cultural traditions underpinning these networks and markets are globally engaged. The success of both the used-clothes trade and *chola paceña* fashions rewrites the scripts of modernity, progress, and contemporaneity and hence functions "to quiet the cacophony of [modernity's] own narratives, its notions of progress, development and civilization" (Jansen 2020, 831), and so to decolonize the imaginary of progress implied in capitalist notions of value. The used-clothes trade is an example of the power of the global market, but it is also a site of resistance where women *de pollera* can sell top labels to wealthy women from La Paz coming to El Alto for a day trip, disrupting the scripts of exploitation that underestimate agency, as well as the cultural map of La Paz, as connections are formed between the informal markets of the north and El Alto and the boutiques of the Zona Sur. The *pollera* sits in its customary position between postcolonial synthesis and marker of indigenous identity and empowerment. However, in its avatar as fashion item it blurs the line between costume and style, antifashion and fashion, tradition and modernity.

The figure of the *chola paceña* designer reconfigures the relationship between the idea of popular, community economies underpinned by indigenous traditions, on the one hand, and the engagement of those markets with modernity and globalization, on the other. The false binary of tradition and modernity rests on a gendered distinction between gift and commodity exchange, with the former increasingly devalued as capital develops. The "traditional," however, has always had its elements of modernity—consumer choice, aesthetic style, and the importance of trend—and these elements have been overlooked in the construction of tradition in opposition to a colonial modernity. *La moda de la chola paceña* represents the empowerment of an aesthetic tradition that underpins the community reciprocity and gift exchange that has generated the market for this trend, in contrast to other examples around the world of co-option of indigenous traditions into mainstream consumption. The confidence that has come with this change in aesthetic frame is shown in the triumphant parades of Gran Poder, but what has triumphed is a parallel aesthetic that has displaced, rather than overturned, previous scripts.

6

Construction
Aesthetics, Recognition, and Urban Mobilities

Evo Morales's time in power was accompanied by a remarkable boom in the construction and real estate sectors. The construction industry outpaced GDP growth both nationally and specifically in La Paz, where laborers saw their wages double between 2010 and 2016 (GAMLP 2015). Real estate values also rose dramatically over this period, provoking concerns in the Banco Central de Bolivia that there was a speculative bubble (Cerezo Aguirre 2014; Vargas Ramos and Villegas Tufiño 2014). In 2015, the peak of the boom, prices "shot up to levels never seen before" (*Correo del Sur* 2019). The Banco Central concluded that the increases in the amount of construction, the costs of construction, and real estate prices were consistent with the economic fundamentals, including government investment in infrastructure and the increased availability of credit for housing (Cerezo Aguirre 2014). However, there was concern that the official figures could not capture the informal sector or the differential effects that these dramatic changes in the built environment were having (Horn 2021). Rumors that investment in real estate, construction, and land was related to money laundering from narcotraffic and other undeclared sources of income were rife (*Urgente Bo* 2016). Investment in real estate on this scale was consistent with increased liquidity, which would be typical of an economy that was overly dependent on natural resources. Furthermore, the high costs of labor and manufacturing for many outweighed the incentives to hire employees and develop businesses. Despite the government's focus on production, high levels of regulation were seen as a burden to productive activity. Analysts of business development in the popular sectors of the economy raised concerns that many people were deciding to close their productive enterprises: "In these stories the innumerable difficulties that they confront in order to produce in this country and the incomparable advantages that commerce and construction offers emerge" (Wanderley 2018). The boom in the construction sector took place despite MAS policies to minimize land speculation and maximize investment in production, and there was concern that the productive sector was attenuated because of the relative attractiveness of real estate as an investment. The rapid expansion, in all directions, of the built environment in La Paz, El Alto, and Bolivia's other cities has for many been the most remarkable change since 2006.

This construction boom, accompanied by fundamental shifts in Bolivian social structures, had dramatic effects on architectural aesthetics. As wealth accumulated in informal markets, an urban environment developed that appealed to the tastes, traditions, aspirations, and livelihood strategies of this emerging Aymara bourgeoisie. El Alto is now characterized not by the corrugated iron and utilitarian bare-bricked housing associated with "slums" but by the brightly colored facades of Freddy Mamani's *cholets*—the townhouses that combine Andean symbols, commercial spaces, and a residential chalet on the top story. The Central Business District and commercial areas of La Zona Sur are now dominated by ever taller high-rise towers, and a city once notorious for *chuto*—undocumented—vehicles and traffic congestion can now be traversed from end to end in an elegant alpine transport system, the Teleférico. The explosion of real estate prices in peri-urban and informal areas of La Paz and El Alto that accompanied these changes was not the intent behind the focus of MAS policy, but the map of La Paz has nevertheless been rewritten in ways that enabled exclusionary colonial barriers to be breached. The La Paz press documented various urban transgressions as an emerging consuming class, led by the wealthy *chola paceña,* took its place in the more luxurious, Westernized spaces in the city, so demonstrating the power of the informal, the cultural, and the feminine in reshaping urban space. While urban expansion is a global phenomenon, La Paz is a spectacular example of a place where the factors so overlooked in urban and economic theory—the informal, the postcolonial, the feminine—gained the power to shape the built environment (Butcher and Maclean 2018; Jazeel 2021; Roy 2016).

The multiple power struggles that have formed La Paz can be read in its urban landscape, and while the logic of capital has underpinned many of these tensions, the racialized dynamics of colonialism, the cultural identities that demarcate the formal and the informal, the competing modes of governance that have jurisdiction over the city, and the gendered struggles that are never only confined to the household have been crucial in shaping the Bolivian capital. The developing urban landscape in La Paz, and related patterns of mobility and displacement, illustrate the story of the ascending wealth and power of informal, indigenous urban areas and the loss of power among traditional elites to the south of the city. Economically, it is predictable that this shift in wealth will result in familiar patterns of displacement: those from wealthy areas use their property as collateral to accumulate more land elsewhere. However, in the case of La Paz this has meant that people from peri-urban areas, mostly of indigenous descent and rural background, are buying real estate in areas associated with traditional elites, who are consequently being displaced to other areas of the city. Accumulation of wealth and related urban displacement are represented in popular culture not by the "fat-cat" white developer or even the traditional criollo class but by an indigenous woman carrying a suitcase of cash.

This chapter proceeds with an analysis of the factors involved in constructing the urban frontiers that divide the center and south of La Paz from the informal settlements on the steep slopes to the north and in El Alto, as well as the political, economic, and cultural forces that have shaped the city and the mobility of its inhabitants. It then examines a place that has become a focal point in local discussions of the way La Paz is changing: the MegaCenter shopping mall in the Zona Sur. The mall could be categorized as a "non-place" (Augé 2009), one of the generic, internationally financed constructions that lend weight to the argument that globalization is rendering the world homogeneous (Chang and Huang 2008). However, the disputes over who belongs in this space and whose expectations of behavior, categorizations, and judgments frame interactions and exchanges within it demonstrate how local, cultural power struggles can be primary in shaping urbanization. To illustrate the cultural struggles that the rise of the Aymara bourgeoisie precipitated, I will examine a satirical image that "went viral" on social media in response to a scandal involving people from El Alto sitting on the floor and eating their own food in the MegaCenter. The meme features a scene from the 2009 film *Zona Sur*—a fictional exploration of the declining fortunes of traditional elites in La Paz—which ends with a wealthy woman *de pollera* offering to buy the protagonist's property in cash, implying that it is only a matter of time before the wealthy *chola paceña* will be offering to purchase the MegaCenter in the same way (see Figure 8).

The incident in the MegaCenter and the response to it uncovers the powerful influence of the informal, the cultural, and the feminine in channeling the flows of capital and shaping urban space.

Urban Boundaries

La Paz is a divided city whose economic geography is neatly expressed in the local aphorism "The higher you live, the poorer you are." The richer, lower areas to the south have high-rise hotels, country clubs, and shopping malls selling international brands. The roads and pavements are generally well maintained, and increasingly this area is home to *urbanizaciones cerradas*—gated communities—which have security at the entrance and are characterized by large, colonial-style mansions and well-irrigated gardens, marking a striking contrast from the arid surroundings. The north of La Paz and El Alto developed from increased rural-to-urban migration in the late twentieth century that created unplanned, "informal" settlements in peri-urban areas on the steep slopes of the city, in a pattern of urban development that is seen across many Andean cities. As one resident from Kollasuyo described the history of the area: "On the slopes you obviously find the most humble people—*la gente chola, campesina*. They would arrive and stake out small properties, with little houses and farms—but of course, they were the poorest people" (interview, La Paz, May 2017). The buildings in El Alto and the *laderas*—slopes—to the north of La Paz are mostly self-built, bare-bricked, and incomplete. Basic infrastructure is inconsistent and improvised, and from the condition of road surfaces it is clear that regulations are not systematically enforced. Characterizing these areas by "lack" and "incompleteness," however, overlooks the place-making and sense of belonging generated by the people who live there who identify with surroundings that reflect rural-urban connections and value the autonomy of communities who have built their own city without reliance on a modernizing state.

The development of La Paz and El Alto is remembered fondly by residents who moved to the city in the 1950s and 1960s, after the revolution. As one woman *de pollera,* Elena, from Kollasuyo, describes:

> Before, this area was full of donkeys. People would come here with their donkeys loaded up with coca and papa and corn from the

countryside. And there were only little adobe houses—not these enormous brick ones—it was lovely. (Interview, May 2017)

New migrants to the city would stake out plots and build their own houses, and it would not be unusual for their families to still live on this land. Water and energy infrastructures were either built by communities themselves or "siphoned" from existing infrastructure. In the 1980s, El Alto was christened and established as a city in its own right, and soon became the fastest growing urban area in Latin America, with the population far outpacing the ability, or willingness, of the state to provide infrastructure or regulate land use and housing. The unfinished houses with rebars protruding from the topmost story—nicknamed *los pelos,* the hairs—add to the impression of informality and exclusion, but they also indicate a hope for fortunes to come. There is always the possibility to rent out rooms to tenants or to give away usufruct rights on an area of the house in return for a lump sum to be paid back—*anticretico.* The rebars also demonstrate incompleteness to the tax authorities, who would charge more for a finished construction, and so are a sign of resistance in this area to state authorities. There is clearly poverty in these neighborhoods, but defining the slopes of La Paz by their lack in comparison to a modern norm—for instance, Mike Davis's description of El Alto as the "Quechua-speaking slum sister of La Paz" (*Socialist Worker* 2006)—is to misunderstand the power dynamics and the meanings that have created this built environment and in which residents, despite the difficulties, feel their history is affirmed.

The built environment of El Alto and the *laderas* of La Paz is an expression of the mobile livelihood strategies that blur the divide between rural and urban and the relationships among household, family, property, and propinquity. Household livelihood strategies require coordination across rural production and urban commerce and necessitate productive units having property in both locations, and areas of El Alto in particular can map onto the rural communities who mostly have property there—for instance, *luribayeños* tend to live in Villa Dolores. Property ownership and entitlement is complicated, as multiple regulatory regimes are at play. The traditional *chachawarmi* two-headed household and bilateral inheritance rights of the Andes has been overlain by modernizing land reforms that allocated a male head of household; competing jurisdictions, some of which recognize community ownership and others not; and the activities of *loteadores,* who buy large areas of un-used land cheaply and divide it into plots to sell individually. Although *loteadores* have been crucial intermediaries for rural-urban migrants and key actors in the growth of El Alto (Diaz 2013), they have become no-torious for practices such as selling the same land twice or not providing appropriate paperwork, to the point that buyers can discover that they have no legal right of ownership (Sheild Johansson 2020; Horn 2021). Despite these complexities, it is still not unusual to find properties that are jointly owned or owned solely by the wife. One resident who had one of the first houses built in the area of Kollasuyo on land given to her by her parents explained:

> It was a strange plot of land—a triangle like this—but I loved it, and I built this house up myself. I ordered the best cement from Chile and designed this house myself. I thought the shape was like a block of cheese, and I wanted it to have fantastic views—from the top you can see right across the mountains. And it was always clear that this house was mine. My husband was terribly abusive—he even tried to get me committed to an asylum—but I got rid of him because I had this house. A lot of it is rented out on *anticretico* now, but this house is mine. (Interview, La Paz, May 2017)

The functionality of many of the houses in the *laderas,* the lack of facade, and the generally ascetic aesthetic aligns with the stereotype of Aymara and Quechua campesinos as miserly; *no van a gastar ni un peso para un foco*—they're not even going to spend a penny for a lightbulb. There is little culture of comfort, and if a family has money to improve a house they will rarely build an indoor bathroom or install heating—they would rather invest in a room that can be rented out to supplement income if need be. There is a rationale to the stereotype, as any conspicu-ous show of wealth in a community dominated by gift exchange, fictive kin, and *compadrazgo* would result in a number of kinfolk asking for contributions and favors. It is often rumored that the old *chola* in worn-out clothes selling on the street will own the building behind her. In contrast, however, the *salones de baile* (dance halls) around these areas of the city—testament to the centrality of the fiesta to Andean culture and economy—are strikingly decorated, recalling the colors and patterns of Andean fabrics. These are spaces where conspicuous consumption has always been permitted within the bounds of community reciprocity, although still mediated by the politics of reputation that guards the delicate balance among gift exchange, cooperation, and competition.

The importance of feeling that one's culture and identity are reflected in the urban environment is evident in the sense of discomfort that residents of northern neighborhoods feel elsewhere in the city. "The boundaries have always been clearly defined," said one resident of Kollasuyo, referring to the sense of "out-of-placeness" she felt when in traditionally middle-class areas in the Zona Sur (interview, May 2017). "I can't come there with you—I'll make you look bad," said an El Alto resident whom I knew socially when I said that I had an appointment in the Zona Sur (July 2006). There is a palpable discomfort when people transgress these invisible boundaries into places that are not their own, which is no less powerful for being intangible, ineffable, and hard to deconstruct (Ahmed 2007). The unease recalls Fausto Reinaga's emphasis on shame—an inculcated sense of doubt that one's own sense of values and ways of behaving can ever be legitimate or adequate, an inherently social sense of self that has long historical roots. The divisions in La Paz were at one time formal and enforced with bans on clothing and language, but the elimination of these formal bans was not enough to change the invisible cultural boundaries that mark the city. The increase in wealth in popular areas was a necessary condition for the changes in the cultural map of La Paz, but it would not on its own have been sufficient. The definitive factor was the ineffable sense of confidence engendered by people of indigenous descent being in power and the centrality of decolonization to the national agenda.

The Zona Sur, the most salubrious area of La Paz inhabited by traditional elites, in many ways feels like a different world. The climate is much more temperate, as its location in the valley between the badlands that define La Paz's skyline protect it from the harsh Altiplano winds and extremes of temperature. It is eight hundred meters lower than El Alto, and it is not unusual for people who live in the Zona Sur to complain of altitude sickness and freezing temperatures when they go up to the neighboring city for the day—which typically would only occur if they were obliged to for work reasons. La Paz's luxury hotels and boutiques are in the Zona Sur, as well as country clubs, tennis clubs, and the exclusive private universities—La Católica and the Escuela Militar de Ingeniería.

However, it would be a mistake to gloss the Zona Sur as being the space solely of the elite. While the wealthiest families live in *urbanizaciones cerradas* and custom-built houses in the hills surrounding the valley, much of the area developed in the 1950s and 1960s as middle-class professionals from the center of La Paz started to move down, attracted by affordable properties. The residential buildings in the Zona Sur adopt either a colonial Spanish or minimalist modernism and reflect a North American imaginary of development. This has produced its own kind of postcolonial sense of inadequacy that Bolivian middle classes feel when looking toward the West. For example, when I asked directions in the Zona Sur to the new multiscreen cinema, I was met with a self-effacing chuckle: "Isn't it amazing! Yes, hard to believe but now even in Bolivia we have these things." Although this area has been better serviced by the state than the informal settlements to the north, there are nevertheless infrastructural inadequacies and environmental hazards. In 2011 a slow landslide took out an entire mountainside in the exclusive area of Irpavi, and residents had to evacuate and watch their detached, often bespoke, houses collapse. In 2016 a drought in the Zona Sur forced residents to queue up for a communal water supply. The irony of seeing traditional elites having to queue for basic services—an activity that is familiar to areas of El Alto—was not lost, but, despite elements of political schadenfreude, the shared hardship also brought about unexpected solidarities (Guzman 2016).

After 2006, the booming economy and rapid changes in political priorities led to a reconfiguration of these divides in the cultural and social map of La Paz and El Alto. The adage that income was inversely related to altitude no longer applied, as wealth in the informal economy increased along with the confidence to show it. Real estate prices in the north of La Paz and El Alto increased steadily between 2006 and 2019, as did the amount of construction, and La Paz also extended southward. Urban development companies increased their construction on land to the south, despite the lack of infrastructure there, and a number of gated communities developed alongside the route from La Paz to Mecapaca. The popular areas of Chasquipampa and Cota Cota to the south of the Zona Sur also developed rapidly over this time (Horn 2018).

In addition to the changing wealth profile, several factors have enabled this expansion, including state and municipal investment in transport networks and a changing cultural sense of belonging. The

Teleférico—a series of ten cable car lines that connect different areas of La Paz and El Alto that began operations in 2014—was developed and implemented by the state government in order to improve the connectivity of excluded areas in the *laderas* to the north and in El Alto. The Teleférico is now the longest urban cable car system in the world and is the first to use rope cable car systems as the primary mode of urban transit (IDB 2018). Bilingual station names and signage establish this transit system as public, inclusive, and part of MAS decolonization policies. It was funded by the national treasury at a cost that was approaching $1 billion U.S. at the end of Morales's administration (Grace 2019), and was constructed by the Austrian company Doppelmayr-Garaventa working directly for the state government. The first lines of the Teleférico linked El Alto with the Zona Sur, and the number of routes increased to ten altogether, forming a complete circuit around La Paz and the cliffs of El Alto. Tickets are subsidized at three bolivianos per trip, and impact studies have suggested that the economic benefits of the Teleférico outweigh the costs, as many passengers, particularly from El Alto, use the line to access income-generating activities (IDB 2018). The journey from El Alto to the Zona Sur before the Teleférico would be undertaken typically in syndicate-run collective forms of transport—minibus, microbus, or *trufi* (fixed-route taxi)—and could easily take upwards of two hours, in cramped conditions and in vehicles that sometimes struggled with the steep inclines of La Paz. The trip on the Teleférico takes forty minutes and is as popular with tourists as it is with residents, with truly outstanding views. For those able to take their journey by cable car, the commute has become an inexpensive delight.

The Teleférico has caused numerous high-profile controversies. In contrast to similar urban transport projects in cities around the world that foregrounded a participatory approach (Maclean 2015), the Teleférico was implemented centrally. Tensions with transport unions, who had the power to bring the city to a standstill with frequent blockades (Burgos 2019), were part of the reason for this, and there was a desire to maintain the project's "merely technical" appearance to avoid political conflict (Vargas Beltrán 2016, 25). However, the placement of these lines was seen as an imposition from the state rather than a participatory process. It is rumored that when the engineers and topographers first arrived in the areas that had been indicated to lay the foundations of the towers, they found that the owners of the houses that would be affected had not been consulted. The green and yellow lines link the center of La Paz with the Zona Sur, and in doing so fly over an exclusive *urbanización cerrada* in the area of Alto Obrajes/Bella Vista. The luxury mansions and swimming pools are in full view of the passing cable cars, which come within ten meters at some points. Residents have complained that land-use regulations have been overlooked, and have specifically cited cases of robberies that they put down to criminals scoping out their properties from the Teleférico (Juárez 2015). These stories are accompanied by a certain glee that the Teleférico represents a public intervention that has damaged the rich and invaded space that had been gated off. Nevertheless, they are also interpreted as evidence of the central state taking more power than was ever considered in the development of the "plural" vision of the economy.

Several public works have been designed explicitly to decolonize the public sphere and reconfigure the relationship between indigeneity, modernity, and power. One of the most striking and controversial changes has been the Casa del Pueblo—House of the People (Figure 7). This high-rise tower with a somewhat "space-agey" aesthetic was built on the main thoroughfare of El Prado to house government offices. It is intended to be a testament to Morales's legacy and weds indigenous iconography with futuristic architecture. The building itself has twenty-nine stories and houses the offices of the president, the vice president, and five other ministries; it also boasts a luxury residence for the head of state (BBC Mundo 2018). It has been nicknamed the Palacio del Evo, and at a cost of $34 million U.S., many commentators suspect that there could have been more effective investments for "the people." The construction of the Casa del Pueblo infringed on municipal planning laws that prevented the construction of high-rise buildings in the center of La Paz, but an exception was voted through by Parliament. To clear the site, historical buildings had to be destroyed, buildings that critics such as classically trained Bolivian architect Juan Carlos Calderón were quick to point out were from the Republican rather than the colonial era (*El Diario* 2017). Morales defended the clearance by emphasizing that the point of the building was precisely to break with the past. As with any architectural innovation, it divided opinion on its aesthetics, and the deliberate choice of a "futuristic" design intentionally broke with accepted tropes. One architect from Kollasuyo who had been involved in a bid for the construction and had pitched a traditional indigenous design concluded that they had not been

FIGURE 7. *La Casa del Pueblo under construction, La Paz, 2017. Author's photograph.*

successful, as "they were precisely going for a design that incorporated indigenous symbols and a modern, even futuristic aesthetic" (interview, May 2017). The Casa del Pueblo is intended as an indelible marker of the right of indigenous people to be at the heart of Bolivian politics and the country's vision of the future. Many people who are of indigenous descent and identify with Morales do not like the building or the destruction it caused, but nevertheless the building marks a transformation of the symbolism of the public sphere and of who has the right to define the aesthetics of taste, power, and the nation.

There have been other architectural innovations that are a product directly of the strength of the economy in previously excluded areas, and the sense of ownership of urban space brought about by the symbolic changes of the Morales years. The *cholets* are a striking symbol of the power and money that has accumulated in informal areas of the city. The brightly colored facades and distinguishing feature of a residential "chalet" on top of a six-story building have become symbolic of the rise in wealth and influence of the Aymara bourgeoisie. These buildings have attracted global attention in the press and in the worlds of art and architecture and have been described variously as "rocketship houses" and "Neo-Andean baroque" (see, e.g., Kim 2015; Mallinson 2017; *New York Times* 2017). In 2018 and 2019, the Fondation Cartier in Paris held an exhibition dedicated to the *cholets* that involved the inside of the gallery in the fashionable 14th arrondissement of Paris being converted into a *cholet*-style interior by Freddy Mamani. Despite this international attention, within Bolivia these buildings have provoked debate in schools of architecture about whether they genuinely constitute a new architectural style and whether Mamani is really an architect, given that he is "untrained." Questions of taste range from the *cholets* being seen as an expression of the colors and symbols of the Andean fiestas to their being dismissed as the garishness of a new rich who disregard quality in favor of cheap, colorful materials imported from China. However, the prominence of these debates demonstrates how the frame of reference in La Paz has changed, with the focus of discussions in art and architectural schools now on innovations from areas previously referred to as slums, constructed by people who have been excluded from those very schools.

The association with the ballroom and fiestas has meant there is now a competition, even within the community bounds of the Aymara economy, of whose *cholet* can be bigger, brasher, and hence more attractive to *festejeros*—partygoers—than the others. When I asked an architect from the north of La Paz who had worked on multiple buildings in El Alto what people tend to want in their *cholet,* he responded, "Whatever their neighbor has—they'll want more, bigger, more luxury in the interior and so on" (interview, May 2017). This phenomenon has resulted in some truly spectacular designs. Some of the most famous and eye-catching *cholets* and *salones de baile* have gone far beyond the Tiwanaku-inspired imagery of Mamani's design, to include images from popular movies including the Transformers and other superhero films (Sagárnaga 2019). One of the most famous is the Iron Man *salon de baile,* which features a huge, constructed effigy of Iron Man leaning out of the facade toward the blue line of the Teleférico. This example plays into debates about *cholets* overall, as it is taken as evidence of "objective" bad taste. One town planner I talked with was particularly clear on this, despite her colleagues' interruptions about Bourdieusian notions of cultural capital: "I don't care—have you seen it? It's awful—that is bad taste, full stop."

There are multiple dimensions to the topography of belonging in La Paz and El Alto, and the changes seen over the period of the MAS government cannot be explained by the rise in wealth alone. The dynamics of identity and recognition, along with culturally situated expectations of how exchange functions, has created flashpoints of contention as identity, belonging, mobility, and markets reconfigure. Prominent examples highlight the systematic tensions identified in the post-neoliberal, pluricultural agenda between colonial, white individual consumerism and indigenous cooperation and reciprocity. However, exploring the prominent role of women *de pollera* in high-profile disputes illustrates the complexities between the familiar and gendered divides between commercial and community exchange.

Urban Transgressions

The radical transformation of the economic, cultural, and political map of La Paz is encapsulated in one meme that circulated on social media in 2014. The controversy it portrays took place soon after the opening of the Teleférico line which connected the neighborhood of Ciudad Satelite in El Alto with the Zona Sur, where the terminal was located next to the Mega-Center mall. Like many such shopping centers around the world, the MegaCenter has a multiscreen cinema that, in accordance with a global norm, offers two-for-one tickets on a Wednesday. People from El Alto came down to take advantage of the offer and brought their own food, which they proceeded to eat while sitting on the floor of the food court area. Photographs taken of the young people dressed in sweatpants and T-shirts and of women *de pollera* sitting on the floor, who did indeed look incongruous against the artificial lighting, bland colors, and inoffensive furnishings of the mall, circulated on social media accompanied by racist slurs describing the behavior as uneducated, gauche, and ignorant. In reaction to this, a meme was generated consisting of a collage of those images juxtaposed with a still from the film *Zona Sur,* in which an indigenous woman, clearly wealthy and dressed in a fashionable *pollera,* is counting out cash from an open suitcase as if to make a purchase. The caption reads "So, how much is your MegaCenter?" (Figure 8).

The film that is referenced—*Zona Sur*—tells the story of the declining fortunes of the traditional elite in La Paz. It traces the struggles of Carola, a blonde, upper-class mother, to maintain her two children in the manner to which they are accustomed while trying to cope with ever diminishing sources of finance and power. The film depicts her

FIGURE 8. *Meme featuring scenes from* Zona Sur *and photographs taken at the MegaCenter. Source: A4000, 2015.*

negotiations with her Aymara servants, whom she has not been able to pay for months, and her efforts to maintain status while negotiating loans and relationships with her social circle. Director Juan Carlos Valdivia grew up in the area and was motivated to make the film from a sense of duty to turn the lens on the elites and his own experiences after reflecting on the ethics of taking the camera into the homes of "the indigenous": "It was encounters with the other that forced me to tell the story of where I'm from" (interview, La Paz, May 2017). He refers to the film as both an "homage and a critique" of the area, which moves away from the caricatures of the upper classes "as the bad guys, the neoliberals, the exploiters," with the intention of decentering the narrative. It is filmed with the camera constantly panning the room, foregrounding the objects in Carola's house both to highlight the insularity of her world and to personify the objects that define and defend her class status. The final scene introduces her Aymara *comadre*, Doña Remedios—a woman *de pollera* and *"con clase"* with whom she shares mutual concerns that their children's friends are of good standing and have professional careers. Both are matriarchs but from different worlds, and after exchanging confidences, Comadre Remedios instructs her assistant to open a suitcase that is full of dollar bills and offers to buy Señora Carola's house to help her get through these hard times. Carola refuses, but the tectonic shift of power between traditional white elites and the Aymara bourgeoisie is established (see Maclean 2018).

The meme and image of the wealth of Comadre Remedios has become a trope that crystallizes the changing political economy of La Paz and its effect on the built environment. The incident in the MegaCenter provoked a wide-ranging debate about the nature of the norms in public space, which in daily conversation was more nuanced than it appeared in media coverage. I interviewed residents of the Zona Sur who disagreed with the condemnation and suggested points of comparison— "In every airport in the world you will see people sitting down on the floor and eating food" (interview, San Miguel, August 2015). In a focus group with business owners in the area, the problem was situated with education: "It's about learning how to behave in public. Some of us have lived in Spain and we know what it's like to be discriminated against and called 'Sudacas,' but you have to learn different ways of behaving" (focus group, San Miguel, August 2015). In response to the controversy, outside the MegaCenter a wide range of people participated in a traditional Andean *apthapi*—a kind of potluck party where everyone brings their own food to share while sitting on the floor—to demonstrate solidarity with those who had been the subjects of that online disparagement.

This incident concentrates the clash of diverse visions of development and economy, and the tropes it draws upon are signs of different mercantile logics and market structures as well as different cultural meanings of economic exchanges. In what follows I explore in more depth how the complexities and entanglements of these different economic worlds have formed the shopping spaces and built environment of La Paz.

Shopping Space

Shopping space brings economic identities to the fore, as the cultural underpinnings of transactions and exchanges that are anything but neutral can trump commercial motivations; that is, people would rather be in a place where they feel comfortable, affirmed, and have good relationships than merely follow price incentives. The meme represents a confrontation of different economic identities that are being renegotiated as the city's cultural boundaries change, and shopping spaces are the key loci of these struggles. The shopping spaces in the Zona Sur are markedly different from those in the north and El Alto. Supermarket chains such as Ketal and Hipermaxi are commonplace in the Zona Sur, whereas they are a rarity in the north. These supermarkets represent the ultimate individualist, regulated consumer space, where produce is packaged and labeled and where there is no need to communicate with anyone besides exchanging minimal niceties with an anonymous cashier. By contrast, popular markets are reliant on relationships. Accessing the best goods relies on cultivating a status as a *casero*—a regular—and goods might be bought to maintain that relationship rather than for need. Markets and supermarkets are both spaces of encounter, however, that attract curiosity and where differences become marked and exoticized. The overcrowded bustle of the Sixteenth July market—the "mall of El Alto"—is a day trip for southern *paceños* who can marvel at the range of goods on display and enjoy the interactions. These trips are accompanied by precautions due to El Alto's reputation for violence, and market sellers joke that they can spot people from the Zona Sur, as they are all wearing the same disguise of sunglasses, baseball hat, and a backpack. It is less common for people from the *laderas* to visit the supermarkets of the Zona Sur, because of the prices and the discomfort they would feel there. But there is the assumption that this packaged produce should be better, and disappointment when it does not seem markedly different from that available in the markets. The relationship between the malls to the south of the city and the popular markets to the north exemplify the gendered and racialized contradictions of development and modernity. Informal markets are sustained by the inability of the consumer logic of supermarkets, malls, and large corporations to provide for an inclusive economy, while the modernization they represent at once others and devalues the contribution of informal vendors (Way 2012).

The MegaCenter mall, the location of the controversy depicted in the meme, was built in 2010 by the Spanish company Grentidem SA and was one of several constructed during the 2010s in the Zona Sur and the center of La Paz. These included the Las Torres mall in the Plaza Isabella Católica in Sopocachi and the sixteen-story Multicine on Avenida Poeta. Such shopping malls—iconic structures of middle-class consumption— have proliferated around the world with the rise in wealth in the global South as increased disposable income and consumption incentivizes international investment (Dávila 2016). Analyses that justify these investments are done purely on monetary terms and are based on the assumption that increased income will transform community into con- sumer relations (McEwan, Hughes, and Bek 2015). The unacknowledged cultural implications of this assumption, however, are clear in the shop- ping spaces of La Paz. While it is simplistic to call these international malls "Western," in the Bolivian context they offer brands that are more in line with the tastes of the white inhabitants of the Zona Sur, and the design of the spaces themselves create expectations of behavior that de- marcate the spaces as traditional middle class (Mamani Ramírez 2015; Casanovas 2018). There are, however, a variety of spaces in La Paz that are shaped by reworking the commercial logic of modernity and complex entanglements of different culturally situated exchanges and meanings.

The consumer logic of international malls contrasts sharply with Andean "community structures [that] have been able to establish an in- stitutionality on their own terms" (Aramayo Cañedo 2015, 54) and are therefore perceived as "disordered." The conflict depicted in the meme is also seen in the resistance to the renovation and formalization of street sellers, which resulted in a transformation of some of the oldest mar- kets in the city where posts have been inherited as well as bought, prices are bargained between *caseros* and the language most heard is Aymara. They are also places where women wield power. *Las vendedoras*—the women sellers—are organized according to the *maestrerío* system (Bar- ragán 2009), a hierarchical system that reflects the vertical relations and responsibilities of a *compadrazgo*—a representative who has earned the trust of those she represents. The municipal government of La Paz, in its Strategic Plan, titled "La Paz, viva, dinámica y ordenada"—La Paz, lively, dynamic and ordered—set out its aims to formalize street sell- ing and move street stalls into two constructed, semi-indoor market spaces in the city center: El Mercado Lanza and El Camacho. The in- tention was to maintain the culture of these tarpaulin-covered stalls while also bringing them off the street and into custom-made build- ings. The stalls were deemed a risk to the vendors and pedestrians, as they encroached on the road, and particular concern had been raised since a notorious hailstorm and flood in 2002 had caused great damage to street stalls and over fifty deaths. The formalization plan was justified on health and safety terms but was also in effect an imposition of a form of governance from the municipality that did not respect the community structures underpinning the market. Construction of the new Mercado Lanza was an arduous process of negotiation that brought out the different visions of mercantile exchange and shopping space held by the vendors and the functionaries from the town hall (Aramayo Cañedo 2015). The *vendedoras*—mostly women *de pollera*—claimed that the move to the new building, a brutalist concrete structure on La Perez, involved the loss of custom, as there would be no passersby, and that it would break down the social relations and responsibilities that were vital to how the market community functioned. After years of delay, the move to the new buildings was completed in 2010 and is generally regarded as an improvement in terms of hygiene and risk. However, it was felt that the community control, which had regulated prices, cooperation, and competition and had "historically given indigenous women power" (Aramayo Cañedo 2015, 65), had been lost.

Emerging developments in consumer spaces, however, show a more complicated picture, as Aymara *comerciantes* have negotiated different configurations of commerce and community, modernity and tradition. For example, the Centro de Moda mall in the fashionable San Miguel commercial area of the Zona Sur is now owned by a woman *de pollera* and her family, who originally made their money importing and retailing goods in the informal areas of La Paz. They redesigned the mall with the explicit aim to combine the dynamics and aesthetics of a street market with an international mall. The son of the family now manages the center, and they live in an *urbanización cerrada* to the south of the Zona Sur. He studied for his MBA in Mexico and has a clear vision of the cultural position of the space: "The business plan was to combine the stalls of the informal market with the comfort of a formal mall, and so we can attract those two groups of customers" (interview, San Miguel, May 2017). This is evident in the way the mall is set up, with tarpaulin-covered stalls in the center, but the relationships underpinning exchange in the informal markets of El Alto—the importance of loyalty, cultivating relationships with *caseros,* and understanding the importance and limits of bargaining within those relationships—do not figure in the exchanges that take place here.

The Arcangel mall in Calle Montenegro of San Miguel has also been bought by a woman *de pollera* who made her wealth in commerce in the informal markets to the north. The upper floors of this mall are dedicated to exclusive fashion boutiques, and the subterranean floors have more affordable clothes and shoe shops, nail salons, jewelry boutiques, and arts and craft stores. Patty, from the north of La Paz, who rented a unit for her Bolivian crafts, explained to me that she had recently moved to the neighborhood of Chasquipampa—an area at the southernmost end of La Paz that was attracting a number of people from the north of the city (Horn 2018). Unlike the Zona Sur, Chasquipampa is inhabited predominantly by people of indigenous descent, and communities there follow the logics of ownership and community of the north—to the chagrin of their neighbors, who frequently complain about the noise from fiestas. Patty explained that her main reasons for moving to this area were to give her daughters access to better schools and for her to be treated better at work. "It's funny, talking to the owner here. Because we're down here, she has to treat me well, but if we were up there, she knows that I know that she'd be yelling at me." Her comment puts pay to some of the romantic notions of Aymara economic communities that erase hierarchy and exploitation, and also indicates the power of place—captured in the dynamic between identity, expectations, perceptions, and reflections—to shape the way people relate to each other.

Real Estate and the Built Environment

The image of Comadre Remedios offering to buy the MegaCenter portrays a phenomenon that was being widely discussed at the time: wealthy women *de pollera* were indeed coming down to the Zona Sur and offering to buy property with suitcases of cash. Local real estate agents were happy to confirm the trend: "Everyone has a story—it happened to me the other day. A *chola* wanted to pay in cash, but the seller refused unless it was a bank transfer, and the sale fell through" (interview, real estate agent, La Paz, August 2015). While sensationalist headlines have described this pattern as an "unstoppable Aymara invasion" or even as "colonization" (Juárez 2014; Mamani Ramírez 2015), those involved in the sales seemed quite sanguine in describing exchanges that had clearly become everyday: "I'm always looking out for them—they're the ones who are most likely to buy" (interview, real estate agent, Obrajes, August 2015). While there is some history of mobility between the areas, the real estate purchases of the Aymara bourgeoisie represent a distinct change in patterns of wealth and mobility: "Before, we generally just used to deal with people from this same area; now people from El Alto have more means and they want to move here for the climate, the schools. . . . A key difference, though, is that the whole family is involved, and it's often the woman doing the negotiating" (interview, real estate agent, Calocoto, Zona Sur, August 2015). One resident of the Zona Sur had a similar story: "I heard a knock at the door and a couple were there asking me if I wanted to sell my house. They offered $400,000 U.S., and when I said no they immediately increased it, but I said no thank you it's not for sale and that was it" (interview, resident, San Miguel, August 2015). According to another resident, "My neighbor sold hers to a woman whose son had just got into university here and wanted a place with a pool so he could fit in and make friends" (personal communication, resident, London and Calocoto, Zona Sur, June 2015). As a consequence of this trend, which started around 2010, real estate prices in the area shot up (Suárez 2018).

The neighborhood of San Miguel in the Zona Sur has changed dramatically as a result of these developments in the real estate market, making it "a laboratory from which the dimensions of change which have been experienced in La Paz can be analyzed" (Suárez 2018, 8). The "Urbanización San Miguel," as it was originally called, was initiated in 1966 by USAID as part of President John F. Kennedy's Alliance for Progress, which financed a project to build over four hundred new "American-style" homes on an old racetrack south of the center of La Paz. According to press coverage at the time, the houses would be "modern and have all basic utilities," and the development would also include the construction of a "civic center, supermarkets, parks, and green areas" (*Presencia* 1966, 6). The original one- and two-story bungalows in the area followed streets that wound around tracing the original path of the racetrack, and mortgages were offered via Mutual La Primera to middle-class professionals from La Paz, with priority given to workers from USAID, W. R. Grace, and members of the Jockey Club that owned the land. The area is hence a prime example of the U.S.-led development and modernization projects of the late twentieth century, and it was pivotal in the development of a property-owning middle class.

By the turn of the century, San Miguel had begun to shift from being primarily residential to a commercial zone particularly known for its restaurants, clubs, and cafés. Many of the original bungalows have been converted and are fronted with colorful and imaginative facades. *Paceña* franchise Alexander Coffee started there in 1996 and has become a chain of restaurants that is definitive of middle- and upper-class La Paz, with branches throughout the Zona Sur and the center. As commerce developed, the area attracted business from elsewhere in the city, which contextualizes the current movement of people characterized in the eponymous film. A feature of the area is the first Andy's supermarket, which started as a small stall in the 1980s and developed into a family business with branches throughout the Zona Sur. The owners, from Uyustus, described how they started their stall there and, by "offering good prices and customer service," developed their business (interview, business owner, San Miguel, May 2017). The owner, perhaps despite origins in the popular markets in the north, advocates a market form of empowerment and now gives courses in El Alto on business and commerce. He has trade links with China and has opened a range of stores across the city selling imported cosmetics at prices attractive to the growing middle class. Similarly, an internet café on Calle 21 in San Miguel was opened by a business family from Calle los Andes in the north of the city. The owner describes the decision to open a branch there in purely business terms—it was where the market was: "We moved the business down here for the market—but my home, family, and surroundings are all in Calle los Andes" (interview, business owner, San Miguel, August 2015).

These formal, commercial entrepreneurs from the north of the city who opened businesses in the south can be distinguished, however, from the popular class that constitutes the current migration to the area, which now stands out for construction more than commerce. A property developer from San Miguel explained the distinction:

> Now it's about property values—those tiny houses are being sold for far more than they are really worth. . . . What's really worth $800 U.S. per square meter constructed is now going for $1,000. The prices are stupidly high, and not really going for their true

value—nothing to do with the actual prices of construction. . . . I
have a friend who is selling at $1,300 U.S. per square meter, which
is ridiculous—there's no way the construction costs are more than
$650 U.S. (Interview, property developer, May 2017)

The bungalows were being bought for the plots of land. Many were de-
molished to build eight- to ten-story tower blocks of flats and offices to
rent out, and some houses were used as storage units for nearby commercial outlets. The tower blocks in San Miguel are notable for their
functional, utilitarian appearance as compared both to the hominess
of the bungalows of San Miguel and the outlandishness of the *cholets*
in the north of the city. The area is covered in construction, with every
street being worked on in multiple plots. A common complaint is that
the towers block the light, which in La Paz also means warmth. Those
who are seeking to leave San Miguel frequently cite the lack of warmth
as a reason for selling and moving farther down the valley—often to Rio
Abajo. There are claims that this constitutes a displacement comparable
to gentrification, but these families generally have other properties, and
many argue that this pattern of mobility is more akin to "white flight"
as Aymara families move in.

Contrary to the headlines, residents of the Zona Sur provided a range
of reactions when I asked them about the phenomenon of people from
the Aymara bourgeoisie making purchases. "Oh please—get one to come
and buy mine" was a frequent response. Two people even offered me a
commission if I could connect them to willing buyers. One retired couple explained to me that they had four children and needed to sell their
property to be able to fairly split the inheritance. Another, formerly a
judge, showed me around the mansion she and her husband had recently
built but which they could no longer afford, as she had lost her job due
to the reforms of the judiciary. They did, however, have other properties
elsewhere. The impression was that the houses being purchased in the
Zona Sur by the new bourgeoisie would be used for socializing rather
than as primary residences: "The property I'm selling now is precisely
oriented to that group—it's got seven bedrooms, it's an event place—
Jacuzzi, swimming pool, and so forth—you could easily take care of
three hundred people there—easily" (interview, property developer,
San Miguel, May 2017).

There is much speculation about what these changes will mean for

Bolivian society, and whether there will eventually be a convergence of culture as well as wealth, especially given the generational aspects of this transformation; the children of wealthy Aymara people are being educated in the best universities, often in the United States, Chile, or Mexico. A recurrent theme is whether there will ever be a *cholet* in the Zona Sur, a question that tends to be met with mocking disbelief, as if it would be impossibly incongruous. "That's weird, though, because the chalets on top of the *cholets* come from there," my research assistant from Kollasuyo explained. "They'd see precisely those little European-style houses and think 'That's what I want,' so that's the house they have on top" (May 2019). However, when I asked one of Freddy Mamani's colleagues what he thought of the possibility of *cholets* in the Zona Sur, he surprised me with the answer: "We've already built one—but it is only a *cholet* on the inside. The client obviously didn't want it looking like that on the outside in that area—*¿que va a pensar la gente?* [what would people think?]" (El Alto, May 2019). Despite the changes in wealth, the sense of not belonging, or of being made to feel ashamed of one's tastes, still demarcates these territories.

Conclusion

A range of financial and economic processes can be read in the meme of Comadre Remedios offering to buy the shopping mall. The exclusionary dynamics that mark the incident at the MegaCenter as a transgression remain, but space has been opened up to allow the relationships between finance, identity, markets, and property to be reconfigured. The overwhelming sense of the image is one of triumph: a bastion of global commerce and middle-class consumption is being purchased by a *chola* and in cash. The *chola* is reclaiming her image as a symbol of Bolivian identity and indigeneity, but not as the exoticized icon of tourist brochures or craft shops, or as the victim of poverty associated with development and NGOs, but as a powerful economic agent. The cash represents the popular economy and community as well as commercial success, but beyond the realms of the "formal." Comadre Remedios's suitcase of cash marks her as coming from a different economic world. She hence still has a subaltern status, and despite her wealth she is still rebelling against and resisting the dominance of global capital. What is not immediately read in the meme, however, is the potential for exploitation within the community, and the multiplicity of economies that lie between the polemic divide between neoliberalism and the *ayllu*. The *apthapi* protest illustrates that the conflicts at the MegaCenter and in other market spaces in La Paz are underpinned by fundamentally different economies. The false neutrality of the international shopping mall naturalizes a commercial, for-profit view of modernity, which is disrupted both economically and culturally by people bringing and sharing their own food. While the protest itself played on the dichotomous analysis of conflict between Western individualism and indigenous cooperation and reciprocity, other examples of place-making in the city represent a more complex view of indigenous modernity and changes in the cultural and economic map of La Paz. The Centro de Moda explicitly blends these visions of a market within a commercial framework, but the dynamics encountered by Patty in the Arcangel mall demonstrate how the hierarchies of community economies are also being transformed. Patty's experience is a reminder that exploitation is also a feature of power in popular markets, something that can be overlooked by commentaries and policies that focus entirely on overturning the iniquities of neoliberalism.

Over the period of Morales's administration, the frame of reference for taste and propriety changed dramatically, and with it the sense of who belongs where and related notions of propriety. The controversies around construction—the *cholets,* the Casa del Pueblo, and the high rises of San Miguel—were enabled not only by the booming economy but also by the profound changes in cultural power that the social movements foregrounding decolonization and the MAS emphasis on plurality had brought about. However, it would also be simplistic to conclude that this is a reversal of colonial oppression and exclusion, as the sense of triumph in the Comadre Remedios meme may imply. The *cholets* do indeed demonstrate a revindication of indigenous aesthetics in Freddy Mamani's Tiwanaku-inspired designs and the confidence of a new rich asserting their heritage in a postcolonial setting dominated by European and occidental-inspired tastes. However, they also show growing ties with China, influence from pop culture, the growing strength of the fiestas industry, and the continued tendency to invest in functional, income-generating properties. The design of the Casa del Pueblo is a vision of an indigenous future and modernity. Although its location manifests a destructive approach toward the regimes of the past, that is not reflected in the wide variety of complex opinion on the new building.

The boom in construction can be explained easily in orthodox economic terms: liquidity has increased, but capital has not found any productive outlets that give it a better return than land or real estate. The patterns of mobility have followed investment and business incentives in commercial areas of El Alto and the Zona Sur, along with other tangible, comparative factors such as climate and the quality of schools. It is striking that investment in land and real estate increased during the MAS administration, whose policies were explicitly designed to bolster production and discourage speculation. Although there was a consensus that greater regulation was needed after the neoliberal period, commentators supportive of the MAS agenda raised concerns about the burden that high levels of regulation placed on productive businesses, including those in areas of high MAS support. The boom in construction and real estate, however, would not have produced the transgressions, controversies, and scandals it did if the changes that were produced were not fundamentally about identity and different culturally demarcated economic worlds.

Conclusion

Processes of Plurality

What if the formulation and operationalization of pluri-economy had taken as its starting point the economic strategies, values, and identities of women earning a living in the popular markets of La Paz and El Alto? Motley diversity would have gone beyond the different historical economic periods referred to in René Zavaleta's theories and taken into account the gendered, culturally situated meanings behind feudal, capitalist, and community exchanges. The logic underpinning identity would have been generated from cooperation and interdependence rather than conflict. Identity categories would have permitted the contradictions and complexities that women *de pollera, cholas, comerciantes,* and market laborers inhabit as they earn a living. These philosophical changes require institutions that permit constant reflection on the identities being generated by the processes and policies being implemented. As Julieta Paredes, Silvia Rivera Cusicanqui, and María Galindo argued from the outset, the new decolonized, post-neoliberal Bolivia would require a constant reflexive process of deconstruction at the heart of power to avoid reiterating the exclusions of a colonial and masculinist hegemony.

In its designation as a political *instrument* of social movements, the MAS was itself an example of the importance of prioritizing process, rather than impact or goals, to defining the kind of power structures a political entity represents. The participatory structures and rotating, cooperative leadership of the rural syndicates and social movements at the heart of the MAS as a "political instrument of social movements" represented a horizontal form of power rather than the vertical, colonial, and masculinist authority of traditional political parties and state institutions. The original vision of the Constitution was built on this model, but the political compromises involved in discussions and the initial need for a strong state to protect Bolivia from neoliberal globalization resulted in Morales leading a highly centralized government. Nevertheless, MAS tactics, negotiations, and the identities they performatively generated indicated as much about the map of the pluri-economy that developed over their period of rule as the declarative content of the institutions and policies that were intended to support different economic worlds. Morales and García Linera's leadership reflected the "tacking back and forth" between different identities—authentic rural indigeneity and popular urban markets—that is associated with *cholaje* (Postero 2010), and so itself belied the essentialist identities apparent in the Constitution. In this context it is perhaps therefore not surprising that despite the limited mention of urban indigeneity and femininity in official discourse, the figure who was most associated with wealth over the thirteen years in question became the urban indigenous *chola*.

The discussions in the Grupo Comuna as well as subsequent MAS electoral strategy and policies illustrate what Arturo Escobar, responding to comments from feminist critics, described as a lack of recognition of the "race and gender position of [MCD] theorising" (Escobar 2007b, 192). As Elina Vuola points out in her comments on the MCD school, "one should always be willing to look at one's own truth claims and positions with the critical eyes of others" (2003, 112). The present analysis has portrayed economic plurality from the point of view of its "others"— the *campesina de pollera* traveling back and forth to peri-urban markets to sell her produce on a weekly basis, the wealthy *chola,* and the workers and *comerciantes* of popular markets—who in different ways represent feminine economic subjects who do not fit into the landscape of the categories of Bolivia's imagined economic plurality. The way their livelihood activities defy the binaries that underpin both orthodox and much critical thinking about the economy—divisions between production and reproduction, nature and culture, risk and care, rural and urban, competition and cooperation—resonates with feminist work on economic diversity. However, indigenous feminist scholarship in Bolivia highlights the importance of a decolonial lens that uncovers the cultural, economic, and epistemic damage done by the humiliation of colonialism which scholarship on economic diversity can underestimate. Their work foregrounds that gender itself is a colonial category, that assumptions around indigeneity can disguise agency, and that embracing multiple culturally situated ways of knowing is key to reimagining the economy. The present study has attempted to address this gap, but the world of experiences of popular markets and the communities and fiestas that drive them are embodied meanings and senses (Rivera

Cusicanqui 2020). Text alone cannot represent the myriad plurality of engagements and encounters that could further rewrite economic scripts by going beyond logocentric confines.

Reflecting on the gendered and racialized positioning of one's own theorizing and thinking demands a reconsideration of the tropes that are implicitly pictured in ideas of value and exchange. Indigeneity and femininity are categories of absence; their defining feature is lack. The act of taking the feminine, the indigenous, or the rural as a starting point is hence inherently destabilizing to conceptual binaries and the logics of identity that underpin them. The indigenous social movements that were the motor behind political change in the early 2000s, however, were driven by claims for autonomy precisely because their worldview had been epistemically alienated by colonialism. The actions and representations of the social movements that had inspired the GC and which were the political power behind the MAS offered discourses of femininity that were far more penetrating than those that would later appear in official texts: gender conceptualized as activity rather than body, and the logic of complementary rather than contradictory difference. While the power and agency of Bartolina Sisa and the iconic status of the *chola* were prominent politically, the *ministras de pollera* faced gendered barriers, exclusions, and representations that forced several high-profile women to surrender their posts. The concerns of violence against women that had so much been a part of Antonia Rodríguez Medrano's rise to power were folded into concerns about decolonization and anti-neoliberalism in government in a way that did not give them full voice. Similarly, the treatment of Nemesia Achacollo, the only minister to resign following the Fondo Indígena scandal, revealed assumptions of a feminine villainy associated more with Eve than with Bartolina Sisa. The discursive tools were present to politicians at the time to reimagine feminine power at the state level, but the political will was not.

Creative Tensions and Disrupting Binaries

The fluidity of indigenous feminine economic strategies disrupts the dichotomous concepts that were implicit in the "creative tensions" frequently cited by García Linera in his publications as vice president. The tensions referred to were principally between Marxist and Indianist thinkers, and they were focused on the dilemma of creating a state powerful enough to protect and redistribute wealth in the context of neoliberal globalization while also respecting autonomy. The other fundamental opposition was between an economistic, class-based analysis of exclusion, on the one hand, and an Indianist analysis that foregrounded identity and, crucially, an epistemology that disrupted the abstractions which falsely separated economy from culture, on the other. Despite the Gramscian framing of these tensions, the economy was still held to be determinant in framing policy, as Zavaleta's categorizations of "motley" diversity illustrate. Indigenous commentators were promptly critical that the importance of autonomy and consultation were falling away from the MAS agenda. However, both Marxist and Indianist thought tended to undervalue feminine labor and the gendered power relations involved in maintaining community identity. The formulation of the creative tensions identified implicitly held on to gendered binaries between local/national, gift/commerce, community/state, modern/traditional, use/exchange, and formal/informal. Foregrounding the messy reality of gendered everyday life itself presents a rethinking of economic categories that would question the assumptions that constituted those tensions.

The notion of scale—the subject of much feminist and postcolonial critique—was at the basis of the pivotal debates between Marxism and Indianism and of the conundrums the MAS would face in government. Collapsing the power-laden distinction between the particular and the universal was a crucial element in pluriversal and feminist thinking, as the sublation of the particular into the universal imposes a modernizing logic. The universal is falsely neutral, and processes that mirror dialectical logic establish a political hierarchy between femininity/indigeneity/rurality and masculinity/whiteness/urbanity. The strategy of "community plus hegemony" aimed to resolve this hierarchy by bringing community dynamics to the scale of the state, the nation, and the public. The notion of a plural nation, the solidarity exchanges between members of ALBA, the original aim to give social movements a formal role in government in the Constitution, and the rotating governance structures adopted in the management of funds and ministries are all examples of bringing community dynamics to government and thus disrupting scale.

For conceptual and political reasons, these attempts to collapse scale did not prevent power from becoming highly concentrated in the state, and social movements could not provide sufficient counterweight to executive power once opposition from the Media Luna had been quelled and the wealth from nationalized industries had exceeded expectations. The horizontal power characterized as "walking while asking questions" did not materialize, and the power centralized in the executive and the persona of Morales would appear to confirm Mujeres Creando's fear that the MAS government would replicate the same "phallic, patriarchal posture" as the neoliberal colonials it had overthrown (Galindo 2006a). Exchanges within ALBA represented a solidarity between powerful men rather than the bonds of care and moral economy of reciprocity that characterize community exchanges. The gendered values underpinning the scaled hierarchy between community/state and local/national were hence replicated in the attempts to create "community plus hegemony."

Gendered constructions of nation and production continued to frame economic strategy, despite their masculinist and modernizing roots. The idea of the plurination was pitted against a strong state from the outset, and it soon became clear, most notably in the TIPNIS dispute, that a state based on extractivism would take priority. Contrary to the impression given in international coverage, the government's extractivist approach did have support within Bolivia because of the sovereignty it represented after years of surrendering the country's resources to global corporations. However, the focus on Bolivia's control over natural resources recreated a value system that would attenuate the power of indigenous autonomies and also restrict the potential to reimagine value in the way promised by the idea of pluri-economy. Along with the phallic ideas of control over nature that are inherent in extractivist models, an economy based on resource extraction adheres to a modernist idea of production. The values generated by defining production as manufacturing something "new" from nature create a gendered and racialized sense of progress and achievement that naturalizes the labor involved in recreative or reproductive activities and, in practical terms, undervalues sectors of the economy dominated by women. This was evident in the list of "productive" activities identified as meriting preferential support from the banks in the 2013 Financial Services Law. However, the economy at the time was awash with examples of ways to collapse these concepts of production and nation that replicated masculinist, colonial ideas of value: for example, the market traders involved in *contrabando hormiga* who were redrawing borders and reinventing quintessentially "Bolivian" markets in the streets of Buenos Aires, and the traders in used clothes who were unpicking designer jumpers to reknit into shawls or ponchos.

The question of scale and the hierarchical distinction between nation and community is related to the distinction between gift and commercial exchange. The gift is inherently particular, whereas commercial exchange and competition can frame neutral rules of the game in liberal constructions of the public. This divide between gift and commerce is definitive of the gendered exclusion created as capital extends and reciprocal labor, which is crucial to economic activity, is rendered unremunerated while profits accrue to market activities. The *bonos* implemented early in Morales's administration were intended to compensate for the gendered invisibility of reproductive labor, but they were based on, and therefore replicated, the gendered construction of reproductive labor. Although the *bonos* were welcome after decades of neoliberalism had increased the burden of reproductive and community labor and exacerbated its invisibility, given that the *chola* is famed for seamlessly negotiating community and competitive markets there could have been a more profound reappraisal of this divide and the values behind which labor is seen as valuable and which is seen as needing support.

The economic strategies of the *chola* reconfigure notions of scale in relation to community reproduction and solidarity rather than commerce and production. There is an implied progression, even in heterodox economics, from gift to profit exchange as capital extends. The conceptual distinction between gift and profit exchange is a useful heuristic device that allows the trajectory from community to capital exchange and its transformative—and potentially corrosive—effects on social relations to be traced. However, a decentered exploration of the values and exchanges that compose the economic strategies of the women *de pollera* who work in rural production while also negotiating the markets of La Paz entwines community and for-profit exchanges. The geography of the divide between community and commercial exchange is expressed in terms of rurality versus urbanity. However, for those traveling back and forth between different rural communities and urban markets on a regular basis, it is a continuum. Households stretch across these divides, as do the community relations that constitute the infrastructure, including transport, that makes these livelihoods possible. The imbricated identity categories rural/indigenous and urban/white which are "produced" by the distinction between community rural production and urban commerce are also part of the performative production of those spatial divides and are generated relationally rather than essentially. They hence can only be represented in process and discussion, rather than static categories. Considering gift and profit as entwined strategies collapses the spatial division between rural and urban that is economically characterized by gift and profit exchange, respectively. It is then conceptually possible to recognize the cooperation that always underpins urban markets as well as the competition that is never far away from rural communities.

The emergence of indigenous fashions and architecture as wealth accumulated in popular sectors of the economy challenged modernizing notions of time. There is a colonial arrogance involved in the Western, urban sense of entitlement to define contemporaneity and therefore construct the "indigenous" as inherently traditional. As an Aymara middle class emerged, however, that arrogance was less challenged than it was ignored, as the culture of fiestas and accompanying fashions in clothes, dance, and music were celebrated on an international stage—including the modern art heartlands of Paris and New York. While Aymara fashion designers and architects offer high-profile—and potentially exoticizable—redefinitions of modernity and contemporaneity, other economic strategies also demonstrated the importance of questioning ideas of time and progress in deconstructing biased notions of value. Assumptions about progress and production that imply placing order on 'natural' chaos also render community, care, and household labor repetitive and natural rather than progressive or technical. Similarly pitting the sale of used clothes against textile-manufacturing industries imposes an idea of which transformations count as productive.

The conceptual space in which these alternatives could be heard was limited by the tacit imaginaries of femininity and indigeneity residing in the foundations of the theories and policies of pluri-economy. Feminist and indigenous scholars commenting on the work of the GC, and later on Morales and García Linera's leadership, emphasized the need for these tacit imaginaries to be explicitly brought to the surface, recognized as culturally specific to the contemporary historical conjuncture, and discussed (Paredes 2010; Regalsky 2010). Despite the complexity of the GC's theorizing and the messiness of the politics of the MAS era, specific feminine tropes emerged as ordering principles focused on maternalism, essentialist visions of community and cultural reproduction, and the betrayal associated with the indigenous woman as intermediary. These ideal types came through despite the evidence of feminine economic power and the warrior iconography of Bartolina Sisa that was so prominent in the activism and work of women *de pollera* in the countryside, the wealthy *chola*, and those working in popular markets. Although the hard work of the indigenous woman was lauded, the dominance of maternalist community ideals and masculinist notions of national production undermined its economic value. Despite the prominent critique of scale, it seemed an overriding notion that the local was coded feminine when it came to economic production, despite the transnational strategies of even modest market *comerciantes*.

The "in-betweenness" that characterizes the *chola* demonstrates the inadequacies of binary categories of identity that frame even critical understandings of economy, production, and nation. The way colonialism created the category of "the indigenous" and erased difference within it can render the indigenous woman as a betrayer of her people in certain imaginaries of Latin American nationhood—a characterization reflected in the work of Fausto Reinaga. The exoticized status of the *chola* as an icon of the nation can recreate this negative sense of the indigenous woman as an acceptable face of indigeneity and as a medium via which to gain power over the colonized. However, in the case of Bolivia under Morales, the political processes behind the MAS as the instrument of social movements built on the power women had in community activism. The icon of Bartolina Sisa, historical descriptions of whom emphasize that her role trading in markets was essential to her development of a power base, foregrounds the combative strengths of indigenous women in their negotiations and their ability to build networks beyond their own communities. The historical figure of Bartolina Sisa, as described by the eponymous social movement, breaks through accepted tropes of femininity—most notably Eve—that are also implicit in economic theory. Breaking with culturally situated imaginaries of permitted indigenous femininities is a precondition for questioning the values that are implicit in the conceptual building blocks behind notions of economy, and therefore in constructing an economy in which all economies fit.

Cash, Clothes, and Construction

The policies to implement a pluri-economy were mainly based on the post-neoliberal, heterodox strand of MAS thinking, but the symbolic decolonization of values that accompanied formal policy also had powerful economic effects. Financial policies to support an inclusive, post-neoliberal economy redirected finance to the productive sector, expanded credit, and insulated Bolivia from the iniquities of transnational capital. Banks were regulated to fulfill a social mission that took priority over the orthodox bottom lines of profit and institutional sustainability. For orthodox commentators MAS policymakers were committing the populist sins associated with resource-rich countries that lacked systems of transparency and accountability and did not go beyond the import substitution industrialization (ISI) policies of the 1960s. The formal policies on finance, however, did not represent a particularly radical approach. For the left they were far too soft, and for indigenous and feminist commentators they were reliant on extractivism. They also had a range of unintended effects. Attempts to divert finance to productive sectors were undercut by the overvalued boliviano, which had in effect been pegged to the dollar. This enabled import commerce—and in particular contraband being sold in peri-urban markets—to flourish. The threat that contraband posed to formal business was compounded by what was widely perceived to be an inconsistent approach to enforcement of tax regulations, despite what was overall a structuralist approach that aimed to bring popular markets into the tax base and formal governance.

Bolivianización was the most dramatic achievement of MAS financial policy. The sharp decline in the use of the U.S. currency returned the sovereignty, both symbolically and politically, that had been lost to the dollar in the structural adjustment of the 1980s. *Bolivianización* had been encouraged by the strength of the boliviano, which also had both economic and symbolic effects. Economically, the strong boliviano encouraged import commerce over national production. While this did not align with the formal national production strategy, it did bolster peri-urban markets based on popular community dynamics. This was seen politically as a correction to the neoliberal system that had favored white, criollo traditional elites. There remained great concerns from commentators internationally and within Bolivia about the dominance of imports in the economy and the imminent risk of devaluation, but the powers involved in the MAS had also created a political landscape that enabled finance to be channeled by community dynamics and different ideas of value and scale.

Although the heterodox approach to production and finance was intended to be a corrective to the commercial, urban, and therefore racial biases implicit in structural adjustment and economic orthodoxy, the MAS's formal financial policies included multiple gender biases. The definition of production favored male-dominated activities, and the scale of the credits given overlooked the female-dominated micro-sector. However, the particular configuration of the symbolic and economic effects of *bolivianización*, the political power of peri-urban markets, and the confidence—in both an economic and a cultural sense—that came with decolonization resulted in the symbol of wealth over this period of time being the *chola paceña* with her suitcase of cash. The character of the wealthy *chola* and the financial subjectivity she represents sheds light on the values and exchanges that need to channel financial flows in order to create a diverse economy. The financial subject of the *chola* can be read as combining gift and for-profit exchange, challenging assumptions about gender, indigeneity, and scale, and offering a script of modernity that does not start from constructions of tradition and time that render the modern indigenous woman a contradiction in terms. It was not the conceptual and theoretical breakthroughs that achieved this, nor explicit attempts to encourage economic plurality, but rather the political need to recognize the strength of the popular markets—a quintessential feminine space—which had for centuries been a locus of power for women in the Andes.

The flourishing of the *moda de la chola paceña* succeeded in quieting "the cacophony of modernity" (Jansen 2020, 831) that had erased the possibility of an indigenous contemporaneity. The commercialization of luxury *polleras* for women whose wealth had been generated in markets predicated on community exchanges and fiestas disrupted the arrow of time implied in the division between gift and profit exchange and is a spectacular demonstration of how the power to define what is "now" can be troubled. Similarly, the flows of used clothes from the retail outlets of the global North reversed the script of "third-world pro-

ducer" and "Western consumer" as high-street-branded items were repurposed and redesigned in the popular markets of El Alto. The trades
both in *pollera* fashions and used clothes demonstrate the messiness of
economic exchanges that defy the division between community gift exchange and commerce. The feminine economic subject represented by
those involved in Aymara high fashions or the *cholas* selling secondhand
designer brands demonstrate the simultaneity of scales as global goods
and materials are repurposed to recreate local traditions. The women
involved in these trades defy the colonial value system that depreciates
the added value of their labor by equating it with natural resources and
extraction or by erasing it from the sphere of production. The national
identity they are recreating stems from the trading networks for which
Aymara markets are famed.

The case for bolstering Bolivian production against the exponential
increases in global textiles and clothing production from Asia was compelling. However, the examples of how Punto Blanco and Enatex collapsed after state intervention could support the neoliberal position
that firms cannot be shackled by regulation and need the flexibility to
react to global markets. Even social commentators sympathetic to the
MAS voiced their concerns that the regulations around wages, bonuses,
and worker takeovers rendered the development of manufacturing and
productive enterprises challenging. This was echoed by concerns from
social movements that the state was becoming too powerful and centralized. Nevertheless, the decimation of the industries over the 1980s and
1990s underscored the need for an institutional landscape that could
protect workers. There was again a dissonance between the economic
vision underpinning MAS policy, its political pragmatism, and the processes that were instituted, regardless of the stated aim of particular
policies. Luis Arce, as minister of economy and public finance throughout the MAS administration, had a clear, heterodox modernizing view
of the actions the state could take. His vision was to bolster the internal
market and regulate firms to consider more than the financial bottom
line, but the political and constitutional checks and balances to prevent
this heterodox vision from tipping into populism were insufficient.
As a result, the overvalued boliviano and prohibitive wage costs led to
commerce flourishing in popular markets. Although this was not the
intended aim, the fact that the people working in popular markets were

of indigenous, rural descent radically changed racialized socioeconomic structures of Bolivia and enabled a decolonization of aesthetics and taste.

The cities of La Paz and El Alto grew exponentially and controversially over the period of MAS rule and were the locus of seismic political and social upheavals. Architecture changed dramatically, both due to state-led decisions about infrastructure and planning and to changes in consumer power and tastes. The Casa del Pueblo is a polemic and striking example of the MAS vision of a decolonized indigenous futurity. The most controversial aspect of this edifice was the destruction of the Republican buildings it replaced in the center of La Paz. This was in itself analogous to the MAS approach of active decolonization, which was reflected in the essentializing language of the 2009 Constitution. The Casa del Pueblo was inspired by the architecture that was already disrupting urban aesthetics and assumptions about indigeneity and modernity. The *cholets* had become a symbol of Aymara modernity and aesthetics, as the new middle class continued the Aymara tradition of investing in land and functional properties but with a renewed aesthetic confidence. The success of architect Freddy Mamani became a symbol of the country's decolonization, as his experience and cultural knowledge trumped the need for formal qualifications from schools that historically had not recognized his skills. However, these dramatic urban changes were also the result of financial incentives that discouraged production and, contrary to intention, incentivized land and real estate speculation.

Mobility around the cities was actively changed by the infrastructure projects led by state and municipal governments. The highest-profile example was the Teleférico, which connected El Alto and the *laderas* to the north with the Zona Sur. Mass-transit systems around the world aim to include excluded neighborhoods, which was indeed the goal and function of transport infrastructures in La Paz and El Alto. The mobility this transport enabled also highlighted the cultural barriers that persisted, as the controversies at the MegaCenter demonstrated—the cultural assumptions about how to sit, eat, and use public toilets were as much barriers as the prior lack of transport connections and affordability. The incident at the MegaCenter, which went viral on social media, highlights the importance of confidence and feeling reflected in one's environment to mobility and belonging. The need to feel recognized justifies the centrality of changing symbolism and language to MAS decolonization policies and recalls Reinaga's emphasis on shame and self-hatred as the primary legacy of colonialism. Questions of shame and taste and a resistance to the cultural map they dictate are shown in the *cholet* in the Zona Sur, which Freddy Mamani's colleague described as "only a *cholet* on the inside."

The controversy at the MegaCenter and the reaction to it demarcate two radically different, culturally situated markets. The *apthapi*—the traditional potluck party set up outside the MegaCenter in protest against the racist comments on social media—was a demonstration of the reciprocity and communal traditions of Aymara market econo-mies, in stark contrast to the global consumer capitalism exemplified by the mall. The *apthapi* demonstrated the vision of post-neoliberal, pluri-cultural markets at the heart of MAS strategy—grounded in community structures that valued reciprocity and solidarity. However, the many markets around La Paz and El Alto demonstrated the complexities of the relationship between gift and consumer exchange that this division evoked. The "mall of El Alto"—the Sixteenth July market fair—dwarfs the MegaCenter in terms of space and the variety of goods that can be consumed. The flow of used designer clothes from the Sixteenth July to the boutiques of the Zona Sur; the contraband in white goods of the Calle Uyustus, which is known throughout both cities as the best place for a tax-free bargain; and the mall in San Miguel owned by a wealthy Aymara family, which explicitly attempts to combine the feel of a street market within a Western consumer setting—all of these demonstrate the complexity of the culturally situated dynamics of competition, coop-eration, reciprocity, and consumption. The maintenance of the polemic between individual consumerism and reciprocal community solidarity at the political level implicitly romanticized feminine community labor, as Galindo and Paredes warned from the outset of the MAS adminis-tration. The reality of markets in La Paz paints a far more penetrating picture of the ambivalences of community and market dynamics and of the feminine subjects that navigate and create them.

Given that the MAS was inspired mostly by rural social move-ments, and that rurality was tightly associated with indigeneity in the Constitution, it is surprising that some of the most prominent devel-opments over this period of time were in urban areas. It was pointed out during negotiations around the Constitution that a conspicuous lacuna in the discourses and texts that started the MAS project was urban indigeneity. This gap was identified from the outset by Rivera Cusicanqui, among others, when it was already evident that the poverty of the cities was worse than in the countryside and that the needs of the urban poor were being overlooked. While the text and theories disregarded urban indigeneity, urban popular markets were a central pillar of support in the water and gas wars and of the MAS. The political and economic forces of global trade, contraband, and an inflated currency combined with the articulations made by the MAS with powerful urban social movements, unions, and market associations, as well as the cultural and symbolic changes that came with decolonization, all came together to potentiate popular urban economies. The feminine economic subject of the *chola*, whose history encompasses an active role in trading and extending cooperative networks, the power of Bartolina Sisa, and the gender dynamics of the Andean household, defies the maternalist construction of the women-targeted welfare programs and the assumptions of community and tradition that accompany feminine indigeneity.

After Evo

The elections of November 2019, which ended Morales's time in power, were surrounded by controversy in Bolivia before they were held. There was great concern that Morales was standing for his fourth term, despite the 2009 Constitution limiting a president to two terms in office. The argument for Morales standing for a third term in 2014 had been that he was granted two terms by the Constitution of 2009 and that this therefore would be only his second term since that constitution had been in effect. Bolivia's Constitutional Court authorized Morales and García Linera to stand for a third term, which for some confirmed fears that the judiciary had been politicized (Cortez Salinas 2014). When Morales's ability to stand again was confirmed it was clear that he would probably win again, due, not least, to a lack of a viable opposition candidate. However, concern was expressed from this point on that Morales had fallen into the trap of the charismatic leader, buoyed by foreign reserves, who was not investing sufficient time in enabling a successor (Mayorga 2017).

By 2019, numerous controversies had led to people losing faith in the overcentralized state and to increasing concerns about authoritarianism, reflecting the initial points raised by feminist and indigenous women's organizations that the MAS and the state would become too powerful and centralized. To stand for a fourth term, Morales had to hold a referendum to overturn the Constitution. This was held in 2016, and the ruling party lost the vote by a margin of 2.6 percent (Achtenberg 2016a). Defeat in the referendum was not entirely unexpected, as results of the 2015 mayoral elections had not been strong for the MAS and opinion polls indicated dissatisfaction (Anria 2016). The result of this referendum, however, was reversed by the Constitutional Court in 2017, on the basis of the argument that term limits violated candidates' human rights (Reuters 2017). This ruling granted Morales the ability to stand again. This caused outrage, and was also surrounded by allegations that potential successors had been actively discouraged from standing. The 2016 referendum had been held on February 21, and a movement that campaigned for the referendum result to be respected took on the moniker 21F in reference to that date. There was a frequently heard proclamation of "and I even voted him in" among the middle class who had become particularly disaffected with the abuses of power of both Morales and García Linera. There was a general concern, however, that the middle classes, who would be crucial to election victory, were underestimating the threat of the return of an overtly racist right. Particularly among the student population there was a recognition that standing for a fourth term was constitutionally incorrect but that they would vote for Morales to prevent a return to far-right, elitist politics.

The 2019 election night itself gained notoriety internationally as a "coup," but the alacrity with which international commentators on the left seized on these proclamations did not reflect the complexity of the debate in Bolivia. Some of the most vocal and long-standing critics of the MAS and of Morales and García Linera's leadership had been feminist and indigenous women's and environmental organizations. The situation rapidly descended, however, into a polarized conflict with those supporting Morales crying "coup" and those against crying "fraud," regardless of evidence and analysis that would emerge presenting a more complex picture (Wolff 2020). This polarization consolidated along familiar classed and racialized lines as anti-Morales demonstrations mustered in southern areas of La Paz and pro-Morales demonstrations in the north. The motivation of many who supported Morales despite acknowledging the tendency to autocracy since 2013 was that the far right would be even worse and would rapidly reverse the gains in terms of equality and standards of living that had been achieved under MAS rule. When I spoke to people at this time whom I had worked with in La Paz, El Alto, Luribay, and Cochabamba, I was struck by how much they emphasized that they just did not want conflict. "They're making me go—if I stay behind they'll fine me, but I really do not want to get shot," texted Noelia from Luribay. The cries of coup and fraud may have been effective political strategies, and they did mirror the counterhegemonic strategies that the MAS had used to gain power. However, these identities instantiate an inherently conflictive logic and, as has become clear around the world in recent years, are not necessarily compatible with the responsibilities of governing, and are themselves preconditions for conflict.

The actions of the interim government of Jeanine Áñez—a senator from the right-wing alliance Plan Progress for Bolivian–National Convergence—quickly realized the fear that the racism of the Catholic right would be reinstated (Zamorano Villarreal 2020). Having become next in line to the presidency after various resignations, Áñez held a Bible as she first entered the Presidential Palace and declared from the balcony, "Thank God, the Bible has returned to the Bolivian government" (*Open Democracy* 2019). Police officers were filmed removing the Wiphala—the flag of indigenous peoples, which had been made the symbol of the plurinational state—and replacing it with the Bolivian red, yellow, and green tricolor (*Página Siete* 2019b). Áñez's first actions as president were to remove the possibility of criminal liability from the police and military with the controversial Decree 4078, which was described as a "carte blanche" for the military to act with impunity (Amnesty International 2019). Shortly afterward, more than thirty people were killed in related protests in El Alto (Pérez 2021). When the new cabinet was initially announced on November 13, 2019, no indigenous people were included (Collyns 2019).

It testified to the power of the cultural decolonization the MAS had achieved that Catholic, colonial symbolism was so swiftly reinstated. This reassertion of colonial traditions was accompanied by proclamations of a "return" to democracy, but one that also implied an erasure of difference that had been so inherent to social movements' idea of the nation. The use of the media by Áñez and her ruling party made it clear that there was a return to a mestizo ideal of the nation that denied racialized hierarchies (Tórrez 2020). The Bolivian tricolor was identified in political campaigns as being the flag of *all* Bolivians, while the Wiphala represented only indigenous peoples. Diversity within Bolivia was presented by the nine departments and their respective costumes, a representation that associated difference with choice rather than the enduring political structures of colonialism (Zamorano Villareal 2020). An element in the growing disaffection with the MAS had been a weariness with the conflict that its political strategies relied on. However, the violent revanchism of the Áñez government and politicians from the Media Luna departments, cloaked in the language of liberal modernity and homogeneous nationhood, exacerbated that conflict and further distanced alternative epistemological approaches to plurality and the pluriverse.

The femininity of Jeanine Áñez—a powerful, right-wing, religious woman—brought to the fore the gendered aspects involved in the revanchism of 2019 Bolivia. As is often the case with female leadership, her abilities in household management were highlighted in electoral campaigns. As the presidential candidate for the party Juntos in the 2020 elections, the metaphor for the nation that was used in her campaign was a ramshackle house that Áñez expertly tidies with the help of a diverse group of people, including a woman *de pollera,* who enthusiastically participates as part of the team. As Gabriela Zamorano Villareal argues:

> The central role and decisiveness of this *blanqueada* ("whitened") woman giving orders to a team of people to clean up a middle-class home, along with the warm and ordered aesthetic of the shots is reminiscent of soap operas, and they do not evoke a political leader so much as the housewife (*patrona*) who knows and accepts the gender role she has been given, which is to keep her house in order. Implicit in this idea of order is a mission to not only "pacify" the country, which she set out in her inaugural speech, but also to establish a moral order in which the family occupies a central position. (2020, 167)

The house they are tidying is identifiably middle class, urban, and white, and there is a denial of power relations within the house between the white woman and the woman *de pollera,* and of the gendered divisions of labor represented, as men fix the electrical wiring while women clean and tidy. The aim is to convey a sense of a traditional order of things rather than the disruptions to the gendered construction of power that a woman president could represent.

Criticism of the MAS from feminist organizations, particularly those of Galindo and Rivera Cusicanqui, were used to bolster the right's campaign against Morales and García Linera. Feminist, indigenous, and environmentalist criticism of the MAS was also drowned out, particularly in international debates, with the polemic developments after the election, which promptly aligned around the conflictive discourses of fraud/coup, tricolor/Wiphala, and Jeanine/Evo (see, e.g., Ollantay 2019). Unsurprisingly, both Galindo (Galindo 2019) and Rivera Cusicanqui (Muñoz Ramírez 2019) made their opposition to the new right-wing government abundantly clear, while also maintaining that the Morales government had lost legitimacy. Rivera Cusicanqui clarified that Morales had committed electoral fraud not only in the 2019 election but also in the 2015 election, and that the level of centralization of the state based on profits from extractivism itself constituted a lack of legitimacy. Galindo shared this view and, despite attempts among MAS supporters to portray this as a betrayal, saw no contradiction between being critical of the MAS's centralization, extractivism, and corruption and opposing the Áñez presidency. In a hard-hitting commentary, she discussed the meaning of Áñez's femininity and humble background in the context of her presidential candidacy:

> Jeanine is the subordinate, she belongs to that giant group of women who the day they contemplate being or are victims of rape decide to negotiate that rape, negotiate their role in the world with rapists, serve as a smokescreen, help cover up crime, survive by placing themselves at the service of the mightiest. (Galindo 2019)

Galindo's commentary highlights the internalized oppression and internalized colonialism of the woman who grew up in Beni and for whom "becoming blonde cannot hide her cheekbones and slanted eyes, of an origin that has placed her in history as the enemy of herself" (Galindo 2019).

One of Áñez's acts during her short presidency was to declare the *chola* a symbol of national heritage. To celebrate the declaration, and as part of her electoral campaign, she hosted a fashion parade of *chola paceña* fashions featuring models from Rosario Aguilar's agency (de Laforcade 2020). The fashion parade illustrated the need to attract an indigenous vote, and how once again the *chola* was the acceptable face of indigeneity to criollo elites. The Santa Cruz–based politician Luis Fernando Camacho also made a point of featuring *chola* women in his political campaigns (Zamorano Villareal 2020). Áñez's campaign was criticized by Yolanda Mamani, a member of Mujeres Creando, for featuring only the face of *cholaje* that was most palatable to a consumer model of integration: "They weren't the *cholas* who need to sell on the streets, or *cholas* in agriculture, they were just catwalk *cholas*, not every day *cholas*" (Radio Deseo 2020). Áñez's event drew out the trope of *chola* as intermediary, but also the changes in indigenous femininity over MAS rule. The social and economic power of the *chola* was showcased, but in such a way that the *pollera* was a costume rather than an item of clothing that encapsulated the interplay of identity, community, and commerce that the *chola paceña* could represent. The finale of the event was the adorning of Áñez with a derby hat and shawl, which resonated more with the image of diversity as cultural choice than structural oppression, or the possibility of a plural economy.

Áñez was featured in a *Forbes* list of women politicians who were leading their countries through the pandemic over the lockdowns of 2020 (Wittenberg-Cox 2020). Bolivia had locked down early, and the measures were some of the strictest on the continent, although this was also to quell civil unrest and criticism from the press (Human Rights Watch 2020). Her management of the pandemic was mired in public procurement scandals which analysts say contributed to her poor showing in the election in October 2020 (Velasquez Guachalla et al. 2021). Covid-19 demonstrated the inadequacies of the healthcare system. At the start of the pandemic there were only thirty-two ventilators in Bolivia, and over the course of the pandemic more than 80 percent of Bolivia's healthcare workers tested positive for the disease (Velasquez Guachalla et al. 2021). The institutional framework and distribution networks needed to provide support during the pandemic entrenched the division between formal and informal sectors, the latter of which were unable to easily access state supports. Those working in the informal sector in Bolivia, as around the world, were more vulnerable during the pandemic, both economically and in terms of exposure to the virus. Those working in markets, transport, and the agricultural sector were designated essential workers (Hummel et al. 2021), despite the fact that their working conditions left them exposed to contamination. Cash transfer programs were bolstered, but as digital payments were not possible, the offices where claims were made were crowded, hence exposing those outside the formal, online banking system to even more risk (Hummel et al. 2021). Nevertheless, both the ingenuity that has helped popular markets survive for centuries and the dependence that government administrations have on supposedly informal markets were demonstrated. Informal crematoria made up for the grisly overcrowding of established services, and market sellers offered masks, hand gel, and PPE for sale, all of which were in short supply.

Data on the gendered impact of the pandemic on informal workers are emerging, but across the region it appears that women have taken on the burden of increased care labor. They represent a greater proportion of the healthcare workers who were disproportionately exposed to the virus, and took on the majority of care within the home. Because of preexisting inequalities, women were more likely to suffer economically. Domestic workers were more likely to lose their jobs than were other laborers, and during the pandemic, as in other crises, the "situation of extreme vulnerability creates a crisis of social reproduction, making more acute the underlying contradiction between the necessity for domestic workers' labour to sustain the economy and their precarious working and living conditions" (Acciari, del Carmen Britez, and del Carmen Morales Pérez 2021, 11). Once again, the systematic invisibility of feminine and feminized labor and the systematic marginalization of the popular markets that are beyond the reach of the state has created unequal gendered impacts.

Luis Arce and his running mate, David Choquehuanca—two high-profile officials in Morales's administration throughout his time in power—won the delayed elections of October 2020. These elections were confirmed as legitimate by international observers, and the results were not contested. Due in part to a fragmented opposition, the MAS comfortably had the highest proportion of votes. Arce was perceived as continuing the MAS legacy, but he had always been a more technocratic minister—perceived as a sensible, safe pair of hands, with a master's degree in economics who had been, as minister of economy and public finance, responsible for healthy economic growth since 2006. However,

as discussed in chapter 4, his approach was one of heterodox modernization rather than plurality in policy terms. One of Arce's first acts was to
reverse changes that the Áñez government had made, including rejoin-
ing ALBA. However, the economic situation Bolivia faces is very different to the years of growth and increasing foreign reserves that Arce had
previously managed. In 2020, reserves were down to $1,803.9 million
U.S. from a peak in 2014 of over $13,000 million U.S. (*Trading Economics*
2021), and the welfare and equality gains of the MAS administration
had been thrown into question by the pandemic. It is expected that Bolivia may have to take on more international debt and that the currency
may have to devalue.

The policy prescriptions that are expected from Arce are a heterodox response to the iniquities of free trade, but in a world where the
international financial institutions behind the neoliberalism that the
MAS railed against in 2006 are losing power on the international stage,
and where the key international relationships are with China and Russia. There seems to be little reason to hope that the preconditions of a
plural economy—a critical eye on the gendered construction of binary
notions underpinning value, production, and scale and of the reflective
processes at the center of government rather than a strong centralized
state—will materialize. It may be that the socioeconomic structures
and political processes in the country have changed to the point that
a more inclusive approach will be demanded by a wealthy indigenous
middle class who are now used to having political command. However, a
conflictive logic of identity—as opposed to the ecological logic of a unity
of contradictions underpinning the pluriverse—predominates in Bolivia and worldwide, in ways that could not have been imagined in 2006.
Populist logics of polarization dominate global political debate, and Bolivia has not been immune to the rhetoric of, for instance, "masking
versus anti-masking" that has further polarized preexisting conflicts.

The epistemology behind ideas of the pluriverse gives us the conceptual tools to imagine an economy in which many economies fit. This
study of pluri-economy has shown that focusing on the economic strategies of those marginalized into categories of absence—in this case,
femininity and indigeneity—can provide further imaginings of how
economies could function that do not figure even in critical theories
of political economy. It has also shown the need to institute processes
that enable constant deconstructive reflection on the identities that are

marshaled politically or used to frame policy. Economic and political circumstances generate the social relations that become crystallized into cultural tropes and identity categories, but these relations can be reread and examined if gendered cultural presumptions about value, production, time, and scale are challenged. Unlearning our assumptions about what counts means finding the space and political commitment for a plurality of economic narratives to be heard. We can then generate new economic scripts, institutions, and processes that are able to recognize the value of the myriad exchanges and relations that bind us together.

Glossary

anticretico: Usufruct rights in exchange for a loan. A tenure agreement in which a tenant pays a large lump sum initially and then can use housing or land for a stipulated time until the loan is repaid.

apthapi: An Aymara tradition of families and communities sharing food.

ayllu: Andean community and economic network linked by kinship ties and traditional leadership structures, and associated with a particular territory.

ayni: Andean principle of reciprocity and commensurate return of goods and favors among community members.

bono: Welfare voucher.

casero/a: A regular customer at a certain stall or, conversely, a customer's favored stall or shop. Can also be used as a friendly address.

chachawarmi: Literally, "man/woman." Encompasses the idea that gender roles are equal and complementary; can also refer to the traditional gender organization of Andean "two-headed" households.

chiflera: Woman who sells items associated with traditional healing or ritual offerings.

chola paceña: An indigenous woman *de pollera* from La Paz, who wears the distinctive pollera from that region.

cholet: Popular name for a style of New Andean architecture most associated with Bolivian architect Freddy Mamani; a fusion of "chalet" and "cholo."

cholo/chola/cholita: Ethnic term for someone of indigenous descent who has migrated to the city. While *cholo* can be perjorative, the term is often used in the feminine—*chola*—to describe urban women *de pollera*. *Cholita* is the diminutive of *chola*, used to refer to a young, unmarried woman *de pollera*.

chota: An indigenous woman who has sold out to Western culture.

comadre/copadre: Godmother/godfather of one's child or mother/father of one's godchild.

comerciante: Market trader.

compadrazgo: System of co-parenting. Relations and institutions pertaining to godparents and godchildren, either in terms of fictive kin or festive sponsorship.

contrabando hormiga: Literally, "ant smuggling." Small-scale smuggling across borders, particularly between Bolivia and surrounding countries.

de pollera: To be *de pollera* denotes an indigenous ethnocultural identity. A women who wears the pollera habitually is a *mujer de pollera*.

de vestido: To wear Western dress. To be *de vestido* is contraposed to being *de pollera* and implies urbanity and whiteness.

entrada: Festival or carnival parade involving folkloric dances in full costume. Often associated with a Catholic saint's day or a town or community's annual festival.

laderas: Literally, "the slopes." Typically the slopes of Andean cities tend to have been built up by rural-urban migration; often lacking in infrastructure, they are associated with poverty.

mayorista: Wholesaler.

Media Luna: The "crescent moon"—used in Bolivian politics to refer to the eastern departments that rejected MAS rule initially and called for autonomy—Santa Cruz, Beni, Pando, and Tarija.

mesa: Ritual offering to the Pachamama, involving brightly colored amulets and wool, coca leaves, and a llama fetus.

mestizaje/mestizo/mestiza: Literally, a person of mixed race.

minorista: Retailer.

la moda de la chola paceña: Luxury pollera fashions associated with the rise of the "indigenous bourgeoisie" in Bolivia.

Pachamama: Andean earth goddess—sometimes translated as Mother Earth. Represents a cosmovision of reciprocity between beings.

pasanaku: Literally, "passes between us." Traditional Andean rotating savings and credit association.

pollera: Andean outfit comprising pleated skirt, blouse, derby hat, and shawl. Associated with indigenous identity, with variations depending on region of provenance.

pongueaje: Peonage–colonial system in the Andes and Southern Cone in
which indigenous tenants were obliged to provide domestic service
for landlords in return for usufruct rights on land.

preste: Lead organizer and sponsor—typically a couple—of a fiesta; also
referred to as *pasante*.

renta dignidad: Unconditional universal basic state pension paid to
those over age sixty.

suma qamaña: Aymara phrase translated as "living well," or "vivir
bien" in Spanish, indicating a relational worldview and ethics of
community and harmony. This phrase has been a central organizing
principle of several Marea Rosa governments, including Bolivia's.

urbanización cerrada: Gated community.

vecino: Literally, "neighbor." The term indicates membership of a town
rather than a rural community.

vivir bien: See **suma qamaña**.

Bibliography

A4000. 2015. *MegaCenter: Ni los alteños son lo que parecen ser, ni los de la Zona Sur son lo que creen ser.* http://a4000.blogspot.co.uk/2015/01/megacenter-ni-los-altenos-son-lo-que.html. Accessed December 2021.

Acciari, L., J. del Carmen Britez, and A. del Carmen Morales Pérez. 2021. Right to health, right to live: Domestic workers facing the COVID-19 crisis in Latin America. *Gender and Development* 29 (1): 11–33.

Achtenberg, E. 2011. Gasolinazo challenges Bolivia's "process of change." *News: NACLA Report on the Americas,* February 28, 2011. https://nacla.org/news/gasolinazo-challenges-bolivia%E2%80%99s-process-change. Accessed December 2021.

Achtenberg, E. 2016a. Evo's Bolivia at a political crossroads: Taking stock of Bolivia's changing political environment after Evo Morales' 2016 referendum defeat. *NACLA Report on the Americas* 48 (4): 372–80.

Achtenberg, E. 2016b. Why Bolivian workers are marching against Evo Morales. *Columns. NACLA Report on the Americas.* May 7, 2016. https://nacla.org/blog/2016/07/05/why-bolivian-workers-are-marching-against-evo-morales. Accessed December 2021.

Adams, D. W., and M. L. Canavesi. 1992. Rotating savings and credit associations in Bolivia. In *Informal finance in low-income countries,* edited by D. W. Adams and D. Fitchett, 313–23. Boulder, Colo.: Westview.

Adkins, K. C. 2002. The real dirt: Gossip and feminist epistemology. *Social Epistemology* 16 (3): 215–32.

Ahmed, S. 2007. A phenomenology of whiteness. *Feminist Theory* 8 (2): 149–68.

Albó, X. 2004. Ethnic identity and politics in the Central Andes: The case of Bolivia, Ecuador, and Peru. In *Politics in the Andes: Identity, conflict, reform,* edited by J. M. Burt and P. Mauceri, 17–37. Pittsburgh: University of Pittsburgh Press.

Albro, R. 1998. Introduction: A new time and place for Bolivian popular politics. *Ethnology* 37 (2): 99–115.

Albro, R. 2000. The populist chola: Cultural mediation and the political imagination in Quillacollo, Bolivia. *Journal of Latin American Anthropology* 5 (2): 30–88.

Albro, R., and M. McCarthy. 2018. Bolivia is not Venezuela—even if its president does want to stay in power forever. *The Conversation,* April 11, 2018. https://theconversation.com/bolivia-is-not-venezuela-even-if-its-president-does-want-to-stay-in-power-forever-93253. Accessed December 2021.

Alexander, J. C. 1995. Analytical debates: Understanding the relative autonomy of culture. *ProtoSociology* 7:35–53.

Allderdice, A., J. Winiecki, and E. Morris. 2007. *Using microfinance to expand access to energy services: A desk study of experiences in Latin America and the Caribbean.*

The SEEP Network. https://seepnetwork.org/files/galleries/597_Energy_ LatAm_FINAL.pdf. Accessed December 2021.

Amnesty International. 2019. *Bolivia: Jeanine Añez must immediately repeal decree giving impunity to armed forces personnel.* Press release, November 18, 2019. https:// www.amnesty.org/en/latest/press-release/2019/11/bolivia-derogar-norma -impunidad-fuerzas-armadas/. Accessed December 2021.

Anria, S. 2013. Social movements, party organization, and populism: Insights from the Bolivian MAS. *Latin American Politics and Society* 55 (3): 19–46.

Anria, S. 2016. Delegative democracy revisited: More inclusion, less liberalism in Bolivia. *Journal of Democracy* 27 (3): 99–108.

Anria, S., and S. Niedzwiecki. 2016. Social movements and social policy: The Bolivian Renta Dignidad. *Studies in Comparative International Development* 51 (3): 308–27.

Anthias, P. 2018. *Limits to decolonization: Indigeneity, territory, and hydrocarbon politics in the Bolivian Chaco.* Ithaca, N.Y.: Cornell University Press.

Aramayo Cañedo, L. 2015. Transformaciones y tensiones: El nuevo mercado Lanza de La Paz. *Tinkazos* 18 (38): 53–69.

Arnold, D. Y., and A. Spedding. 2005. *Mujeres en los movimientos sociales en Bolivia, 2000–2003.* La Paz, Bolivia: Centro de Información y Desarrollo de la Mujer.

Artaraz, K. 2011. New Latin American networks of solidarity? ALBA's contribution to Bolivia's National Development Plan (2006–10). *Global Social Policy* 11 (1): 88–105.

Asher, K. 2013. Latin American decolonial thought, or making the subaltern speak. *Geography Compass* 7 (12): 832–42.

Asher, K. 2017. Spivak and Rivera Cusicanqui on the dilemmas of representation in postcolonial and decolonial feminisms. *Feminist Studies* 43 (3): 512–24.

Augé, M. 2009. *Non-places: Introduction to an anthropology of supermodernity.* Translated by John Howe. London: Verso. First published 1992.

Avendaño, T. R. 2009. El sumak kawsay en Ecuador y Bolivia: Vivir bien, identidad, alternativa. *Icaria Editorial* 37:15–19.

AWID. 2011. *Women's movements present alternatives at the World Social Forum.* https://www.awid.org/news-and-analysis/womens-movements-present -alternatives-world-social-forum. Accessed December 2021.

Babb, F. 1989. *Between Field and Cooking Pot: The Political Economy of Market Women in Peru.* Austin: University of Texas Press.

Bailey, F. G., ed. 1971. *Gifts and poison: The politics of reputation.* New York: Schocken.

Baker, P. 2015. The phantom, the plebeian, and the state: Grupo Comuna and the intellectual career of Álvaro García Linera. *Viewpoint Magazine,* February 25, 2015. https://viewpointmag.com/2015/02/25/the-phantom-the-plebeian-and -the-state-grupo-comuna-and-the-intellectual-career-of-alvaro-garcia-linera/. Accessed December 2021.

Barnett, C. 2005. The consolations of "neoliberalism." *Geoforum* 36 (1): 7–12.

Barragán, R. 2009. Más allá de lo mestizo, más allá de lo aymara: Organización y representaciones de clase y etnicidad en el comercio callejero en la ciudad de La Paz. In *Historia social urbana: Espacios y flujos,* edited by E. Kingman, 293–322. Quito, Ecuador: FLACSO.

Bartolina Sisa. n.d. Nuestro trabajo. https://www.bartolinasisa.org/nuestro
-trabajo/. Accessed December 2021.

Bastien, J. W. 1979. Land litigations in the Andean ayllu from 1592 until 1972.
Ethnohistory 26 (2): 101–31.

Bateman, M., and K. Maclean, eds. 2017. *Seduced and betrayed: Exposing the contemporary microfinance phenomenon.* Santa Fe: University of New Mexico Press.

Baudoin, M. 2016. Colour bars: Traditional clothing is still a sign of social status
in Bolivia and wearing often leads to discrimination. *Index on Censorship* 45 (4):
18–20.

BBC. 2006. In pictures: Evo Morales' sweater. January 20, 2006. http://news.bbc
.co.uk/1/hi/in_pictures/4630396.stm. Accessed December 2021.

BBC Mundo. 2018. Cómo es la imponente y polémica "Casa Grande del Pueblo,"
la nueva sede del gobierno de Bolivia construida por Evo Morales. August
18, 2018. https://www.bbc.com/mundo/noticias-america-latina-45229290.
Accessed December 2021.

Bolivia Impuestos. 2021. *Régimen simplificado en Bolivia y lo que debes saber.*
https://boliviaimpuestos.com/regimen-simplificado-en-bolivia/. Accessed
September 2022.

Bromley, R. 1990. A new path to development? The significance and impact of
Hernando de Soto's ideas on underdevelopment, production, and reproduction. *Economic Geography* 66 (4): 328–48.

Burgos, C. 2019. El transporte público, un negocio en manos de pocos que
acumulan dinero y poder. *Los Tiempos*, July 1, 2019. https://www.lostiempos
.com/especial-multimedia/20190701/transporte-publico-negocio-manos
-pocos-que-acumulan-dinero-poder. Accessed December 2021.

Butcher, M., and K. Maclean. 2018. Gendering the city: The lived experience of
transforming cities, urban cultures, and spaces of belonging. *Gender, Place, and
Culture* 25 (5): 686–94.

Butler, J. 1998. Merely cultural. *New Left Review* 227:33–44.

Butters, R. 2012. Political femicide. *Bolivian Express,* August 14, 2012. https://
bolivianexpress.org/blog/posts/political-femicide. Accessed December 2021.

Calhoun, C. J., ed. 1992. *Habermas and the public sphere.* Cambridge: MIT Press.

Calle Sarmiento, A. C. 2018. Analysis of the ownership of financial products:
Evidence to contribute to financial inclusion in Bolivia. In *Financial decisions of
households and financial inclusion: Evidence for Latin America and the Caribbean,*
edited by M. J. Roa and D. Mejia, 15–50. https://scioteca.caf.com/bitstream/
handle/123456789/1189/2016-jrp.pdf?sequence=1#page=39. Accessed December 2021.

Camargo, E. 2019. Gender inequality and intimate partner violence in Bolivia.
Revista Colombiana de Sociología 42 (2): 257–77.

Cameron, J., and J. K. Gibson-Graham. 2003. Feminising the economy: Metaphors, strategies, politics. *Gender, Place, and Culture* 10 (2): 145–57.

Canessa, A. 2010. Dreaming of fathers: Fausto Reinaga and indigenous masculin-
ism. *Latin American and Caribbean Ethnic Studies* 5 (2): 175–87.

Casanovas, N. 2018. *Pollera y ojos verdes: Racismo en la interacción pública rutinaria.*
La Paz, Bolivia: Plural Editores.

Castree, N. 2003. Commodifying what nature? *Progress in Human Geography* 27 (3): 273–97.

CEDLA. 2015. *Boletín OBESS: El doble aguinaldo y la realidad de los trabajadores.* https://cedla.org/publicaciones/obess/boletin-obess-el-doble-aguinaldo -y-la-realidad-de-los-trabajadores/. Accessed September 2022.

Cerezo Aguirre, S. 2014. Boom en el sector inmobiliario en Bolivia: ¿Burbuja o fundamentos económicos? *Banco Central de Bolivia Revista de Análisis* 76 (20): 75–118. https://www.bcb.gob.bo/webdocs/publicacionesbcb/revista_analisis/ ra_vol20/articulo_3_v20.pdf. Accessed December 2021.

Cerrato, M. 2015. Nation form, community form: Nationalisation and dialectic in García Linera's thought. *Culture, Theory, and Critique* 56 (3): 333–48.

Chang, T. C., and S. Huang. 2008. Geographies of everywhere and nowhere: Place-(un)making in a world city. *International Development Planning Review* 30 (3): 227–47.

Chatterton, P., and A. Pusey. 2020. Beyond capitalist enclosure, commodification, and alienation: Postcapitalist praxis as commons, social production, and useful doing. *Progress in Human Geography* 44 (1): 27–48.

Chipana, W. 2013. Tasas de interés para créditos productivos continúan elevadas. *La Razon,* June 2, 2013. http://www.la-razon.com/economia/Tasas-creditos -productivos-continuan-elevadas_0_1843615718.html. Accessed December 2021.

Choque Quispe, M. E. 2007. *Equidad de género en las culturas aymaras y qhichwa.* http://machaca.cebem.org/documents/capacitacion_2007_equidad_genero .pdf. Accessed May 2013.

Coen, S. E., N. A. Ross, and S. Turner. 2008. "Without tiendas it's a dead neigh-bourhood": The socio-economic importance of small trade stores in Cocha-bamba, Bolivia. *Cities* 25 (6): 327–39.

Collyns, D. 2016. Sex, lies, and paternity claims: Bolivia's president reels amid tumultuous scandal. *The Guardian,* June 24, 2016. https://www.theguardian .com/world/2016/jun/24/bolivia-evo-morales-press-freedom-gabriela -zapata-child#comments. Accessed December 2021.

Collyns, D. 2019. Bolivia president's initial indigenous-free cabinet heightens polarization. *The Guardian,* November 14, 2019. https://www.theguardian .com/world/2019/nov/14/bolivia-president-jeanine-anez-cabinet-indigenous. Accessed December 2021.

Committee on Foreign Affairs. 2009. U.S.–Bolivia relations: Looking ahead. *Hearing before the Subcommittee on the Western Hemisphere of the Committee on Foreign Affairs, House of Representatives.* March 3. https://www.govinfo.gov/ content/pkg/CHRG-111hhrg47827/html/CHRG-111hhrg47827.htm. Accessed December 2021.

Constitution of 2009. Bolivia (Plurinational State of)'s Constitution of 2009. Translated by Max Planck Institute. Constitute Project. Oxford University Press. https://www.constituteproject.org/constitution/Bolivia_2009.pdf. Accessed April 2023.

Corcoran-Tadd, N. 2016. "Is this the gold that you eat?": Coins, entanglement, and early colonial orderings in the Andes (AD 1532–ca. 1650). In *Archaeology of entanglement,* edited by L. Der and F. Fernandini, 49–76. London: Routledge.

Correo del Sur. 2019. El mercado inmobiliario podría comenzar a descender

durante 2019. January 8, 2019. https://correodelsur.com/capitales/20190108_
el-mercado-inmobiliario-podria-comenzar-a-descender-durante-2019.html.
Accessed December 2021.

Cortez Salinas, J. 2014. El Tribunal Constitucional Plurinacional de Bolivia: Cómo
se distribuye el poder institucional. *Boletín Mexicano de Derecho Comparado* 47
(139): 287–96.

Craik, J., and M. A. Jansen. 2015. Constructing national fashion identities. *International Journal of Fashion Studies* 2 (1): 3–8.

Cusack, A. 2014. The Bolivarian Alliance for the Peoples of Our America (ALBA):
The birth of post-neoliberal regionalism? PhD thesis, University of Sheffield,
Department of Politics.

Cusack, A. 2018. *Venezuela, ALBA, and the limits of postneoliberal regionalism in
Latin America and the Caribbean.* New York: Palgrave Macmillan.

Dash, A. 2017. A study on socio-economic effect of demonetization in India. *International Journal of Management and Applied Science* 3 (3): 13–15.

Dávila, A. 2016. *El mall: The spatial and class politics of shopping malls in Latin America.* Oakland: University of California Press.

Davis, M. 2006. *Planet of slums.* London: Verso.

El Deber. 2013. Subsidiarán aguinaldo de microempresas para mitigar impacto del
doble bono. December 17, 2013. https://eju.tv/2013/12/subsidiarn-aguinaldo
-de-microempresas-para-mitigar-impacto-del-doble-bono/. Accessed September 2022.

El Deber. 2018. Gobierno pone en la mira a cuatro empresas para traspasarlas a los
fabriles. May 3, 2018. https://eldeber.com.bo/68892_gobierno-pone-en-la-mira
-a-cuatro-empresas-para-traspasarlas-a-los-fabriles. Accessed December 2021.

de la Cadena, M. 1995. Women are more Indian: Ethnicity and gender in a community near Cuzco. In *Ethnicity, markets, and migration in the Andes: At the crossroads of history and anthropology,* edited by B. Larson and O. Harris, 329–48.
Durham: Duke University Press.

de Laforcade, G. 2020. Indigeneity, gender, and resistance: Critique and contemporaneity of Bolivian anarchism in the historical imagination of Silvia Rivera
Cusicanqui. *Anarchist Studies* 28 (2): 19–53.

DeLanda, M. 2008. Deleuze, materialism, and politics. In *Deleuze and politics,* edited by I. Buchanan and N. Thoburn, 160–77. Edinburgh: Edinburgh University
Press.

de la Torre, A., A. Ize, and S. L. Schmukler. 2011. *Financial development in Latin
America and the Caribbean: The road ahead.* Washington, D.C.: The World Bank.

Deere, C. D., and M. León. 2001a. Disjuncture in law and practice: Women's
inheritance of land in Latin America. In *Gender perspectives on property and
inheritance: A global sourcebook,* edited by S. J. R. Cummings, H. van Dam,
A. Khadar, and M. Valk, 19–32. Amsterdam: Kit Publishers.

Deere, C. D., and M. León. 2001b. Who owns the land? Gender and land-titling
programmes in Latin America. *Journal of Agrarian Change* 1 (3): 440–67.

Deere, C. D., and M. León. 2002. Individual versus collective land rights: Tensions
between women's and indigenous rights under neoliberalism. In *The spaces of
neoliberalism: Land, place, and family in Latin America,* edited by J. Chase, 53–84.
Bloomfield, Conn.: Kumarian Press.

Delta Financiero. 2016. Destacan el Pasanaku en Bolivia como medio de préstamo y ahorro. October 3, 2016. http://deltafinanciero.com/436-Destacan-el-Pasanaku -en-Bolivia-como-medio-de-prestamo-y-ahorro. Accessed December 2021.

El Diario. 2011. "Transnacionales aún controlan recursos hidrocarburíferos." November 28, 2011. https://eju.tv/2011/11/transnacionales-an-controlan -recursos-hidrocarburferos/. Accessed September 2022.

El Diario. 2017. Casa colonial convertida en "Casa del pueblo" provoca polémica. July 31, 2017. https://www.eldiario.net/noticias/2017/2017_07/nt170731/ metrocuadrado.php?n=55&-casa-colonial-convertida-en-casa-del-pueblo -provoca-polemica. Accessed December 2021.

Diaz, M. P. (2013). La periferia de la ciudad de El Alto y la apropiación de los migrantes rurales (1996–2012). *X Jornadas de Sociología.* Facultad de Ciencias Sociales, Universidad de Buenos Aires, Buenos Aires.

Díaz Carrasco, M. A. 2013. De empleada a ministra! Despatriarcalización en Bolivia. *Íconos: Revista de Ciencias Sociales* 45:75–89.

Dürr, E., and J. Müller. 2019. *The popular economy in urban Latin America: Informality, materiality, and gender in commerce.* Lanham, Md.: Lexington Books/ Rowman & Littlefield.

Dussel, E. 2003. *Philosophy of liberation.* Translated by A. Martinez and C. Morkovsky. Eugene, Ore.: Wipf and Stock.

Dussel, E. 2012. Transmodernity and interculturality: An interpretation from the perspective of philosophy of liberation. *Transmodernity: Journal of Peripheral Cultural Production of the Luso-Hispanic World* 1 (3): 28–59.

Eaton, K. 2014. Recentralization and the left turn in Latin America: Diverging outcomes in Bolivia, Ecuador, and Venezuela. *Comparative Political Studies* 47 (8): 1130–57.

Ellner, S. 2019. Pink-tide governments: Pragmatic and populist responses to challenges from the right. *Latin American Perspectives* 46 (1): 4–22.

Escobar, A. 1992. Imagining a post-development era? Critical thought, development, and social movements. *Social Text,* nos. 31/32:20–56.

Escobar, A. 2007a. The "ontological turn" in social theory: A commentary on "Human Geography without Scale," by Sallie Marston, John Paul Jones II, and Keith Woodward. *Transactions of the Institute of British Geographers* 32 (1): 106–11.

Escobar, A. 2007b. Worlds and knowledges otherwise: The Latin American modernity/coloniality research program. *Cultural Studies* 21 (2–3): 179–210.

Escobar, A. 2010. Latin America at a crossroads. *Cultural Studies* 24 (1): 1–65.

Escudero Pérez, I., C. Heras, and A. Campaignolle. 2018. La artesana que dirigió un ministerio y encaró al machismo en su ciudad. *Pikara,* February 28, 2018. https://www.pikaramagazine.com/2018/02/la-artesana-que-dirigio-un -ministerio-y-encaro-al-machismo-en-su-ciudad/. Accessed December 2021.

Fabricant, N., and N. Postero. 2015. Sacrificing indigenous bodies and lands: The political–economic history of lowland Bolivia in light of the recent TIPNIS debate. *Journal of Latin American and Caribbean Anthropology* 20 (3): 452–74.

FAO [Food and Agriculture Organisation]. 2013. *Discurso de la Excma. Sra. Nemesia Achacollo Tola, Ministra de Desarrollo Rural y Tierras, Estado Plurinacional de*

Bolivia. http://www.fao.org/quinoa-2013/press-room/news/quinoa-bolivia -speech/fr/?no_mobile=1. Accessed December 2021.

Farthing, L. 2007. Everything is up for discussion: A 40th anniversary conversation with Silvia Rivera Cusicanqui. *NACLA Report on the Americas* 40 (4): 4–9.

Farthing, L. 2019. An opportunity squandered? Elites, social movements, and the government of Evo Morales. *Latin American Perspectives* 46 (1): 212–29.

Farthing, L., and B. Kohl. 2014. *Evo's Bolivia: Continuity and change*. Austin: University of Texas Press.

Featherstone, M. 1995. *Undoing culture: Globalization, postmodernism, and identity*. London: Sage Publications.

Feldman, I. 2015. The re-encounter of Indianismo and Marxism in the work of Álvaro García Linera. *Viewpoint Magazine*, February 25, 2015. https://www .viewpointmag.com/2015/02/25/the-re-encounter-of-indianismo-and-marxism -in-the-work-of-alvaro-garcia-linera/. Accessed December 2021.

Ferrufino Goitia, R. 2009. Análisis crítico de los preceptos económicos establecidos en la nueva Constitución Política del Estado. In *Reflexión crítica a la nueva Constitución Política del Estado*, edited by S. Käss and I. Velásquez Castellanos, 517–55. La Paz, Bolivia: Fundación Konrad Adenauer.

Filomeno, M. 2017. Punto Blanco, la empresa que sus trabajadores sacan a flote. *Página Siete*, June 4, 2017. https://www.paginasiete.bo/economia/2017/6/4/ punto-blanco-empresa-trabajadores-sacan-flote-139927.html. Accessed December 2021.

Financial Services Law. 2013. https://servdmzw.asfi.gob.bo/circular/leyes/ Ley393ServiciosFinancieros.pdf.

Forero, J. 2006. The fashion of the populist. *New York Times*, February 2, 2006. https://www.nytimes.com/2006/02/02/fashion/thursdaystyles/the-fashion -of-the-populist.html. Accessed December 2021.

Foronda, H. D. 2009. Bolivia digna, pero vestida con ropa usada. *El Diario*, March 14, 2009. https://www.eldiario.net/noticias/2009/2009_03/nt090314/1_05opn.php. Accessed December 2021.

Fraser, N. 1990. Rethinking the public sphere: A contribution to the critique of actually existing democracy. *Social Text*, nos. 25/26:56–80.

Fraser, N. 2009. *Scales of justice: Reimagining political space in a globalizing world*. New York: Columbia University Press.

Fraser, N., A. Honneth, and J. Golb. 2003. *Redistribution or recognition? A political-philosophical exchange*. London: Verso.

Frazier, B. J., M. Bruss, and L. Johnson. 2004. Barriers to Bolivian participation in the global apparel industry. *Journal of Fashion Marketing and Management: An International Journal* 8 (4): 437–51.

Freeland, A. 2019a. Motley society, plurinationalism, and the integral state: Álvaro García Linera's use of Gramsci and Zavaleta. *Historical Materialism* 27 (3): 99–126.

Freeland, A. 2019b. The national-popular in Bolivia: History, crisis and social knowledge. *Postcolonial Studies* 22 (3): 275–82.

Freeman, C. 2001. Is local:global as feminine:masculine? Rethinking the gender of globalization. *Signs: Journal of Women in Culture and Society* 26 (4): 1007–37.

Gago, V. 2017. *Neoliberalism from below: Popular pragmatics and baroque economies.* Translated by L. Mason-Deese. Durham: Duke University Press.

Galindo, M. 2006a. Evo Morales y la descolonización fálica del estado boliviano. *Ephemera* 6 (3): 323–34.

Galindo, M. 2006b. No saldrá Eva de la costilla de Evo. *El Viejo Topo* 218:78–79.

Galindo, M. 2019. Jeanine: ¿Usurpadora, sustituta, subalterna? *Página Siete,* December 18, 2019. https://www.paginasiete.bo/opinion/maria-galindo/2019/ 12/18/jeanine-usurpadora-sustituta-subalterna-240715.html. Accessed December 2021.

Galindo, M., and J. Paredes. 2000. *Machos, varones, y maricones: Manual para conocer tu sexualidad por ti mismo.* La Paz, Bolivia: Ediciones Mujeres Creando.

Gallop, J. 1994. The translation of deconstruction. *Qui Parle* 8 (1): 45–62.

GAMLP [Gobierno Autónomo Municipal de La Paz]. 2015. *El sector de la construcción en la municipalidad de La Paz.* Report, Programa de Análisis e Investigación Municipal. La Paz, Bolivia.

Gandy, M. 2005. Cyborg urbanization: Complexity and monstrosity in the contemporary city. *International Journal of Urban and Regional Research* 29 (1): 26–49.

García-Escribano, M. M., and S. Sosa. 2011. *What is driving financial de-dollarisation in Latin America?* International Monetary Fund. https://www.elibrary.imf.org/ view/journals/001/2011/010/article-A001-en.xml. Accessed December 2021.

García Linera, Á. 2003. Movimientos sociales y democratización política. In *Democracias en riesgo en América Latina,* edited by R. Salazar Pérez, E. A. Sandoval Forero, and D. de la Rocha Almazan, 139–206. Buenos Aires: LibrosEnRed.

García Linera, Á. 2008a. Sindicato, multitud, y comunidad: Movimientos sociales y formas de autonomía política en Bolivia. In *La potencia plebeya: Acción colectiva e identidades indígenas, obreras, y populares en Bolivia,* edited by P. Stefanoni, 347–420. Bogotá, Colombia: Siglo del Hombre Editores y Clacso. First published 2001.

García Linera, Á. 2008b. Los tres pilares de la nueva Constitución Política del Estado. *Revista de Análisis: Reflexiones sobre la coyuntura, número 4.* La Paz, Bolivia: Vicepresidencia del Estado Plurinacional.

García Linera, Á. 2009 . *Forma valor y forma comunidad.* La Paz, Bolivia: Muela del Diablo. First published 1995.

García Linera, Á. 2011. *Las tensiones creativas de la revolución: La quinta fase del proceso de cambio.* La Paz, Bolivia: Vicepresidencia del Estado Plurinacional.

García Linera, Á. 2013. *El "oenegismo," enfermedad infantil del derechismo (O cómo la "reconducción" del Proceso de Cambio es la restauración neoliberal).* La Paz, Bolivia: Vicepresidencia del Estado Plurinacional.

García Linera, Á. 2014. Indianism and Marxism: The disparity between two revolutionary rationales. In *Plebeian power: Collective action and indigenous, working-class, and popular identities in Bolivia,* 305–21. Leiden: Brill. First published 2005.

García Linera, Á., R. Gutiérrez, R. Prada, and L. Tapia. 1999. *El fantasma insomne: Pensando el presente desde el Manifiesto comunista.* La Paz, Bolivia: Muele del Diablo.

Garrett, R., S. B. Stewart, G. S. Koch, C. M. Mueller, W. D. Rogers, and A. R. Sarabia. 1965. Organizing and financing businesses in Latin and South America. *Business Lawyer* 21 (1): 5–42.

Geddes, M. 2016. What happens when community organisers move into government? Recent experience in Bolivia. In *Class, inequality, and community development*, edited by M. Sham and M. Mayo, 121–36. Bristol: Policy Press.

Gibson-Graham, J. K. 1996. *The end of capitalism (as we knew it): A feminist critique of political economy*. Oxford: Blackwell.

Gibson-Graham, J. K. 2005. Surplus possibilities: Postdevelopment and community economies. *Singapore Journal of Tropical Geography* 26 (1): 4–26.

Gibson-Graham, J. K. 2006. *A postcapitalist politics*. Minneapolis: University of Minnesota Press.

Gibson-Graham, J. K. 2008. Diverse economies: Performative practices for other worlds. *Progress in Human Geography* 32 (5): 613–32.

Gil, K. 2010. No es facil instalar nuevas empresas. *Página Siete*, May 30, 2010. http://2.bp.blogspot.com/_nsMceH5htks/TAUQ7KfSSJI/AAAAAAAAABI/_DSeHQvOP6A/s1600/entrevista+ministra+Rodr%C3%ADguez.jpg. Accessed December 2021.

Gill, L. 1993. "Proper women" and city pleasures: Gender, class, and contested meanings in La Paz. *American Ethnologist* 20 (1): 72–88.

Gill, L. 1997. Creating citizens, making men: The military and masculinity in Bolivia. *Cultural Anthropology* 12 (4): 527–50.

Glassman, J. 2003. Rethinking overdetermination, structural power, and social change: A critique of Gibson-Graham, Resnick, and Wolff. *Antipode* 35 (4): 678–98.

Godoy, R., and M. De Franco. 1992. High inflation and Bolivian agriculture. *Journal of Latin American Studies* 24 (3): 617–37.

Gómez Ramírez, E., and C. Handland. 2021. *The informal economy and coronavirus in Latin America*. European Parliamentary Research Service Briefing. https://www.europarl.europa.eu/RegData/etudes/BRIE/2021/690587/EPRS_BRI(2021)690587_EN.pdf. Accessed December 2021.

González-Vega, C., M. Schreiner, R. L. Meyer, J. Rodriguez-Meza, and S. Navajas. 1997. BancoSol: The challenge of growth for microfinance organizations. In *Microfinance for the poor?*, edited by H. Schneider, 129–70. Paris: Organization for Economic Co-operation and Development.

Gonzalo Chávez, A. 2016. Ametex, Enatex, Jodatex. *Página Siete*, July 3, 2016. https://www.paginasiete.bo/opinion/gonzalo-chavez/2016/7/3/ametex-enatex-jodetex-101558.html. Accessed December 2021.

Grace, M. 2019. Bolivia's aerial transit system casts shadow on elections. *Al Jazeera*, October 18, 2019. https://www.aljazeera.com/ajimpact/bolivias-aerial-transit-system-casts-shadow-elections-191018195656239.html. Accessed December 2021.

Graham, D. H., and C. González-Vega. 1995. State-owned agricultural development banks: Lessons and opportunities for microfinance. *Ohio State University Economics and Sociology Occasional Paper* No. 2245.

Grisaffi, T. 2017. From the grassroots to the presidential palace: Evo Morales and the coca growers' union in Bolivia. In *Where are the unions? Workers and social movements in Latin America, the Middle East, and Europe,* edited by S. Lazar, 44–63. London: Zed Books.

Grosfoguel, R. 2007. The epistemic decolonial turn: Beyond political-economy paradigms. *Cultural Studies* 21 (2–3): 211–23.

Grosfoguel, R. 2011. Decolonizing post-colonial studies and paradigms of political-economy: Transmodernity, decolonial thinking, and global coloniality. *Transmodernity: Journal of Peripheral Cultural Production of the Luso-Hispanic World* 1 (1): 1–25.

Guardian. 2016. Bolivia's cholita climbers scale highest mountain yet: "I cried with emotion." April 21, 2016. https://www.theguardian.com/world/2016/apr/21/bolivia-mountain-climbers-women-cholita-aymara-illimani-peak-summits. Accessed December 2021.

Gustafson, B. 2011. Flashpoints of sovereignty: Territorial conflict and natural gas in Bolivia. In *Crude domination: An anthropology of oil,* edited by A. Behrends, S. P. Reyna, and G. Schlee, 220–42. New York: Berghahn Books.

Gustafson, B. 2017. Oppressed no more? Indigenous language regimentation in plurinational Bolivia. *International Journal of the Sociology of Language* 246: 31–57.

Gustafson, B. 2020. *Bolivia in the age of gas.* Durham: Duke University Press.

Guzman, K. 2016. All dried up. *Bolivian Express.* December 29, 2016. https://bolivianexpress.org/blog/posts/all-dried-up. Accessed April 2023.

Hale, C. R. 2002. Does multiculturalism menace? Governance, cultural rights and the politics of identity in Guatemala. *Journal of Latin American Studies* 34 (3): 485–524.

Hale, C. R. 2004. Rethinking indigenous politics in the era of the "indio permitido." *NACLA Report on the Americas* 38 (2): 16–21.

Hall, S. 1980. Cultural studies: Two paradigms. *Media, Culture, and Society* 2 (1): 57–72.

Hardt, M. 2008. Multitud y sociedad abigarrada. In *Imperio, multitud, y sociedad abigarrada,* edited by T. Negri, M. Hardt, G. Cocco, J. Revel, Á. García Linera, and L. Tapia, 41–43. La Paz, Bolivia: Comuna and Muela del Diablo Editores.

Harten, S. 2011. *The rise of Evo Morales and the MAS.* London: Zed Books.

Harvey, D. 1989. *The condition of postmodernity: An enquiry into the origins of cultural change.* Malden, Mass.: Blackwell.

Heng, D. 2015. *Impact of the new financial services law in Bolivia on financial stability and inclusion.* IMF Working Paper No. 15/267. https://ssrn.com/abstract=2733576. Accessed December 2021.

Herrera, T., and A. Leonardo. 2018. Empoderamiento campesino con base étnica: Relaciones políticas CSUTCB-Gobierno. *Temas Sociales* 42:147–78.

Hicks, D. L., B. Maldonado, B. Piper, and A. G. Rios. 2018. Identity, patronage, and redistribution: Economic inequality in Bolivia under Evo Morales. *Journal of Economics, Race, and Policy* 1 (1): 26–41.

Hirsch, C. 2019. Between resistance and negotiations: Indigenous organisations and the Bolivian state in the case of TIPNIS. *Journal of Peasant Studies* 46 (4): 811–30.

Holloway, J. 2010. *Crack capitalism.* London: Pluto Press.

Honig, B. 1993. *Political theory and the displacement of politics*. Ithaca, N.Y.: Cornell University Press.

Hope, J. 2021. Driving development in the Amazon: Extending infrastructural citizenship with political ecology in Bolivia. *Environment and Planning E: Nature and Space* 5 (2): 520–42.

Horn, P. 2018. Indigenous peoples, the city, and inclusive urban development policies in Latin America: Lessons from Bolivia and Ecuador. *Development Policy Review* 36 (4): 483–501.

Horn, P. 2021. The politics of hyperregulation in La Paz, Bolivia: Speculative peri-urban development in a context of unresolved municipal boundary conflicts. *Urban Studies* 59 (12): 2489–505.

Howard, R. 2010. Language, signs, and the performance of power: The discursive struggle over decolonization in the Bolivia of Evo Morales. *Latin American Perspectives* 37 (3): 176–94.

Human Rights Watch. 2020. *Bolivia: COVID-19 decree threatens free expression*. https://www.hrw.org/news/2020/04/07/bolivia-covid-19-decree-threatens-free-expression. Accessed December 2021.

Hummel, C., F. M. Knaul, M. Touchton, V. X. Velasquez Guachalla, J. Nelson-Nuñcz, and C. Boulding. 2021. Poverty, precarious work, and the COVID-19 pandemic: Lessons from Bolivia. *The Lancet Global Health* 9 (5): e579–e581.

IBCE [Instituto Boliviano de Comercio Exterior]. 2005. *Impacto de la importación de ropa usada en Bolivia*. La Paz, Bolivia: IBCE.

IDB [Inter-American Development Bank]. 2018. *Getting u lift: The impact of aerial cable cars in La Paz, Bolivia*. https://publications.iadb.org/publications/english/document/2018DEC11_Getting_a_Lift.pdf. Accessed December 2021.

IMF [International Monetary Fund]. 2016. *Bolivia: Staff report for the 2016 Article IV Consultation*. https://www.elibrary.imf.org/view/journals/002/2016/387/article-A001-en.xml. Accessed December 2021.

IP Nicaragua. 2020. ¿Qué pasó con el SUCRE, la moneda de los países del ALBA? June 20, 2020. https://ipnicaragua.com/que-paso-con-el-sucre-la-moneda-de-los-paises-del-alba/. Accessed December 2021.

Jansen, M. A. 2020. Fashion and the phantasmagoria of modernity: An introduction to decolonial fashion discourse. *Fashion Theory* 24 (6): 815–36.

Jazeel, T. 2021. The "city" as text. *International Journal of Urban and Regional Research* 45 (4): 658–62.

Jessop, B. 2008. Dialogue of the deaf: Some reflections on the Poulantzas-Miliband debate. In *Class, power, and the state in capitalist society: Essays on Ralph Milliband*, edited by P. Wetherly, C. W. Barrow, and P. Burnham, 132–57. London: Palgrave Macmillan.

Juárez, I. 2014. Comerciantes del Gran Poder ganan terreno en San Miguel. *Página Siete*, February 1, 2014. http://www.paginasiete.bo/economia/2014/2/2/comerciantes-gran-poder-ganan-terreno-miguel-12940.html. Accessed December 2021.

Juárez, I. 2015. El efecto de vivir debajo del Teleférico en La Paz. *Página Siete*, June 14, 2015. https://www.paginasiete.bo/gente/2015/6/15/efecto-vivir-debajo-teleferico-59948.html. Accessed December 2021.

Justo-Chipana, M., and M. Moraes. 2015. Plantas medicinales comercializadas por las chifleras de La Paz y El Alto (Bolivia). *Ecología en Bolivia* 50 (2): 66–90.

Kanahuaty, C. 2015. El campo intelectual en Bolivia: El Grupo Comuna. *Ecuador Debate* 94:159–70.

Kehoe, T. J., C. G. Machicado, and J. Peres-Cajías. 2019. *The monetary and fiscal history of Bolivia, 1960–2017.* NBER Working Paper No. 25523. Cambridge, Mass.: National Bureau of Economic Research.

Kempf, M. 2019. Gobierno: Ley de Empresas Sociales no atenta contra la propiedad privada. *El Deber,* January 9, 2019. https://eldeber.com.bo/20330_gobierno -ley-de-empresas-sociales-no-atenta-contra-la-propiedad-privada. Accessed December 2021.

Kim, J. 2015. Bolivia's "spaceship architecture" showcases the new wealth of indigenous people. *Quartz,* February 21, 2015. https://qz.com/338877/ flamboyant-spaceship-architecture-in-bolivia-makes-sure-indigenous -people-keep-their-traditional-culture/. Accessed December 2021.

Knaack, P. 2020. Bolivia, pulling in two directions: The developmental state and Basel standards. In *The political economy of bank regulation in developing countries: Risk and reputation,* edited by E. Jones, 239–59. Oxford: Oxford University Press.

Kohl, B. 2002. Stabilizing neoliberalism in Bolivia: Popular participation and privatization. *Political Geography* 21 (4): 449–72.

Kohl, B. 2003. Democratizing decentralization in Bolivia: The law of popular participation. *Journal of Planning Education and Research* 23 (2): 153–64.

Kohl, B. 2006. Challenges to neoliberal hegemony in Bolivia. *Antipode* 38 (2): 304–26.

Laframboise, N. 2017. Bolivia: Preservando los avances. *IMF Blog,* September 20, 2017. https://blog-dialogoafondo.imf.org/?p=8313. Accessed December 2021.

Lagos, M. L. 1994. *Autonomy and power: The dynamics of class and culture in rural Bolivia.* Philadelphia: University of Pennsylvania Press.

Laing, A. F. 2015. Resource sovereignties in Bolivia: Re-conceptualising the relationship between indigenous identities and the environment during the TIPNIS conflict. *Bulletin of Latin American Research* 34 (2): 149–66.

Laing, A. F. 2020. Re-producing territory: Between resource nationalism and indigenous self-determination in Bolivia. *Geoforum* 108:28–38.

Larner W. 2003. Guest editorial: Neoliberalism? *Environment and Planning D: Society and Space* 21: 509–12.

Larner, W., and M. Molloy. 2009. Globalization, the new economy, and working women: Theorizing from the New Zealand designer fashion industry. *Feminist Theory* 10 (1): 35–59.

Larson, B., and O. Harris, eds. 1995. *Ethnicity, markets, and migration in the Andes: At the crossroads of history and anthropology.* Durham: Duke University Press.

Lat Fem. 2020. Cholitas escaladoras: "Jamás nos hemos sacado las polleras." November 27, 2020. https://latfem.org/cholitas-escaladoras-jamas-nos -hemos-sacado-las-polleras/. Accessed December 2021.

Latin News. 2015. Bolivia: More heads roll over Fondioc corruption scandal. September 1, 2015. https://www.latinnews.com/component/k2/item/66171 -bolivia-more-heads-roll-over-fondioc-corruption-scandal.html. Accessed December 2021.

Lazar, S. 2002. Cholo citizens: Negotiating personhood and building communities in El Alto, Bolivia. Doctoral thesis, Goldsmiths, University of London.

Lazar, S. 2006. El Alto, ciudad rebelde: Organisational bases for revolt. *Bulletin of Latin American Research* 25 (2): 183–99.

Lazar, S. 2007. In-betweenness at the margins: Collective organisation, ethnicity, and political agency among Bolivian street traders. In *Livelihoods at the margins: Surviving the city,* edited by J. Staples, 237–56. Walnut Creek, Calif.: Left Coast Press.

Lazar, S. 2008. *El Alto, rebel city: Self and citizenship in Andean Bolivia.* Durham: Duke University Press.

Lister, R. 1997. *Citizenship: Feminist perspectives.* Basingstoke: Palgrave.

Little, B. 2016. Indigenous "chola" clothing comes to fashion week. *National Geographic,* September 19, 2019. https://www.nationalgeographic.com/culture/article/fashion-week-new-york-chola-clothing-bolivia. Accessed December 2021.

Lucero, J. A. 2008. Fanon in the Andes: Fausto Reinaga, indianismo, and the black Atlantic. *International Journal of Critical Indigenous Studies* 1 (1): 13–22.

Lugones, M. 2010. Toward a decolonial feminism. *Hypatia* 25 (4): 742–59.

Luján Chávez, R. M. 2012. *De-dollarizing the Bolivian economy: An empirical model approach.* Quinto Encuentro de Economistas de Bolivia. https://www.bcb.gob.bo/eeb/sites/default/files/paralelas5eeb/jueves/Dolarizacion/Ramiro%20Lujan.pdf. Accessed December 2021.

Lundvall, J., S. Garriga, A. Bonfert, E. Tas, and M. Villegas-Otero. 2015. *Bolivia: Challenges and constraints to gender equality and women's empowerment.* Washington, D.C.: World Bank Group. https://openknowledge.worldbank.org/handle/10986/23829. Accessed December 2021.

Maclean, K. 2007. Translation in cross-cultural research: An example from Bolivia. *Development in Practice* 17 (6): 784–90.

Maclean, K. 2010. Capitalizing on women's social capital? Women-targeted microfinance in Bolivia. *Development and Change* 41 (3): 495–515.

Maclean, K. 2013. Gender, risk, and micro-financial subjectivities. *Antipode* 45 (2): 455–73.

Maclean, K. 2014. Chachawarmi: Rhetorics and lived realities. *Bulletin of Latin American Research* 33 (1): 76–90.

Maclean, K. 2015. *Social urbanism and the politics of violence: The Medellín miracle.* Basingstoke: Palgrave Macmillan.

Maclean, K. 2016. Gender, risk, and the Wall Street alpha male. *Journal of Gender Studies* 25 (4): 427–44.

Maclean, K. 2018. Envisioning gender, indigeneity, and urban change: The case of La Paz, Bolivia. *Gender, Place and Culture* 25 (5): 711–26.

Maclean, K. 2019. Fashion in Bolivia's cultural economy. *International Journal of Cultural Studies* 22 (2): 213–28.

Mallinson, H. 2017. Inside the vibrant suburb that looks like a video game: The $1 million technicolour towers that are transforming a Bolivian city. *Mail Online,* March 3, 2017. https://www.dailymail.co.uk/travel/travel_news/article-4274424/The-colourful-Bolivian-town-looks-like-video-game.html. Accessed December 2021.

Malloy, J. M. 1991. Democracy, economic crisis, and the problem of governance:

The case of Bolivia. *Studies in Comparative International Development* 26 (2): 37–57.

Mamani Ramírez, P. 2015. Robando papel higiénico en el MegaCenter. *Página Siete*, February 12, 2015. https://www.paginasiete.bo/ideas/2015/2/15/sociedad-robando-papel-higienico-megacenter-47148.html. Accessed December 2021.

Mamani Ramírez, P. 2017. "Estado Plurinacional" autoritario del siglo XXI. *Religacion: Revista de Ciencias Sociales y Humanidades* 2 (6): 68–95.

Marston, S., J. P. Jones, and K. Woodward. 2005. Human geography without scale. *Transactions of the Institute of British Geographers* 30:416–32.

Martínez Novo, C. 2018. Ventriloquism, racism, and the politics of decoloniality in Ecuador. *Cultural Studies* 32 (3): 389–413.

Mayorga, F. 2017. El liderazgo carismático de Evo Morales y el proyecto político de Mas: Nacionalismo e indigenismo. In *Geografía del populismo: Un viaje por el universo del populismo desde sus orígenes hasta Trump,* edited by A. Rivero, J. Zarzalejos, and J. del Palacio, 161–70. Madrid: Tecnos—FAES.

McEwan, C., A. Hughes, and D. Bek. 2015. Theorising middle class consumption from the global South: A study of everyday ethics in South Africa's Western Cape. *Geoforum* 67:233–43.

McFarlane, C. 2019. Thinking with and beyond the informal–formal relation in urban thought. *Urban Studies* 56 (3): 620–23.

McGuire, J. W. 2013. Conditional cash transfers in Bolivia: Origins, impact, and universality. Paper prepared for the 2013 Annual Meeting of the International Studies Association, San Francisco, April 3–6. http://jmcguire.faculty.wesleyan.edu/files/2013/08/McGuire2013cBolivianCCTs.pdf. Accessed December 2021.

McKay, B. M. 2018. The politics of convergence in Bolivia: Social movements and the state. *Third World Quarterly* 39 (7): 1247–69.

McNelly, A. 2017. The contours of Gramscian theory in Bolivia: From government rhetoric to radical critique. *Constellations* 24 (3): 432–46.

McNelly, A. 2020a. The incorporation of social organizations under the MAS in Bolivia. *Latin American Perspectives* 47 (4): 76–95.

McNelly, A. 2020b. Neostructuralism and its class character in the political economy of Bolivia under Evo Morales. *New Political Economy* 25 (3): 419–38.

McRobbie, A. 2011. Reflections on feminism, immaterial labour, and the post-Fordist regime. *New Formations* 70 (70): 60–76.

Meagher, K. 2013. *Unlocking the informal economy: A literature review on linkages between formal and informal economies in developing countries.* WIEGO Working Paper 27. Cambridge, Mass.: WIEGO.

Medina, L., and M. F. Schneider. 2018. *Shadow economies around the world: What did we learn over the last 20 years?* International Monetary Fund, January 24, 2018. https://www.imf.org/en/Publications/WP/Issues/2018/01/25/Shadow-Economies-Around-the-World-What-Did-We-Learn-Over-the-Last-20-Years-45583. Accessed December 2021.

Melhuus, M., and K. A. Stølen, eds. 1996. *Machos, mistresses, madonnas: Contesting the power of Latin American gender imagery.* London: Verso.

Méndez, A. 2014. La banca y la Ley de Servicios Financieros. *La Patria,* February 17, 2014. https://impresa.lapatria.bo/noticia/173638/la-banca-y-la-ley-de-servicios-financieros. Accessed April 2023.

Méndez, C. 2019. Ropa usada causa pérdidas de $US 100 millones anuales al sector textil. *Página Siete*, August 7, 2019. https://www.paginasiete.bo/economia/2019/8/7/ropa-usada-causa-perdidas-de-us-100-millones-anuales-al-sector-textil-226652.html. Accessed December 2021.

Mendoza Hernández, A. 2020. Bolivianización: Causas y mecanismos de propagación en el rescate de la soberanía monetaria. *Ola Financiera* 13 (35): 99–116.

Mignolo, W. 2000. (Post)occidentalism, (post)coloniality, and (post)subaltern rationality. In *The pre-occupation of postcolonial studies*, edited by F. Afzal-Khan and K. Seshadri-Crooks, 86–118. Durham: Duke University Press.

Mignolo, W., and A. Escobar, eds. 2013. *Globalization and the decolonial option*. London: Routledge.

Molyneux, M. 2006. Mothers at the service of the new poverty agenda: Progresa/Oportunidades, Mexico's conditional transfer programme. *Social Policy and Administration* 40 (4): 425–49.

Monasterios, K. 2007. Bolivian women's organizations in the MAS era. *NACLA Report on the Americas* 40 (2): 33–37.

Moody's. 2015. Moody's assigns Ba3 deposit rating to Banco de Desarrollo Productivo S.A.M. (Bolivia). https://www.moodys.com/research/Moodys-assigns-Ba3-deposit-rating-to-Banco-de-Desarrollo-Productivo--PR_329726. Accessed December 2021.

Moore, H. 2011. *Still life: Hopes, desires, and satisfactions*. Cambridge, UK: Polity Press.

Morales, J. A. 2004. Dollarisation of assets and liabilities: Problem or solution? The case of Bolivia. *Money Affairs* 17 (2): 103–35.

Moreiras, A. 2015. Democracy in Latin America: Álvaro García Linera, an introduction. *Culture, Theory, and Critique* 56 (3): 266–82.

Morris, M. 1992. The man in the mirror: David Harvey's "Condition of Postmodernity." *Theory, Culture, and Society* 9 (1): 253–79.

Moser, C. O. 2010. *Ordinary families, extraordinary lives: Assets and poverty reduction in Guayaquil, 1978–2004*. Washington, D.C.: Brookings Institution Press.

Mouffe, C. 1999. Deliberative democracy or agonistic pluralism? *Social Research* 66 (3): 745–58.

Mouffe, C. 2005. *On the political*. London: Routledge.

El Mundo. 2008. Acusan a un ministro boliviano de estar implicado en un caso de contrabando. December 9, 2008. https://www.elmundo.es/elmundo/2008/12/09/internacional/1228857353.html. Accessed December 2021.

Muñoz Ramírez, G. 2019. La sociedad boliviana "no ha renunciado a su derecho, a su memoria y a su autonomía": Silvia Rivera Cusicanqui. *Desinformémonos*, November 24, 2019. https://desinformemonos.org/la-sociedad-boliviana-no-ha-renunciado-a-su-derecho-a-su-memoria-y-a-su-autonomia-silvia-rivera-cusicanqui/. Accessed December 2021.

Musto, M. 2010. Revisiting Marx's concept of alienation. *Socialism and Democracy* 24 (3): 79–101.

Nagar, R., V. Lawson, L. McDowell, and S. Hanson. 2002. Locating globalization: Feminist (re)readings of the subjects and spaces of globalization. *Economic Geography* 78 (3): 257–84.

Naqvi, N. 2018. State-directed credit in a world of globalised finance: Developmental policy autonomy and business power in Bolivia. *The Global Economic*

Governance Programme. Working Paper 139. University of Oxford. https://www
.geg.ox.ac.uk/sites/geg.bsg.ox.ac.uk/files/2018-11/GEG%20WP%20139%20
State%20directed%20credit%20in%20a%20world%20of%20globalised%20
finance%20Natalya%20Naqvi.pdf. Accessed December 2021.

Naqvi, N. 2021. Renationalizing finance for development: Policy space and public
economic control in Bolivia. *Review of International Political Economy* 28 (3):
447–78.

Negri, A., and M. Hardt. 2004. *Multitude: War and democracy in the age of empire*.
New York: Penguin Press.

New York Times. 2017. Step inside Bolivia's psychedelic dream homes. November
22, 2017. https://www.youtube.com/watch?v=wlodF_DjhIA. Accessed December 2021.

Ollantay, I. 2019. ¿Por qué algunos intelectuales indigenistas y feministas negaron
el Golpe de Estado en Bolivia? *TeleSur,* December 12, 2019. https://www
.telesurtv.net/bloggers/Por-que-algunos-intelectuales-indigenistas-y
-feministas-negaron-el-Golpe-de-Estado-en-Bolivia-20191212-0001.html.
Accessed December 2021.

Ollman, B. 1976. *Alienation: Marx's conception of man in a capitalist society*. 2nd ed.
Cambridge, UK: Cambridge University Press.

Open Democracy. 2019. The Bible makes a comeback in Bolivia with Jeanine Añez.
November 20, 2019. https://www.opendemocracy.net/en/democraciaabierta/
qui%C3%A9n-es-jeanine-a%C3%B1ez-y-por-qu%C3%A9-desprecia-los-pueblos
-ind%C3%ADgenas-de-bolivia-en/. Accessed April 2023.

Oporto, H. 2013. República plurinacional. *Página Siete,* December 19, 2013. https://
www.paginasiete.bo/ideas/2013/12/22/republica-plurinacional-9152.html.
Accessed December 2021.

Otramérica. 2011. "No se puede descolonizar sin despatriarcalizar." June 27, 2011.
http://otramerica.com/temas/no-se-puede-descolonizar-sin-despatriarcalizar/
361. Accessed September 2022.

Página Siete. 2014a. Policía detiene al dueño de la empresa textil Punto Blanco. August 30, 2014. https://www.paginasiete.bo/sociedad/2014/8/31/policia-detiene
-dueno-empresa-textil-punto-blanco-30932.html. Accessed December 2021.

Página Siete. 2014b. Silvia Rivera: No hay ningún gobierno indígena en América.
January 4, 2014. https://www.paginasiete.bo/nacional/2014/1/5/silvia-rivera
-ningun-gobierno-indigena-america-10474.html. Accessed December 2021.

Página Siete. 2015. Evo dice que admira "honestidad" de Nemesia Achacollo.
August 31, 2015. https://www.paginasiete.bo/nacional/2015/8/31/dice-admira
-honestidad-nemesia-achacollo-68501.html. Accessed December 2021.

Página Siete. 2016a. Desfile de modas La Chola Paceña: Tradición nuestra.
August 7, 2016. http://www.paginasiete.bo/flash/2016/8/7/desfile-modas
-chola-pacena-tradicion-nuestra-104961.html. Accessed December 2021.

Página Siete. 2016b. Enatex cierra sus 4 plantas y solo ofrecerá servicios. May 16,
2016. https://www.paginasiete.bo/economia/2016/5/16/enatex-cierra
-plantas-solo-ofrecera-servicios-96621.html#. Accessed December 2021.

Página Siete. 2019a. Empresas sociales sobreviven al contrabando y con eventuales. July 19, 2019. https://www.paginasiete.bo/economia/2019/7/19/

empresas-sociales-sobreviven-al-contrabando-con-eventuales-224648
.html#ancla-comentarios. Accessed December 2021.

Página Siete. 2019b. En el balcón la whipala, la Biblia, y la segunda mujer presidenta del país. November 12, 2019. https://www.paginasiete.bo/nacional/2019/11/12/en-el-balcon-la-whipala-la-biblia-la-segunda-mujer-presidenta-del-pais-237203.html. Accessed December 2021.

Paredes, J. 2010. Hilando fino desde el feminismo indígena comunitario. In *Aproximaciones críticas a las prácticas teórico-políticas del feminismo latinoamericano,* ed. Y. Espinosa Miñoso, 117–20. Buenos Aires: En la Frontera.

Paredes, J. 2012. En enero comienza la clausura definitiva de negocios por evasion. *La Razón,* December 14, 2012. https://www.la-razon.com/lr-article/en-enero-comienza-la-clausura-definitiva-de-negocios-por-evasion/. Accessed December 2021.

Paulson, S. 1996. Familias que no "conyugan" e identidades que no conjugan: La vida en Mizque desafía nuestras categorías. In *Ser mujer indígena, chola, o birlocha en la Bolivia postcolonial de los años 90,* edited by S. Rivera Cusicanqui, 85–154. La Paz, Bolivia: Ministerio de Desarrollo Humano, Secretaría de Asuntos Étnicos, de Género y Generacionales.

Peres-Cajías, J. A. 2014. Bolivian public finances, 1882–2010: The challenge to make social spending sustainable. *Revista de Historia Económica/Journal of Iberian and Latin American Economic History* 32 (1): 77–117.

Pérez, K. 2021. El Decreto 4078, la carta blanca para que militares y policías actúen "blindados" en las massacres. *La Razón,* August 17, 2021. https://www.la-razon.com/nacional/2021/08/17/el-ds-4078-carta-blanca-para-que-militares-y-policias-actuen-blindados-en-las-masacres/. Accessed December 2021.

Phillips, A. 1993. *Democracy and difference.* University Park: Penn State University Press.

Pickerill, J., and P. Chatterton. 2006. Notes towards autonomous geographies: Creation, resistance and self-management as survival tactics. *Progress in Human Geography* 30 (6): 730–46.

Postero, N. 2010. Morales's MAS government: Building indigenous popular hegemony in Bolivia. *Latin American Perspectives* 37 (3): 18–34.

Postero, N. 2017. *The indigenous state.* Oakland: University of California Press.

Potter, G. A., and L. Zurita. 2009. The peasant women's movement in Bolivia: Bartolina Sisa and COCAMTROP. In *Rural social movements in Latin America: Organizing for sustainable livelihoods,* edited by C. D. Deere and F. S. Royce, 229–46. Gainesville: University Press of Florida.

Prada Alcoreza, R. 2008. Análisis de la nueva Constitución Política del Estado. *Crítica y Emancipación: Revista Latinoamericana de Ciencias Sociales* 1:35–50.

Presencia. 1966. 450 viviendas serán construidas en Calacoto con ayuda de Alianza. February 18, 1966. http://biblioteca.lapaz.bo/ul/PR19660218.pdf?fbclid=IwAR1Tq5CYeIlHV23Ct76SuA4rdKfu7rm2Ui82Bk89jLvLeWXt6pPN7x VmuZw. Accessed December 2021.

Puente, R. 2015. Fondioc y Nemesia Achacollo. *Página Siete,* September 17, 2015. https://www.paginasiete.bo/opinion/2015/9/18/fondioc-nemesia-achacollo-70434.html. Accessed December 2021.

Querejazu, A. 2016. Encountering the pluriverse: Looking for alternatives in other worlds. *Revista Brasileira de Política Internacional* 59 (2): e007.

Quiroga, C. 2012. Bolivia's Morales seeks to tap reserves to boost industry. Reuters, February 14, 2012. https://www.reuters.com/article/bolivia-reserves/update-2-bolivias-morales-seeks-to-tap-reserves-to-boost-industry-idU SL2E8DDEAY20120214. Accessed December 2021.

Radio Deseo. 2020. Añez y la barbieficación de la chola: Análisis con Yola Mamani (La Chola Bocona). January 28, 2020. https://www.youtube.com/watch?v= OGP8bBHW4jI. Accessed December 2021.

Rakowski, C. A. 1994. Convergence and divergence in the informal sector debate: A focus on Latin America, 1984–92. *World Development* 22 (4): 501–16.

Ramírez Terceros, W. 2011. Nacionalización o adecuación de los contratos petroleros. *El Diario*, April 12, 2011. https://eju.tv/2011/04/nacionalizacin-o-adecuacin -de-los-contratos-petroleros/. Accessed September 2022.

La Razón. 2011. Raúl Prada: "El gobierno está en contra del proceso." June 6, 2011. https://eju.tv/2011/06/ral-prada-el-gobierno-est-en-contra-del-proceso/. Accessed September 2022.

Regalsky, P. 2010. Political processes and the reconfiguration of the state in Bolivia. *Latin American Perspectives* 37 (3): 35–50.

Reinaga, F. 1969. *La revolución india.* La Paz, Bolivia: Partido Indio boliviano.

Reuters. 2017. Bolivian court clears way for Morales to run for fourth term. November 28, 2017. https://www.reuters.com/article/us-bolivia-politics/bolivian -court-clears-the-way-for-morales-to-run-for-fourth-term-idUSKBN1DS2ZX. Accessed December 2021.

Revista Warmi. 2014. https://issuu.com/revistawarmi. Accessed December 2021.

Rhyne, E. 2001. *Mainstreaming microfinance: How lending to the poor began, grew, and came of age in Bolivia.* Bloomfield, Conn.: Kumarian Press.

Rivera Cusicanqui, S., ed. 1996. *Ser mujer indígena, chola, o birlocha en la Bolivia postcolonial de los años 90.* La Paz, Bolivia: Ministerio de Desarrollo Humano, Secretaría de Asuntos Étnicos, de Género y Generacionales.

Rivera Cusicanqui, S. 2008. El potencial epistemológico y teórico de la historia oral: De la lógica instrumental a la descolonización de la historia. *Temas Sociales* 11: 49–64.

Rivera Cusicanqui, S. 2010. The notion of "rights" and the paradoxes of postcolonial modernity: Indigenous peoples and women in Bolivia. *Qui Parle: Critical Humanities and Social Sciences* 18 (2): 29–54.

Rivera Cusicanqui, S. 2012. Ch'ixinakax utxiwa: A reflection on the practices and discourses of decolonization. *South Atlantic Quarterly* 111 (1): 95–109.

Rivera Cusicanqui, S. 2015. Strategic ethnicity, nation, and (neo)colonialism in Latin America. *Alternautas* 2 (2): 10–20.

Rivera Cusicanqui, S. 2020. Sociology of the image: A view from colonial Andean history. In *Ch'ixinakax utxiwa: On decolonising practices and discourses,* 12–45. Cambridge, UK: Polity Press.

Rodriguez Fernandez, G. V. 2020. Neo-extractivism, the Bolivian state, and indigenous peasant women's struggles for water in the Altiplano. *Human Geography* 13 (1): 27–39.

Rojas, R. 2010. Diez mujeres, en el gabinete de Evo Morales. *La Jornada,* January 24, 2010. http://www.jornada.unam.mx/2010/01/24/mundo/019n2mun. Accessed December 2021.

Rojas, R. 2014. Punto Blanco es otra afectada por la crisis textil en Bolivia. *La Prensa*, July 12, 2014. https://eju.tv/2014/07/punto-blanco-es-otra-afectada -por-la-crisis-textil-en-bolivia/. Accessed December 2021.

Romero, R., and A. Nolacea Harris, eds. 2005. *Feminism, nation, and myth: La Malinche*. Houston: Arte Público Press.

Rosales, A., M. Cerezal, and R. Molero-Simarro. 2011. *SUCRE: A monetary tool toward economic complementarity*. SOAS. Discussion Paper 31. London: Research on Money and Finance. https://core.ac.uk/download/pdf/6258882.pdf. Accessed April 2023.

Rousseau, S. 2011. Indigenous and feminist movements at the constituent assembly in Bolivia: Locating the representation of indigenous women. *Latin American Research Review* 46 (2): 5–28.

Roy, A. 2016. Who's afraid of postcolonial theory? *International Journal of Urban and Regional Research* 40 (1): 200–209.

Sagárnaga, R. 2019. Revolución "transformer": Del cholet a la casa de Iron Man. *Los Tiempos*, April 15, 2019. https://www.lostiempos.com/oh/tendencias/ 20190415/revolucion-transformer-del-cholet-casa-iron-man. Accessed December 2021.

Santos, B. de Sousa. 2004. The World Social Forum: Toward a counter-hegemonic globalization (Part I). In *The World Social Forum: Challenging empires*, edited by J. Sen, A. Anand, A. Escobar and P. Waterman, 235–45. New Delhi: The Viveka Foundation.

Santos, B. de Sousa. 2015. *Epistemologies of the South: Justice against epistemicide*. London: Routledge.

Schilling-Vacaflor, A. 2011. Bolivia's new constitution: Towards participatory democracy and political pluralism? *European Review of Latin American and Caribbean Studies/Revista Europea de Estudios Latinoamericanos y del Caribe* 90:3–22.

Schipani, A. 2014. Bolivia's indigenous people flaunt their new-found wealth. *Financial Times*, December 4, 2014. https://www.ft.com/content/9265426c -7594-11e4-a1a9-00144feabdco. Accessed December 2021.

Sheild Johansson, M. 2020. Taxes for independence: Rejecting a fiscal model of reciprocity in peri-urban Bolivia. *Social Analysis* 64 (2): 18–37.

Shultz, J. 2003. Bolivia: The water war widens. *NACLA Report on the Americas* 36 (4): 34–37.

Simone, A. 2019. Contests over value: From the informal to the popular. *Urban Studies* 56 (3): 616–19.

Socialist Worker. 2006. Mike Davis on a *Planet of Slums*: The rising tide of urban poverty. May 12, 2006. https://socialistworker.org/2006-1/588/588_06_ MikeDavis.php. Accessed December 2021.

Socolow, S. M. 2015. *The women of colonial Latin America*. 2nd ed. New York: Cambridge University Press.

Soliz Rada, A. 2014. García Linera y la "república etnocida." *Página Siete*, April 12, 2014. https://www.paginasiete.bo/ideas/2014/4/13/garcia-linera-republica -etnocida-18707.html. Accessed December 2021.

Spivak, G. C. 1994. Can the subaltern speak? In *Colonial discourse and postcolonial theory: A reader,* edited by P. Williams and L. Chrisman, 66–111. London: Routledge.

Stefanoni, P. 2012. ¿Y quién no querría "vivir bien"? Encrucijadas del proceso de cambio boliviano. *Crítica y Emancipación, CLACSO* 4 (7): 9–25.

Stephenson, M. 1999. *Gender and modernity in Andean Bolivia.* Austin: University of Texas Press.

Stewart, F. 1992. Can adjustment programmes incorporate the interests of women? In *Women and adjustment policies in the Third World,* edited by H. Afshar and C. Dennis, 13–45. London: Palgrave MacMillan.

Suárez, H. J. 2018. *La Paz en el torbellino del progreso: Transformaciones urbanas en la era del cambio en Bolivia.* Mexico City: Universidad Nacional Autónoma de México, Instituto de Investigaciones Sociales.

Supreme Decree 1842. 2015. https://www.asfi.gob.bo/images/MARCO_ NORMATIVO/SERV_FINAN_/DS_1842.pdf.

Svampa, M. 2019. *Neo-extractivism in Latin America: Socio-environmental conflicts, the territorial turn, and new political narratives.* Translated by M. E. Essimel. Cambridge, UK: Cambridge University Press.

Swinehart, K. 2018. Gender, class, race, and region in "bilingual" Bolivia. *Signs and Society* 6 (3): 607–21.

Tambakaki, P. 2014. The tasks of agonism and agonism to the task: Introducing "Chantal Mouffe: Agonism and the Politics of Passion." *Parallax* 20 (2): 1–13.

Tassi, N. 2017. *The native world-system: An ethnography of Bolivian Aymara traders in the global economy.* New York: Oxford University Press.

TeleSur. 2018 ¿Qué es la Ley de Empresas Sociales de Bolivia? June 6, 2018. https://www.youtube.com/watch?v=_awjro6REFQ. Accessed December 2021.

Thomson, S. 2019. Self-knowledge and self-determination at the limits of capitalism: Introduction to René Zavaleta Mercado's *Towards a History of the National-Popular in Bolivia: 1879–1980. Historical Materialism* 27 (3): 83–98.

Thoumi, F. E., and M. Anzola. 2010. Asset and money laundering in Bolivia, Colombia, and Peru: A legal transplant in vulnerable environments? *Crime, Law, and Social Change* 53 (5): 437–55.

Los Tiempos. 2010. Sectores sociales descontentos con nuevo gabinete de Evo. January 23, 2010. https://www.lostiempos.com/actualidad/nacional/20100123/ sectores-sociales-descontentos-nuevo-gabinete-evo. Accessed December 2021.

Los Tiempos. 2016. Enatex, el desenlace de un fracaso que se anticipaba. May 22, 2016. https://www.lostiempos.com/actualidad/economia/20160522/ enatex-desenlace-fracaso-que-se-anticipaba. Accessed December 2021.

Toranzo, C. 1991. A manera de prólogo: Burguesía chola y señorialismo conflictuado. In *Max Fernández, la política del silencio: Emergencia y consolidación de Unidad Cívica Solidaridad,* edited by F. Mayorga, 13–29. La Paz, Bolivia: Universidad Mayor de San Simón/Instituto Latinoamericano de Investigaciones Sociales.

Toranzo, C. 2020. Burguesías cholas y capitalismo boliviano. *Journal de Comunicación Social* 10 (10): 167–90.

Tórrez, Y. 2020. Lo simbólico de la restauración oligárquica en Bolivia. *Blog— Hurgando el avispero.* https://hurgandoelavispero1.wordpress.com/2020/08/26/ lo-simbolico-de-la-restuaracion-oligarquica-en-bolivia-por-yuri-f-torrez/. Accessed December 2021.

Trading Economics. 2021. Bolivian foreign exchange reserves. https://trading economics.com/bolivia/foreign-exchange-reserves. Accessed December 2021.

Ugarte Quispaya, R. 2015. Análisis sobre la baja capacidad recaudatoria del IVA en el sector de los pequeños contribuyentes: El caso de Bolivia. *Revista de Administración Tributaria* 38:92–105. https://www.ciat.org/Biblioteca/Revista/Revista_38/espanol/2015_ugarte_quispaya.pdf. Accessed December 2021.

Uharte Pozas, L. M. 2017. Una década del gobierno del MAS en Bolivia: Un balance global. *Barataria: Revista Castellano-Manchega de Ciencias Sociales* 22:131–48.

UN-HABITAT. 2008. *Housing finance mechanisms in Bolivia*. https://unhabitat.org/sites/default/files/download-manager-files/Housing%20Finance%20Mechanisms%20in%20Bolivia.pdf. Accessed December 2021.

El Universo. 2004. Miss Bolivia niega que hiciera declaraciones racistas. May 31, 2004. https://www.eluniverso.com/2004/05/31/0001/1065/0CB63023F65B4D6189F1F215D5709EBF.html. Accessed December 2021.

UNODC [United Nations Office on Drugs and Crime]. 2018. *Bolivia: Monitoreo de cultivos de coca 2017*. https://www.unodc.org/documents/bolivia/2017_Bolivia_Informe_Monitoreo_Coca.pdf. Accessed December 2021.

UNODC [United Nations Office on Drugs and Crime]. 2020. *Estado Plurinacional de Bolivia: Monitoreo de cultivo de coca 2019*. https://reliefweb.int/sites/reliefweb.int/files/resources/Bolivia_Informe_Monitoreo_Coca_2019.pdf. Accessed December 2021.

Urgente Bo. 2016. Bolivia es vulnerable para el lavado de dinero del narco. May 29, 2016. https://urgente.bo/noticia/bolivia-es-vulnerable-para-el-lavado-de-dinero-del-narco. Accessed December 2021.

USTR: The Office of the United States Trade Representative. 2022. *2021 Review of notorious markets for counterfeiting and piracy*. https://ustr.gov/about-us/policy-offices/press-office/press-releases/2022/february/ustr-releases-2021-review-notorious-markets-counterfeiting-and-piracy. Accessed September 2022.

Vaca, M. 2009. ALBA: Sucre sí, alianza militar no. BBC Mundo, October 17, 2009. https://www.bbc.com/mundo/america_latina/2009/10/091017_2012_alba_final_jrg. Accessed December 2021.

Vaca, M. 2010. Bolivia: 10 mujeres en el gabinete. BBC Mundo, January 23, 2010. https://www.bbc.com/mundo/america_latina/2010/01/100123_1814_bolivia_gabinete_gm. Accessed December 2021.

Van Cott, D. L. 2003. From exclusion to inclusion: Bolivia's 2002 elections. *Journal of Latin American Studies* 35 (4): 751–75.

Van Cott, D. L. 2005. *From movements to parties in Latin America: The evolution of ethnic politics*. New York: Cambridge University Press.

Van Vleet, K. 2003. Partial theories: On gossip, envy, and ethnography in the Andes. *Ethnography* 4 (4): 491–519.

Vargas Beltrán, D. 2016. La planificación sin participación ciudadana en proyectos de transporte público en La Paz. Unpublished master's thesis, Universitat Politècnica de Catalunya. Escola Tècnica Superior d'Arquitectura de Barcelona. https://cpsv.upc.edu/es/shared/tesis/tmbarch16presentacio_vargas.pdf. Accessed December 2021.

Vargas Ramos, J., and M. Villegas Tufiño. 2014. *Seguimiento al mercado inmobiliario y al crédito de vivienda que realiza el BCB para la detección de señales de burbujas.*

Banco Central de Bolivia. https://www.bcb.gob.bo/webdocs/publicacionesbcb/
2016/06/31/12-Mercado%20inmobiliario.pdf. Accessed December 2021.

Velasco, C., and R. Marconi. 2004. Group dynamics, gender, and microfinance in
Bolivia. *Journal of International Development* 16 (3): 519–28.

Velasquez Guachalla, V. X., C. Hummel, J. Nelson-Nunez, and C. Boulding. 2021.
Compounding crises: Bolivia in 2020. *Revista de Ciencia Politica* 41 (2): 211–37.

Villarroel P., and W. Hernani-Limarino. 2015. Evaluando el impacto de micro-
créditos en Bolivia: Evidencia del Crédito Productivo Individual—Banco de
Desarrollo Productivo. *Latin American Journal of Economic Development*, 233–82.

VOA News. 2019. Bolivia: An island of economic stability, but storm clouds gather.
July 1, 2019. https://www.voanews.com/economy-business/bolivia-island
-economic-stability-storm-clouds-gather. Accessed December 2021.

Vuola, E. 2003. Option for the poor and the exclusion of women: The challenge of
postmodernism and feminism to liberation theology. In *Opting for the margins:
Theological and other challenges in postmodern and postcolonial worlds,* edited by
J. Reiger, 105–26. New York: Oxford University Press.

Wade, P. 2005. Rethinking mestizaje: Ideology and lived experience. *Journal of
Latin American Studies* 37 (2): 239–57.

Walker, A. 2014. Cholets. *Bolivian Express.* July 25, 2014. https://bolivianexpress
.org/blog/posts/cholets. Accessed April 2023.

Walsh, C. E. 2009. *Interculturalidad, estado, sociedad: Luchas (de) coloniales de nuestra época.* Quito, Ecuador: Ediciones Abya-Yala.

Wanderley, F. 2008. Género, etnicidad, y trabajo en Bolivia: Insumos conceptuales
para el diseño de políticas de promoción del empleo en el marco de la equidad.
Revista Umbrales 18:145–69.

Wanderley, F. 2018. La pérdida de capacidad productiva en Bolivia. *Página Siete,*
November 29, 2018. https://www.paginasiete.bo/opinion/fernanda-
wanderley/2018/11/29/la-perdida-de-capacidad-productiva-en-bolivia-201562
.html#. Accessed December 2021.

Way, J. T. 2012. *The Mayan in the mall: Globalization, development, and the making of
modern Guatemala.* Durham: Duke University Press.

Webber, J. R. 2011. *From rebellion to reform in Bolivia: Class struggle, indigenous
liberation, and the politics of Evo Morales.* Chicago: Haymarket Books.

Webber, J. R. 2015. Burdens of a state manager. *Viewpoint Magazine,* February 25,
2015. https://viewpointmag.com/2015/02/25/burdens-of-a-state-manager/.
Accessed December 2021.

Webber, J. R. 2016. Evo Morales and the political economy of passive revolution in
Bolivia, 2006–15. *Third World Quarterly* 37 (10): 1855–76.

WFTO [World Fair Trade Organisation]. n.d. *Antonia Rodriguez Medrano: A story of
an Agent for Change.* https://wfto.com/news/antonia-rodriguez-medrano-story
-agent-change. Accessed December 2021.

Wittenberg-Cox, A. 2020. 8 (more) women leaders facing the coronavirus crisis.
Forbes, April 22, 2020. https://www.forbes.com/sites/avivahwittenbergcox/
2020/04/22/8-more-women-leaders-facing-the-coronavirus-crisis/?sh=16c
83c2d288f. Accessed December 2021.

Wolff, J. 2013. Towards post-liberal democracy in Latin America? A conceptual
framework applied to Bolivia. *Journal of Latin American Studies* 45 (1): 31–59.

Wolff, J. 2020. The turbulent end of an era in Bolivia: Contested elections, the ouster of Evo Morales, and the beginning of a transition towards an uncertain future. *Revista de Ciencia Política* 40 (2): 163–86.

World Bank. 2015. *Bolivia: Challenges and constraints to gender equality and women's empowerment*. Washington, D.C.: World Bank. http://documents1.worldbank.org/curated/en/339531468190181959/pdf/103087-WP-P154195-Box394854B-OUO-8-Bolivia-Gender-Report-ENGLISH-WEB.pdf. Accessed December 2021.

Wright, M. W. 2010. Gender and geography II: Bridging the gap—feminist, queer, and the geographical imaginary. *Progress in Human Geography* 34 (1): 56–66.

Wynter, S. 2003. Unsettling the coloniality of being/power/truth/freedom: Towards the human, after man, its overrepresentation—An argument. *CR: The New Centennial Review* 3 (3): 257–337.

Wynter, S., and K. McKittrick. 2015. Unparalleled catastrophe for our species? Or, to give humanness a different future: Conversations. In *Sylvia Wynter: On being human as praxis*, edited by K. McKittrick, 9–89. Durham: Duke University Press.

Yuval-Davis, N. 1997. *Gender and nation*. London: Sage.

Zamorano Villarreal, G. 2020. Indigeneity, race, and the media from the perspective of the 2019 political crisis in Bolivia. *Journal of Latin American Cultural Studies* 29 (1): 151–74.

Zavaleta Mercado, R. 2002. *Lo nacional-popular en Bolivia*. La Paz, Bolivia: Muela del Diablo. First published 1986.

Zibechi, R. 2005. Survival and existence in El Alto. *Counter Punch*, October 15, 2005. https://www.counterpunch.org/2005/10/14/survival and existence in -el-alto/. Accessed September 2022.

Zibechi, R. 2010. Governments and movements: Autonomy or new forms of domination? *Socialism and Democracy* 24 (2): 1–7.

Index

accumulation, 10–12, 37, 45, 57, 76; in informal markets, 144, 146–47, 165, 177
Achacollo, Nemesia: Fondo Indígena and, 95–96, 115; as minister of rural development and land, 95; resignation of, 7, 203
aesthetics: architectural, 29, 113, 175; of Casa del Pueblo, 184–85, 212; of *cholets*, 176, 198, 212; of fashion, 149, 166. *See also* Neo-Andean baroque
agonism, political theory of, 40
Aguilar, Rosario, 172, 219
ALBA (Alternativa Bolivariana para los Pueblos de Nuestra América), 6, 117, 132–34, 144, 204–5, 221; Social Movements Council of, 133–34; Structural Convergence Fund of, 133–34; trade in textiles and, 150, 151, 154–55, 172
Albro, Robert, 103
alcohol, 100, 106, 112
Alexander Coffee, 195
alienation, 33, 35–42, 47–48, 148
Alliance for Progress, USAID program (1966), 194
alpaca wool, 94, 153
Altiplano, the: extractive mining and, 119; migration from, to Chapare, 62
América Textil SA (Ametex), 151, 153–58
Andean communitarianism, 45
Andean community economic structures: *cholaje* and, 103; fiesta and, 180; gift exchange and, 126; history of, 104, 116; introduction of capital to, 118–19, 126; principles underpinning, 11, 52, 79, 130, 146, 191. *See also ayllu; ayni*
Andean cosmovision, 2, 33
Andean ideas of gender, 102; as activity, 99, 203; complementary but equal, 4, 82, 87, 90; equal right to political participation, 83. *See also chachawarmi*

Andean lending mechanisms, 130. *See also anticretico; pasanaku*
Andean textiles, 150–51, 172
Andean Trade Promotion and Drug Eradication Act (ATPDEA), 156
Andy's Supermarket, 195
anticretico, 130, 179–80, 223
antifashion, 166, 174
Áñez, Jeanine, 216–19, 221
Apaza, Gregoria, 92
apthapi, 189, 198, 213, 223
Arce, Luis: as minister, 139; as president, 211, 220
architecture: of Aymara Bourgeoisie, 13, 24, 29, 105, 113, 165, 207; boom in construction and, 176–77, 212; of Casa del Pueblo, 184–87, 212; in El Alto and the north of La Paz, 178–80; in San Miguel, 194–97. *See also cholets*; Mamani, Freddy; Neo-Andean baroque
Argentina, 110
Arias, Iván, 69
Asociación Artesanal Boliviana Señor de Mayo (ASARBOLSEM), 93
Assembly for the Sovereignty of the Peoples (1995), 62
assimilationism: liberal, 86–87; MNR and, 80
autonomy: indigenous movements' demands for, 3, 8, 31–34, 48, 203, 204; Media Luna demands for, 71; plurinational state and, 1, 15; territorial, 57–58, 64–67, 73–75; as theorized by the Grupo Comuna, 44, 48, 57–58, 61
ayllu: Andean cooperative organization and, 79, 80, 198; colonialism and, 119–20; universalized, 49
Aymara and Quechua, dominance over lowland groups, 68, 82, 87

Aymara bourgeoisie: architecture and, 13, 29, 105, 176, 185–87, 189; fashion and, 13, 146, 147, 166, 170, 172; narcotraffic and, 14, 170; in popular culture, 24, 177, 187–89; popular markets and, 143–47, 176; property and, 23, 193–97; urban change and, 19, 23, 177, 194–96
Aymara culture: icons of, 92; stereotypes of, 27, 67, 111, 112. *See also* Katari, Tomás; Katari, Túpac; Sisa, Bartolina
Aymara fashion: designers, 13, 28, 166, 168, 172, 207; models, 166. *See also* fashion; *moda de la chola paceña*
Aymara, language, 7, 17, 36, 98, 108, 121, 158
ayni, 101, 112, 130, 223

Babb, Florence, 103
Banco de Desarrollo Productivo (BDP), 27, 138
banking reforms, 138–43. *See also* Financial Services Law
banks: Banco Sol, 128; Central, 127, 128, 135–37; commercial, 127–28; development, 128; Inter-American Development, 129; Mutual La Primera, 129, 194–95; mutuals, 127–29; state-owned, 128, 138. *See also* financial institutions; *fondos financieros privados*; microfinance
Bartolinas, Las, 62, 64–65, 91, 95
Batt, clothing outlet, 163
Beni, 70, 218, 224
Bible, 216
Bolivianización, 135–38, 209
boliviano, currency, 15, 127, 132–37, 147, 209
bonos (welfare vouchers), 70–72, 206
Brazil: goods from, 104, 106, 110, 154, 159; pink tide and, 5; trade with, 155
Bretton Woods, 133
Buenos Aires, 21, 51, 110, 206
business: elites, 70–77; regulation of, 77–78, 161; in San Miguel, 194–95; small and medium, 94, 133, 160–61

cabinet, *chachawarmi*, 90, 95–96
cabinet, ministerial: of Evo Morales, 83; of Jeanine Añez, 216
cable car. *See* Teleférico
Calderon, Juan Carlos, 184

Calle de las Brujas, La Paz, 105
Calle Linares, 105
Camacho, El, 191
Cardénas, Victor Hugo, 64
care: labor, 36, 38, 39, 100, 163, 220; risk and, 124–25, 129, 202; valorization of, 4, 35, 39, 41, 42, 56, 84, 207
Carola (protagonist of *Zona Sur*). See *Zona Sur* (film)
Casa de la Moneda, 119
Casa del Pueblo, 184, 185, 198, 212
casero/a, 22, 106, 112, 113, 190, 223
Catholic symbolism, 216
Cementerio, 20, 126, 168
Central Bank, 127, 128, 135, 136, 137
Central Business District, 176
centralization, 7, 75, 218
Central Obrera Boliviana (COB), 62, 67, 71, 155–58
Central Obrera Regional (COR), 66, 67
Centro de Moda, 192, 198. *See also* shopping malls
Cervantes, Miguel de, 119
chachawarmi, 4, 20, 98, 101, 114–15, 179, 223; cabinet, 90, 95–96
Chamber of Commerce, 159
Chapare, 20, 62, 65
Chasquipampa, 182, 193
chifleras, 105
Chile, 19, 23, 104, 106, 157, 159, 180, 197
China, 16, 95, 131, 195, 198, 221; imports from, 152, 186; textiles and clothing production in, 154–57, 162
ch'ixi, 52
chola, 102–6; defined, 54, 67, 102; as icon, 92, 96, 105, 197, 203, 208, 218–19; as intermediary, 67, 92, 102–3, 208, 219; as market trader, 12–13, 66–67, 82, 92, 111, 143; suspicion of, 111, 146, 148; wealth of, 5, 118, 144–48, 176, 177, 202, 208, 210
cholaje, 54, 67, 82, 202, 219
chola paceña beauty contests, 171
cholets, 23, 165, 168, 186, 197, 213
cholo, 47, 54, 223
Choquehuanca, David, 220
chota, 104, 162, 223
Christianity, 92
civil society, 3, 8, 34, 43–49, 60, 73, 133
civil unrest, 31, 219
class: as basis for revolt, 3, 26, 32, 35, 44,

59, 60, 71; criollo, 57, 121, 177, 209, 219;
ethnicity and, 25, 45–47, 50, 119–21;
upper, 37, 150, 164, 187–89, 195;
working, 7, 49, 155, 164. *See also* middle
classes
class-based analyses, 3; economism of, 36,
37, 41; feminism and, 40–41; fragmentation and, 40, 42, 50–52; Indianism
and, 32, 44–49, 61, 204; MNR and, 31
clientelism, 61, 66, 147, 148
coca: eradication, 62; unions, 20,
60–62, 66. *See also* counter-narcotics
measures
cocaine, 14, 145. *See also* narcotraffic
Cochabamba, 64, 65, 99, 216
collateral, 127, 129–30, 131, 138, 147, 177;
definition of, under 2013 Financial
Services Law, 140–43; microfinance
and, 122–24
collective interest, 76
colonial elites, 121
colonialism: capitalism and, 43, 48, 49,
50–51, 107, 118, 119–26; environmental, 8; gender and, 37–38, 55–56, 82–85,
124, 208; internalized, 91, 218; in Latin
America, 1, 53–54, 79, 119–26; state
and, 22, 42; violence and, 3, 37. *See also*
modernity/coloniality/decoloniality
Comadre Remedios (character from *Zona
Sur*), 189, 193, 197, 198
comerciantes. See chola
Comité de la Coordinación de las Seis
Federaciones, 62
commerce: Aymara bourgeoisie and,
193, 195, 197, 209; credit and, 117–20,
127–29, 141; fashion and, 166; gift
exchange and, 90, 106, 204–7, 211;
incentives to invest in, 117, 128, 137,
143, 166, 175, 179, 195, 211; production
and, 51, 78, 117, 127, 141
communitarianism, 40–41, 44–45, 48, 78,
110, 137
"Community of Communities," 42
compadrazgo, 107, 116, 147, 168, 180,
191, 224. *See also* festive sponsorship;
fictive kin
competition: from imports, 137, 153–58,
161; liberal rationality and, 3, 38–39,
206
Comuna Group. *See* Grupo Comuna
Conditional Cash Transfers, 70

Confederación de Pueblos Indígenas de
Bolivia, 64
Confederación Sindical de Colonizadores
de Bolivia, 62, 65
Confederación Sindical Única de Trabajadores del Campo de Bolivia, 62
confidence: cultural identity and, 7,
144–48, 168, 174, 181, 182, 198; economic factor of, 80, 86–87, 113, 147–48,
181, 210, 212; national, 136, 144
Consejo Nacional de Ayllus y Markas del
Qullasuyo, 83
Constituent Assembly, 1, 26, 32, 58, 59,
72–74, 87; social movements involvement in, 55, 72–74, 82; territorial
autonomy and, 64, 73–74
constitution, 2009, 1–5, 7, 72–85, 87,
111, 155, 212, 214; gender and, 4–5,
59, 82–85, 87; identity and, 55, 58, 60,
78–82; pluri-economic subject and, 58,
73, 78–82; pluri-economy as defined in,
1–5, 26, 43, 59, 73–76, 86–87; state and,
7, 74–78
Constitutional Court, 214–15
consumers: Andean women as, 27, 89,
111–15, 158, 164, 167, 210–11; economic
role of, 27, 53, 158, 160, 167; fashion
and, 149, 150, 158, 167, 169–74, 219
consumir lo nuestro, 158
consumption: alienation and, 39–40;
base, 113, 144, 155; conspicuous, 13,
111–13, 144–46, 165, 180–81; internal,
28, 154–55; middle class and, 191, 197
contemporaneity, 149, 166–70, 173, 207,
210
contraband, 9, 158, 209, 213, 214; suspicion of, 104; in used clothes, 16, 28,
155, 159–60, 173
contrabando hormiga, 110, 116, 206, 224
cooperation: Andean principles of, 11,
130, 198; pluri-economy and, 1–5, 172
cooperative banking, 129
cooperatives, 76, 125, 141, 143, 150–52,
162; banking, 129, 139; knitting, 93–94,
152, 162, 164. *See also* banks: mutuals
co-optation, 47, 64, 66, 71, 166, 168
Coordinadora de Mujeres Campesinas del
Tropico de Cochabamba, 64, 65
Coordinadora de Pueblos Étnicos de
Santa Cruz (CPESC), 64
Correa, Rafael, 5, 133, 134

corruption, 7, 28, 96, 145–47, 159, 218
cosmovision, 6, 20, 33, 224
Cota Cota, 182
counter-narcotics measures, 156
coup, 215–18
Covid-19, 219–21
CRECER, 122, 129
credit, 120, 122, 125, 129
credit unions, 127
criollo, 57, 121, 177, 209, 219. *See also* class
Cuba, 6, 132, 134, 155
cultural plurality, 2
currency. *See* boliviano, currency; bolivianización; devaluation; dollar, U.S.; SUCRE

dance, 18, 113, 169, 180, 207
dance halls, 180, 186
Davis, Mike, 179
debt relations, 119
decentralization, 39, 53, 75
decolonization: cultural, 91, 209–14, 216; demands for, 8, 59, 65, 136, 172, 198; gender and, 4, 38, 65, 84–85, 91, 102, 115, 202–3
dedollarization, 27, 136, 137
del Granado, Juan, 68
depatriarchalization, 115
dependency theory, 45
de pollera: discrimination against women *de pollera*, 103–4, 122, 167–68; as identity, 28, 103–4, 149, 169, 171, 201–2. See also *ministras de pollera*
de Soto, Hernan, 122
de Sousa Santos, Bonaventura, 35
devaluation, currency, 126–27, 137, 146, 210
displacement, 141, 168, 177, 196
dollar, U.S., 106, 117, 127, 128, 132–37, 189, 209
dollarization, 135, 136
domestic violence, 100
Doppelmayr-Garaventa, 183

East Asia, 28, 166, 169
Ecuador, 5, 6, 133, 134, 156
education, 65, 189
Ejército Guerrillero Túpac Katari, 64
El Alto: architecture in, 186; built environment of, 175–77, 178–80, 212; fieldwork in, 17–24; history of, 9, 63,

178–80; "in betweenness" and, 66; MAS political support in, 82, 131; NGOs and social movements in, 66–67, 93–94, 161; political culture of, 63, 67; protests in, 66–68, 216; real estate in, 5, 29, 182; rural-urban mobility and, 8, 12, 66; Teleférico and ,182–83, 187, 212
El Diario, 69, 184
elections: presidential 2002, 69; presidential 2005, 8, 59, 61, 69, 71, 131; presidential 2015, 218; presidential 2019, 214–15, 218, 219, 220; presidential 2020, 217, 219, 220
Empresa Pública Nacional Textil (Enatex), 28, 151–58, 172–73, 211
environmental organizations, 215
epistemology: decolonial, 12, 16–17, 32, 37, 41–43, 56, 202–4; plurality of, 2, 217, 221
Escaladoras, 167–68
Escobar, Arturo, 25, 35, 202
Estenssoro, Víctor Paz, 54
ethnicity: class and, 25, 45–47, 50, 119–21; clothes and, 28, 149, 166; colonialism and, 31, 45–46, 50; gender and, 14, 46–47, 119–20; in the 2009 Constitution, 55, 82; urbanity and, 55, 82, 121. See also *cholaje; mestizaje;* mestizo; whiteness
Eve, 4, 92, 203, 208
extractive industries, 3, 13, 60
extractivism, 67, 119, 205, 209, 218

Fanon, Franz, 46
Fantasma Insomne, El (García Linera et al.), 32
far right, 20, 215
fashion: shows, 5, 13, 24, 165–68, 171, 218–19; modernity and, 13, 149–50, 165–66, 168–71, 174, 207. See also *moda de la chola paceña*
Federación de Juntas Vecinales (FEJUVE), 66
Federación de Trabajadores Gremiales, (FTG), 66
Federación Nacional de Mujeres Campesinas de Bolivia "Bartolina Sisa." *See* Bartolinas, Las
Felipe Quispe, 64
femininity: Jeanine Añez and, 217–19;

construction of in 2009 Constitution, 5, 26, 57, 59, 72, 74, 82–87; Grupo Comuna theorizing and, 33–34, 46–49, 57, 203, 207; ideals of, 5, 27, 92, 203; motherhood and, 2, 46; power of, 176–78, 208; scale and, 13, 125, 208
feminist: organizations, 4–5, 8, 26, 59, 80, 84, 92; criticism of the MAS, 33–34, 42, 44, 56–57, 209, 214–15, 218. *See also* Galindo, María; Paredes, Julieta; Mujeres Creando
fertilizer, 120, 121
festive sponsorship, 18, 107, 112, 120, 224
feudalism, 52
fictive ethnicity, 48
fictive kin, 101, 110, 121, 180, 224
fiestas, 18, 20, 112, 113, 169, 180, 225
financial crisis, 29, 128, 129
financial institutions: Andean, 129–30; in Bolivia, 118, 126–31; in Luribay, 119–24; international, 113, 127, 131, 221. *See also* banks; *fondos financieros privados*; International Financial Institutions; microfinance
financial regulation, 117
Financial Services Law, 27, 117, 138–42, 205
flags, 7, 216–18. *See also* tricolor; Wiphala
focus groups, 16, 18, 24
Fondation Cartier pour l'Art Contemporain, Paris, 24
Fondo Indígena, 7, 95, 115, 203
fondos financieros privados (FFPs), 127
food sovereignty, 65, 138
foreign reserves, 15, 133, 137, 221
Forma Valor, Forma Comunidad, (García Linera), 49
Fundación para Alternativas de Desarrollo (FADES), 129

Gago, Veronica, 10, 45, 51–52
galerías, 165, 168. *See also* shopping space
Galindo, María, 4, 5, 55, 72, 166, 201, 205, 213, 218; "No saldrá Eva de la costilla de Evo," 4
García Linera, Alvaro: development of the MAS and, 64, 69; *El Fantasma Insomne*, 32; *Forma Valor, Forma Comunidad*, 49; Grupo Comuna and, 25, 32–33, 44, 46–51, 56; leadership with Evo Morales, 60, 72, 202, 207, 214, 215, 218;

publications of, 32, 49, 70, 203; *Las Tensiones Creativas de la Revolución*, 70; TIPNIS dispute and, 8, 67–68
gasolinazo, 9
gas wars, 10, 32, 66, 68, 145, 214
gated communities, 178, 182
Gav Sport, 163
GDP, 133, 136, 158, 175
gender: colonial imposition of, 4, 38, 91, 202, 203; complementarity and, 91, 96, 98, 102; conceptualized as activities, 98–99, 203; equality, discourses of, 4, 65, 83, 91, 106; in the 2009 Constitution, 82–85. *See also chachawarmi*
gender-based violence, 83, 93, 100
gendered binaries, 12, 33, 38–39, 116, 129, 147, 204, 205
gentrification, 196
global corporations, 10, 43, 143, 205
gossip, 101, 107, 112
Gramsci, Antonio, 3, 34, 43–47, 56, 61, 204
Gran Poder, 20, 168, 169, 174
Gregoria Apaza, 92
group identity, 101
Grupo Comuna: criticism of, 33–34, 207; formation of, 32; MCD school and, 33; members of, 32, 44; 2009 Constitution and, 59–61, 86; vision of plurieconomy and, 25, 35, 44–58
Gutiérrez Aguilar, Raquel, 10, 44

hacienda system, 100
hamlets, 17, 112, 120, 121, 122, 123
Herbalife, 107, 108
heteronormativity, 4
Highly Indebted Poor Countries, 131
Hipermaxi, 190
Homo economicus, 36–37, 114, 115, 148
households: Andean, 4, 17, 87, 214; division of labor in, 100–103, 114, 207; extending across rural/urban space, 17, 52, 66, 103, 179, 206–7; headship, 84–85, 99, 124, 179; ideals of, 4, 13, 27, 38, 101, 102, 179, 217; liberalism and, 38–39, 42; livelihood strategies of, 179. *See also chachawarmi*
Hu Jintao, 152
human/nature relations, 3
Hurtado, Melva, 7
hydrocarbons, 1, 15, 60, 70, 71, 137, 138, 158
hyperinflation, 6, 127. *See also* inflation

Iberkleid, Marcos, 155
identity documents, 65
illegality, 22, 49, 51–52, 104
illiteracy. *See* literacy
import substitution industrialization,
　209
import tariffs, 155, 156
Indianism, 25, 61, 79, 89, 137, 153, 203,
　204; Grupo Comuna theorizing and,
　31–35, 40, 43, 44–48, 55, 56
indigenista, 46
indigenous women: ideals of, 5, 27, 57,
　84–85, 89, 164, 208; Indianism and,
　46–47; as intermediaries, 61, 66, 67, 92,
　96, 139, 208, 219; in the MAS govern-
　ment, 90–96; modernity and, 28, 59,
　177, 210; poverty and, 14, 156–57. See
　also *cholas, escaladoras*
indigenous women's social movements,
　59, 64–65, 82, 90, 115, 215
individual, abstract, 2, 35, 37, 39, 79, 146.
　See also *Homo economicus*
individualism, 18, 19, 82, 83, 115, 149,
　190, 198
industrial action, 156
inflation, 6, 127, 136, 138, 146
informality: debates around term, 11–12;
　neoliberal approaches to, 52, 109–10,
　122, 144; neoliberal versus structur-
　alist approaches to, 9–10, 159–60;
　popular markets and, 9–14; structural-
　ist approaches to, 78, 107, 109, 110–11,
　118, 143, 209; used clothes trade and,
　159–65
informal sector, size of in Bolivia, 6, 14,
　143
inheritance rights, 65, 98, 99, 124, 140,
　179
Instituto Boliviano de Comercio Exterior,
　(IBCE), 105, 159, 163
integral state, 43, 49
intellectuals, 31–35, 47, 89
Inter-American Development Bank,
　(IDB), 129
interest rates, 117
internal consumption, 154
international development, 13, 111. *See
　also* non-governmental organizations;
　USAID
International Financial Institutions, 113,
　127, 131, 221

International Monetary Fund (IMF), 128,
　131, 135, 137, 143
international press, 113, 152
intersectionality, 25, 56, 59, 82
Intiwara, 161
Iquique, Chile, 104, 159

Katari, Tomás, 46
Katari, Túpac, 91, 93
Kataristas, 31, 48, 64
Kennedy John, F., 194
Ketal Supermarket, 190
Keynes, John Maynard, 133
kinship, 96, 101, 107, 112, 121, 223
Klein, Naomi, 132
Kollasuyo, neighborhood of La Paz: con-
　struction in, 178, 180, 184, 197; fashion
　boutiques in, 165, 168–69; fieldwork
　in, 19–25

laborers, 89, 96, 106, 175, 201
La Ceja, El Alto, 126
La Coordinadora de Defensa del Agua y
　de la Vida, 50
laderas, 178–80, 183, 190, 212, 224
La Feria 16 de Julio. *See* Sixteenth July
　Market Fair
land: capitalization and, 119–22, 124, 127,
　130; gender and, 65, 83, 89, 96–102,
　107–8; investment in, 29, 146, 175, 196,
　199, 212; laborers, 93, 122; ownership,
　65, 75–76, 83, 89, 98–102, 108, 112, 130,
　179–80; reform, 31, 70, 179; regula-
　tions, 179, 184; speculation, 175–76,
　212. See also *anticretico*; *loteadores*
landlessness, 107, 123
landslide, 182
languages: original, 36; trivalent, 36.
　See also Aymara, language; Quechua,
　language
La Paz: built environment of, 29, 176, 177,
　193–99, 212; fieldwork in, 15–24; mayor
　of, 68, 166; municipal government of,
　191–92. *See also* Kollasuyo, neighbor-
　hood of La Paz; San Miguel, neighbor-
　hood of the Zona Sur; Zona Sur
La Rodríguez, market in La Paz, 126
La Salada, market in Buenos Aires, 21, 51,
　52, 110
laundering, 15, 145, 146, 148, 170, 175
Law of Capitalization, 75

Law of Popular Participation, 75
leadership, 66, 86, 96, 202, 207, 215;
  autocratic, 215; co-operative, 201;
  of Evo Morales, 60, 62; female, 217;
  male-dominated, 65; masculinist,
  116; personal, 153; personalized, 72;
  traditional, 223
Ley de Empresas Sociales, 155
Ley de Servicios Financieros. *See* Financial Services Law
liberal: individual, 2, 35, 37, 39, 146–47;
  institutions, 36, 63
liberalism: false neutrality of, 74, 83,
  86–87, 206, 217–18; feminist and
  decolonial critique of, 35–44
liberalization, 150, 151
literacy, 65, 109
llama fetuses, 106
llama leather, 152
localism, 49
lodgers, 20
logic: dialectical, 2, 32, 45, 204; of complementarity, 79; of production, 45;
  reciprocal, 42; vertical, 66; western, 2.
  See also rule of noncontradiction
logic of identity, 25, 35, 36, 56, 201, 203;
  complementary, 79; conflictual, 36, 40,
  42, 79, 221; ecological, 45, 79, 80, 221
logic of plurality, 33, 36, 49, 61
loteadores, 179–80
lowland indigenous groups, 55, 68
Lugones, Maria, 38
Luribay: fieldwork in, 17–25; finance in,
  118–24; governance in, 63; rural production in, 97–100; women's livelihood
  strategies and, 97–100, 108, 121–24

machismo, 4, 65, 92, 115
maestrerío system, 191
Magníficas, Las, 172
Malinche, La, 92
Mamani, Freddy, 29, 113, 176, 197, 198, 212,
  213; Exhibition in Paris of, 13, 24, 186
Mamani, Yolanda, 219
manufacturing: disincentives to invest in,
  175, 211; gender and, 125, 205; policies
  supporting, 139, 141–43; of textiles,
  28, 150–59, 162, 175, 207
mañaneras, 162–64
marea rosa. *See* pink tide
marianismo, 93

market associations, 23, 67, 106, 214
mayoristas, 106–7
Mbeki, Thabo, 152
Media Luna, 70–71, 72, 205, 217, 224
MegaCenter mall, 113, 177–78, 189–91,
  193, 213; meme featuring, 177, 187–89,
  197–98
Mercado Lanza, El, 191–92
mesa, 106, 224
mestizaje: gender and, 46–47, 90–91, 92;
  nation and, 34, 80, 216; urbanity and,
  54. *See also cholaje*
mestizo: citizen, 34, 46, 54; identity,
  48–49, 54–55, 57, 120; urban, 57. *See
  also* assimilationism; fictive ethnicity;
  Malinche, La; Reinaga, Fausto
methodology. *See* research methodology
microcredit, 127, 142
microfinance, 16–18, 121–24, 128–29, 138,
  140
middle classes: as consumers, 113–15, 150,
  158, 160, 163–64, 167–68, 190–91, 195,
  197; in La Paz, 129, 181–82, 194–95;
  support for the MAS and, 68–69, 87,
  215. *See also* Aymara bourgeoisie
ministras de pollera, 90–94
minoristas, 89, 106
moda de la chola paceña, 24, 28, 149,
  150–51, 165–74, 210
modernity: capitalism and, 13, 38, 79, 108,
  119, 149, 198; fashion and, 166, 170–74;
  gender and, 57, 125, 148, 151; indigenous, 3, 29, 104–5, 171, 184, 198–99,
  212; Latin American scholarship on, 2;
  scripts of, 19, 151, 173, 210, 217; time
  and, 13, 149–50, 166, 207. *See also*
  modernity/coloniality/decoloniality
modernity/coloniality/decoloniality, 33,
  42–43, 118, 119, 202
modernization: extractivism and, 6, 8,
  10, 67; gender and, 8, 57, 71–72; MAS
  approach to, 6, 10, 14, 27, 60, 67, 71,
  220–21; MNR and, 31–32, 80, 139;
  projects, 7, 76, 194–95
modernizing state, 86, 173, 178
Morales, Evo: background of, 20, 46–47,
  62; cabinet of, 90–91, 95, 96; leadership of, 7, 60, 62–64, 72, 152–53, 201–2,
  205, 207; legacy of, 184, 185, 214–15;
  scandals and, 7, 95–96, 214–15; support
  for, 20, 23, 60–61, 82, 131, 144, 218

motley society, 34, 44, 45, 48, 88
Mouffe, Chantal, 40
Movimiento Nacional Revolucionario
  (MNR), 31, 34, 44–46, 54, 71, 80, 84,
  139
Movimiento sin Miedo, 68
muchedumbre, 51, 107, 109
Mujeres Creando, 41, 42, 55, 73, 166, 205,
  219
multiculturalism, 2, 37, 39, 45, 53, 74, 79,
  82
multilevel marketing schemes, 107
multiscreen cinema, 182, 187
multitude, the, 51, 53
Mutual La Primera, 129, 194

Nacional-popular en Bolivia, Lo,
  (Zavaleta Mercado), 34, 46
narcotraffic, 14, 104, 145, 170, 175
narrative, 11, 40, 57, 130, 149, 156, 164,
  188
nation: gender and, 86, 116, 151, 160,
  205–6, 208; Indianism and, 47; indigenous, 75–76, 81, 84, 86, 87; mestizo
  ideal of, 80, 216–17
nation-state, 28, 40, 44, 45, 48–50, 64, 86,
  132, 173
National Development Plan, 131, 138
national identity, 105, 116, 163, 211
nationalization, 1, 60, 69, 71, 137, 138, 158
national populism, 54, 60
national production: as central to MAS
  policy, 27, 117, 137–39, 144, 147, 150,
  209–12; definitions of, 150–51, 154,
  162, 205; resource extraction and, 69,
  105; scale and, 11–12; of textiles, 28,
  159–62; threats to, 28, 78, 110, 116, 132,
  152, 159–64, 211
national sovereignty, 9, 75, 137
natural resources: boom in, 16, 28, 131,
  137; disputes over, 32, 43, 65, 73;
  exploitation of, 32, 43, 76, 132, 170–71,
  211; nationalization of, 1, 60, 69, 116,
  137, 205; rights to, 65, 73–76. See also
  TIPNIS
neighborhood associations, 17
neighbors/peasants distinction, 120
Neo-Andean baroque, 186
neo-extractivism, 14, 15
neoliberalism: colonialism and, 43; effects
  of on Bolivia's industries, 151–52, 153,

159, 172; entrepreneurialism and, 57;
  inequality and, 44, 78, 128, 143, 198,
  206; informality and, 51–52, 78, 143;
  reductionism of, 115; rejection of, 3, 5,
  16, 40, 60, 151–52, 203, 221
neoliberal multiculturalism, 53
non-governmental organizations
  (NGOs): income generation programs
  of, 107, 108, 161; liberal feminism and,
  65, 82; reproductive and sexual rights
  and, 84; García Linera's criticism of,
  68; microfinance provision and, 129
nonproductive sector as defined in FSL,
  141, 142
No saldrá Eva de la costilla de Evo
  (Galindo), 4
notorious markets, 22

obligatoriness, 63
ontology: of the pluriverse, 115; of reciprocal exchange, 101; relational, 49, 56;
  of scale, 12
Oriente, the, 70, 71
ownership: collective rights of, 75;
  community, 179; documentation of,
  140; of land, 112; legal right of, 180; of
  property, 179

Pachamama, 46, 81, 106, 224
Paco Paredes, Eliana, 13, 24, 165, 168, 169
pandemic. See Covid-19
Pando, 70, 224
Paredes, Julieta, 4, 73, 201
Paris, 13, 24, 186, 207
particularism, 38
pasanaku, 130, 224
pastoral ideal, 3, 79
patriarchy, 4, 91, 96, 205
patronage, 95, 147, 148
Patzi, Felix, 54, 63
peasants, 17, 53, 67, 103, 112, 120, 127.
pensions. See Renta Dignidad
Pérez de Urdininea, President, 120
peri-urban: areas, 8, 10, 25, 52, 96, 100,
  122, 131; markets, 9–12, 26, 50–51, 59,
  90, 104, 144, 202, 209, 210; settlements, 177–78. See also laderas
Peru, 9, 105, 106, 126, 136, 154, 156, 157
petty commerce/trade, 51, 106–11
petty traders, 49–51, 89, 106–11, 143,
  162–64, 205–6

pink tide, 5–6, 26, 132
Plan Progress for Bolivian–National
    Convergence, 216
plurality: of epistemology, 2, 217; of iden-
    tity, 15, 26, 33–34, 42, 44, 53–56, 58, 79;
    permitted subjects of, 53–56; process
    and, 60, 79–80, 201–14; as recognized
    in 2009 Constitution, 2, 43, 73, 79,
    83; state and, 15, 29, 85–87, 138, 198;
    theories of, 2, 26, 39, 45–48, 70
pluri-economy: as defined in constitu-
    tion, 2–3, 26, 36, 78–81; gender and, 4,
    26, 28–29, 33, 44, 56, 72, 115, 207, 221;
    historical context for, 26, 59–72, 73, 86;
    informality and, 9, 13, 29, 44, 110–11
plurinational state, 1, 2, 44, 72, 216
pluriverse, 2, 25, 33–36, 43, 57, 86, 217, 221
police, 162, 216
political: participation, 84; parties, 26, 59,
    60, 71, 73, 201; subject, the, 28–29, 50,
    57, 82, 83
pollera: as "anti-fashion," 166–67; ban of,
    168; as costume, 168, 170–72, 174, 219;
    defined, 5; escaladoras and, 167–68; as
    everyday dress, 169–71; as symbol of
    empowerment, 168. See also de pollera
pollera fashions. See moda de la chola
    paceña
pongueaje, 31, 225
popular culture, 24, 91
populism, 5, 60, 211; logic of, 66
Postero, Nancy, 86
postmodernity, 33
Potosí, 93, 119
Prada Alcoreza, Raúl, 44, 69, 80
pragmatic left, 69
precarity, 52, 106–7
Presidential Palace, 216
prestes, 169
private property, 60, 76
private sphere, 37–38
privatization of water, 50
procesos de cambio, 14, 90
proletariat, 9
Pro Mujer, 129
property: as collateral, 124, 127, 140–42,
    177; investment in, 112, 156; ownership
    of, 101, 179; private, 60, 76; rights to,
    70, 74–76, 130. See also real estate
property owning democracy, 126, 129–30,
    195

protectionism, 134–35, 153–54
protests: against global corporations, 10,
    32, 50–51, 59, 66, 68–69; against the
    MAS, 9, 67–68, 161; debt, 128, 140;
    following 2019 election, 215–16; social
    movements and, 32, 63–67. See also
    apthapi; gasolinazo; gas wars; TIPNIS;
    water: wars
public sphere, 37–39, 184, 185
Pueblos Originarios, 83
Punto Blanco, 151–55, 172, 211

Quechua, language, 7, 36, 112
quinoa, 95
Quintana, Juan Ramon, 159
Quiroga, José Antonio, 69
Quispe, Rafael, 83

Ramírez Terceros, Wilfredo, 69
Ramos, Veronica, 158
real estate: boom in, 15, 175–76; built en-
    vironment and, 5, 193–97; as collateral,
    141; defined as non-productive, 142;
    development of in San Miguel, 194;
    in El Alto, 105; investments in, 156,
    199; money laundering and, 145, 175;
    prices of, 19, 29, 106, 175, 176, 182, 194;
    speculation and, 76, 175, 212
real estate agents, 193, 194
rebars, 179
reciprocity: Andean principle of, 130, 223;
    as characteristic of a rural/agricultural
    economy, 120; community labor and,
    35, 205; logics of, 103; pluri-economy
    and, 3–4, 33; regional trade and, 133;
    as related to competition, 124, 146; at
    scale of government, 96, 115–16
recognition, 6, 31, 33, 45, 54, 57, 64, 175
redistribution, 1, 3, 6, 14, 33, 75–78, 79–80
reductionism, 36, 49, 83, 58, 118
referendum, Bolivian Constitutional
    2009, 1
referendum, Bolivian Constitutional
    2016, 215; 21F Movement formed in
    response to, 215
regulation: by communities of market,
    52; of creditors' rights, 128; financial,
    27, 78, 117, 127–28, 131–43; of formal
    business and employment, 76–78, 161,
    175, 178, 211; informality, 117, 151, 178;
    of land use, 184; tax, 143–44, 209

Reinaga, Fausto, 34, 44–47, 54, 55, 181, 208, 213; La Revolución India, (Reinaga), 34
relationality, 2, 13, 20, 36, 43
relationships: abusive, 101; community labor and, 40, 101; loans and, 122–23; popular markets and, 113, 190, 192, 193; wealth, and, 114. See also *compadrazgo*; kinship
Renta Dignidad, 70–71
reproduction, social, 4, 45, 50, 87–88, 114, 171, 220
reproductive labor: in Andean rural communities, 98, 101–2, 114; GC theorizing and, 47, 52–53, 57; gendered, 5, 26, 59, 74, 92–93, 98, 101–2, 114, 206; as recognized in the 2009 Constitution, 74, 81, 84; value and, 13, 35–38, 41, 124–25, 205–6
reproductive and sexual rights, 84
reputation, 18, 97, 98, 101, 102, 116, 122, 128, 181, 190
research methodology, 14–25
residentes, 121
retailers, 67, 106, 163; of clothing, 151, 163
revolution: class-based, 32, 59, 60; the everyday and, 55; MNR and, 54; in 1952, 44, 121, 178; rationales of, 44; Fausto Reinaga and, 46
Revolución India, La (Reinaga), 34
rights: collective, 75; cultural, 80; demanded by indigenous women's organizations, 65; employment, 87; family, 84; group, 37, 74; indigenous, 81, 82, 85; individual, 92; labor, 77; to natural resources, 60, 65, 75; to prior consultation, 76; to private property, 60; reproductive, 84; social, 8, 67, 70, 75, 77, 78; universal, 37; women's, 83
Rio Abajo, 196
risk: assessment, 125; care and, 124, 202; colonial construction of, 125; Covid-19 pandemic and, 220; entrepreneurial, 124–25; financial, 135; informality and, 109, 191–92, 220; involved in rural production, 122; loans and, 140; to financial institutions, 124, 140; value and, 27, 38, 39, 74, 125
rituals, 20, 64, 80, 81, 86, 105, 117, 130
Rivera Cusicanqui, Silvia: criticism of

the MAS, 47, 56–57, 201, 218; criticism of 2009 Constitution, 55, 85, 213–14; "permitted Indian" and, 53, 153; René Zavaleta Mercado and, 45
roads: construction and maintenance of, 68, 178; in Kollasuyo, 20; in Luribay, 17–18; TIPNIS dispute and, 8, 67
Rodríguez, Casimira, 91
Rodríguez Medrano, Antonia: knitting co-operative and, 93–94, 162; as minister of productive development and plural economy, 93–95, 115, 203. *See also* Asociación Artesanal Boliviana Señor de Mayo
Rodríguez Zapatero, José Luis, 152
ROSCAs, rotating savings and credit associations, 130
Rousseau, Stéfanie, 82
rule of noncontradiction, 2
rural areas, 7–8, 54, 66–67, 142
rural credit, 120–22, 129, 142
rurality, 2, 5, 8, 202, 207, 212–13
rural-urban: alliances, 66; boundaries, 15, 51, 68, 110, 116, 179, 202, 207; migration, 11, 178, 180; mobility, 64, 104

salones de baile. See dance halls
Sánchez de Lozada, Gonzalo, President, 54
San Miguel, neighborhood of the Zona Sur, 192–98
Santa Cruz, 6, 42, 70, 131, 145, 166, 172, 219
scale: capital and, 125, 137; exchange and, 206–7; gender and, 89–90, 105, 116, 125, 139, 147, 206–10, 221; government and, 49, 93–94, 96, 115–16, 204–5; informal livelihoods and, 105, 108, 116; local versus global/universal, 37, 43, 56; Ministra Antonia Rodríguez's approach to, 93–95; theories of, 11–13, 50, 53, 56. *See also* universal, as opposed to particular
scandal, 95, 96, 153, 177, 203
self-built houses, 20
self-employed, 81
Seligman, Linda, 103
Senatex, 158
shopping malls, 16, 131, 177, 191, 197
shopping space, 189–93
silver, 119

Sisa, Bartolina, 62, 90–93, 103, 203, 208, 214
Sixteenth July market fair, 20–22, 105–8, 113, 150, 159, 163–65, 190, 213
slums, 176, 179, 186
small and medium sized enterprises (SMEs), 133, 138, 139, 142, 161
social capital, 130
social collateral, 130
social control, 63
social movements: Constituent Assembly and, 1, 72, 74, 204; feminist, 80; Grupo Comuna and, 43, 48, 56; indigenous, 32, 47, 50, 55, 56, 61, 65, 66, 71, 85, 203; indigenous women's, 59, 65, 82, 90, 91, 92, 93; MAS and, 6, 62–71, 75, 173, 208, 211–14; MAS as political instrument of, 26, 59, 62, 75, 86, 201; protests in early 2000s, 10, 32, 50, 143, 145, 203; relationship with the state, 64, 74, 203, 205; women's participation in, 4, 55, 64–65, 82–83
social networks, 101, 106, 111, 112
social reproduction, 4, 45, 50, 114, 171, 220
sociedad abigarrada. See motley society
sociology of absences, 42
solidarity: within ALBA, 6, 117, 132–33, 173, 204; national production and, 173; as principle of pluri-economy, 4, 78–79; as recognized in 2009 Constitution, 3, 75
sovereign wealth fund, 137
Spain, 108, 119, 152, 189
state: banks, 127, 128, 138; enterprises, 95, 150, 151, 134; extractivism, 10, 43, 117, 138, 218; regulation, 10, 77, 135, 154, 179, 94; subsidies, 9, 77, 127, 151
state, the: apparatus of, 26, 59; Grupo Comuna theorizing and, 44, 47, 49, 50, 56, 173; Marxist and Indianist visions of the, 34, 61; MNR and, 80; paternalism and, 72, 84; redistribution and, 33, 43, 75, 117, 204; role in pluri-economy, 3, 75, 78, 83; transitory role of, 48, 86; 2009 Constitution and, 2, 3, 72–78, 79; as universalized ayllu, 49
state of nature, 37
street sellers, formalization of, 191–92
strikes, 6, 158

structural adjustment, 54, 77, 83–84, 127–28, 135, 209–10
Suazo, President, 127
subsistence, 26, 39, 45, 52–53, 63, 100, 120
SUCRE (Sistema Unificado de Compensación Regional de Pagos), 27, 117, 132–35, 137, 144
suit and tie, 153
suma qamaña, 3
supermarkets, 190, 194–5
Supreme Decree 1842, 139
sweatshop, 149, 157
symbolism, 7, 81, 158, 172, 185, 212, 216
syndicates, 62, 67, 183

Taller de Historia Oral Andina, 55
Tapia, Luis, 44, 45
Tarija, 70, 224
Tarque, Jaqueline, 165
taxation, 62, 69, 71, 77, 143; authorities, 179; avoidance, 104; collection of, 144; payment of in informal sector, 144
tax regulations: enforcement of, 14, 148, 161, 209; general and simplified regime of, 144
Teleférico, 6, 176, 183, 184, 186, 187, 212
Tensiones Creativas de la Revolución, Las (García Linera), 70
term limits, 215
territorial authorities, 76. See also autonomy: territorial
textiles. See ALBA: trade in textiles and; Andean textiles; China: textiles and clothing production in; manufacturing: of textiles; national production: of textiles
time: arrow of, 13, 149, 160, 210; assumptions about, 13, 222; capitalist construction of, 149, 151, 160, 207, 210; as key economic concept, 2, 5; value and, 13, 207, 210
TIPNIS (Territorio Indígena y Parque Nacional Isiboro Sécure), 8, 67, 76, 205
Tiwanaku, 186, 198
trade: agreements, 132, 134, 151; with China, 195; deals with the United States, 134, 155, 156; global, 116, 132, 159, 166, 173, 214; guilds, 67, 78; illicit, 145; intraregional, 133; regional, 154; in white goods, 104. See also ALBA;

Andean Trade Promotion and Drug Eradication Act
traditional healers, 105
traditional lending mechanisms, 130. See also *anticretico*; *pasanaku*
transmodernity, 43
transport: infrastructure, 7, 176, 182–83, 206, 212–13; ownership of, 18, 106–7; rural production and, 96–97, 102–4, 113–14; unions, 9, 183. *See also* Teleférico
tricolor, 7, 216, 218

union of opposites, 52
unions: agrarian, 17, 18, 62, 65, 101, 122; coca, 20, 60–62, 66; definitions of labor and, 53; fragmentation of, 50, 152; MAS relationship with, 60, 61–63, 66, 71, 214; rural, 8, 50, 95, 201; trade unions, 71; transport, 9, 183; women's participation in, 4, 45, 65, 82–83, 123
United States: capital flight to, 127; coca-eradication policies and, 62, 65; funding from, 126, 129; imports from, 5, 19, 28, 104, 150, 152, 160; trade agreements and, 132, 134, 155–56
Unity Pact, 74
universal, as opposed to particular, 12, 15, 33, 36–37, 49–51, 56, 204, 210
Universidad Católica Boliviana, 19
Universidad Pública de El Alto (UPEA), 145
urban: development companies, 182; indigeneity, 9, 10, 26, 31, 33, 60, 81, 202, 214; *urbanizaciones cerradas*, 178
USAID (United States Agency for International Development), 129, 194
used clothes, 16, 150–52, 159–65, 169, 172–74, 205–7, 210–11; research project on, 19–23; as threat to national production, 28, 105, 154. *See also* *mañaneras*
usos y costumbres, 63
usufruct rights, 127, 130, 179, 225
Uyustus, Avenida de, 104, 195, 213

Valdivia, Juan Carlos, 24, 188
Varda, Raúl, 154, 155

Vargas, Rubén, 155
vecinos, 17, 120
Vega Camacho, Oscar, 32
Venezuela, 5, 6, 95, 131, 132, 134
vertical integration, 28, 154, 156, 157
vicuña, 170
Villa Pabón, neighborhood of La Paz, 109
vivir bien, 3, 8, 225
Vuola, Elina, 35, 202

Walisuma, 161
Warmi, magazine, 165
war on drugs, 62, 65
water: infrastructure, 179; supply, 18, 121, 182; wars, 10, 32, 64, 66, 68, 214
welfare, 70, 72, 80, 87, 155, 214, 221
white goods, 104, 105, 143, 213
whiteness, 21, 204, 224
white women, 150
wholesalers, 67, 106
Wiphala, 7, 216–18
women's rights, 65, 93
workers: care, 19, 219; collective action and, 50–51; domestic, 108–9, 220; formal, 71; home, 152; industry, 50; informal, 9, 110–11, 115–16, 136, 147, 202, 220; non-syndicalized, 57; precarious, 50; protections, 77–78, 84–85, 211; takeovers, 151, 154–58. *See also* Central Obrera Boliviana; Central Obrera Regional; strikes
W. R. Grace, 194
Wynter, Silvia, 37

Zamorano Villareal, Gabriela, 217
Zapata, Gabriela, 7
Zapatistas, 2, 57, 63
Zavaleta Mercado, René, 10, 34, 44–47, 50–51, 119, 201, 204
Zona Sur: changing profile of, 23–24, 176–77, 181–84, 189, 199, 212–13; connections with El Alto, 164, 166, 174, 182–84, 187, 190, 199, 212; real estate purchases in, 193–97; shopping spaces in, 177, 190–93; support for MAS in, 68. *See also* MegaCenter mall; Teleférico
Zona Sur (film), 24, 177, 187–89

Kate Maclean is associate professor at the Institute for Global Prosperity, The Bartlett, University College London. She is author of *Social Urbanism and the Politics of Violence: The Medellín Miracle* and coeditor of *Seduced and Betrayed: Exposing the Contemporary Microfinance Phenomenon*.